ESSENTIALLY EQUIVALENT TO A DIVIDEND

PAUL D. SEGHERS
MEMBER OF THE NEW YORK BAR
AND
CERTIFIED PUBLIC ACCOUNTANT

WILLIAM J. REINHART
MEMBER OF THE NEW YORK BAR

SELWYN NIMAROFF
MEMBER OF THE NEW YORK BAR

THE RONALD PRESS COMPANY , NEW YORK

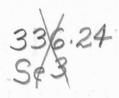

Library of Congress Catalog Card Number: 60-7772

PRINTED IN THE UNITED STATES OF AMERICA

To Our Wives

PREFACE

Corporate distributions to or for the benefit of a stockholder carry federal income tax implications of major consequence to today's businessman. Sound business requires a constant awareness of the potential tax effect of such distributions and the utilization of every available provision of the tax law—the statutes, the regulations, the rulings, and the cases—in order to mitigate the impact of the "tax bite."

This area of the tax law is of great concern both to the stockholder and to the corporation. The different tax treatment accorded to capital gains and to dividends requires that the stockholder be concerned as to whether money or other property he receives, actually or constructively, from a corporation is to be treated, for tax purposes, as a capital gain or as a dividend distribution—or, if he is so fortunate, as a nontaxable return of capital. And the corporation, in computing its taxable income, must be concerned as to whether the payment which it is making is to be treated as a deductible expense or as a nondeductible dividend distribution.

The discussion of all of the facets of this problem is the subject matter of this book. Chapter 1 introduces the problem and presents the history of the relevant statutory provisions; Chapter 2 discusses the principles evolved by the courts, illustrated by quotations from their decisions; Chapter 3 contains a digest of every representative published case in which the problem has been considered, giving both the taxpayer's position and the court's holding as to each argument; and finally, Chapter 4 contains suggestions as to what to do and what not to do in order to avoid or minimize the tax which might otherwise result from the receipt of a benefit from a corporation. In addition, there is a table of Cases Cited; an Index to Laws, Regulations, and Rulings; and a Bibliography.

The material covered in this book is so marshaled that each of the many issues involved can readily be found, and the applicable law with respect to each such issue can readily be ascertained. The judicial decisions have been summarized and classified. Thus, with each of the issues separately treated, the study which may be required is narrowed to the particular issue which is involved and to the body of law with respect thereto.

The material is presented in such a way as to be of value both to the taxpayer whose concern is with a *fait accompli* and to the taxpayer who is contemplating a prospective transaction. For the lawyer, accountant, or other adviser who may be assisting the taxpayer, the time which ordinarily must be devoted to the necessary research will be substantially conserved, and the detailed planning which may be required will be considerably minimized.

The authors cannot miss this opportunity to express their deep appreciation to Mary Dyczynski for her devoted cooperation and her untiring effort in typing not only the entire manuscript but the several drafts and multitude of changes therein which preceded the final typing.

PAUL D. SEGHERS
WILLIAM J. REINHART
SELWYN NIMAROFF

New York City
May, 1960

CONTENTS

ESSENTIALLY EQUIVALENT TO A DIVIDEND

Chapter 1

THE PROBLEM

Any receipt of cash or other property from a corporation may, for Federal income tax purposes, constitute income taxable to a stockholder as a dividend, even though the payment is not declared or designated as a dividend by the paying corporation. In certain circumstances, all or a portion of amounts received, actually or constructively, in redemption of stock; as forgiveness of indebtedness; as excessive profits on the sale of goods by a stockholder to the corporation; as a bargain purchase of property from the corporation; and the actual or constructive receipt, under many other forms, of property or benefits, may be taxable as ordinary dividend income. Hence, anyone who owns shares of stock may be vitally concerned with the answer to the question: *When does a distribution or transfer of cash or other property to or for the benefit of a stockholder constitute, in whole or in part, income taxable as a dividend?*

This question is one of the most difficult among the maze of problems which beset transactions coming within the scope of the "reorganization" provisions of the often-criticized Subchapter C of the Internal Revenue Code of 1954,[1] and of the corresponding provisions of prior law. It also arises in connection

---

[1] Officially, Subchapter C, Chapter 1, Subtitle A of the Internal Revenue Code of 1954 (comprising Sections 301 through 395 of the said Code), but generally spoken of simply as "Subchapter C." Wherever the phrase "the 1954 Code," or simply "the Code" is used herein, the reference is to the Internal Revenue Code of 1954, and all references to sections are, unless otherwise indicated, to sections of that Code.

with transactions falling within the scope of numerous other sections of the Code.

All these questions and problems fall within the body of law dealing with the determination of what is commonly spoken of as "essentially equivalent to a dividend." Actually, that phrase, used in the Code, Section 302(b)(1) [but not in Section 356(a) (2)], is misleading—it will be seen that *no* "distribution" or other transfer of property to or for the benefit of a shareholder is taxable *as* a "dividend" except to the extent, if any, that it *is*, in fact, a *"dividend,"* as that word is defined in the Code.

Judicial recognition of the maze of problems in this field is found in *Wilson v. United States,* 154 F. Supp. 341 (D.C. N.Y., 1958), wherein the court stated: "This action to recover substantial moneys paid pursuant to an assessment of additional income tax claimed to be erroneous and illegal presents the nightmarish problem that arises from the terms of Section 115(g), Internal Revenue Code of 1939, 26 U.S.C.A. §115(g). ... It has taken several weeks of study to gain a fair comprehension of the applicable law from the myriad of judicial writings on this intricate statute. It makes one shudder to realize that ordinarily a question of this kind is to be considered as an ultimate question of fact to be submitted to a jury if a jury is insisted upon."

As the House Ways and Means Committee has said, in speaking of the provisions of the Internal Revenue Code of 1939: "Existing law with respect to corporate distributions, liquidations, mergers, consolidations, separations and other transactions is so confused that taxpayers cannot plan transactions with any degree of certainty. .... In many cases taxpayers and the Government can ascertain the tax consequences of these transactions only after protracted and expensive litigation." (H.R. Rep. No. 1337, 83d Cong.) The same condition exists under the 1954 Code, as amended to date.

Simply stated, the problem is: in what circumstances may all or some portion of a distribution or transfer of cash or other property, including a forgiveness of indebtedness or a bargain sale, to or for the benefit of a shareholder of a corporation be taxable to such shareholder as a dividend? The corollary—in what circumstances can it be shown that a distribution or transfer gives rise either to no taxable income or to income taxable only as a capital gain rather than as a dividend?—covers too wide a scope, as it would include *all* the problems of the "reorganization" provisions of Subchapter C of the Internal Revenue Code and more besides. Hence, the corollary will not be dealt with exhaustively herein, although it will necessarily and constantly demand, and receive, attention.

The importance of the problem can best be appreciated by a realization of the fact that every distribution by a corporation to, or for the benefit of, a stockholder thereof is a dividend, taxable as such to such stockholder, unless such "distribution" comes within some provision of the Internal Revenue Code providing for different treatment.

Legislative History. The phrase "essentially equivalent to the distribution of a taxable dividend" first appeared in our taxing statutes in Section 201(d) of the Revenue Act of 1921. In its inception it was comparatively narrow in scope, but it has become the basis for what is now an extensive field of law in our tax-gathering structure. And, with the recent advent of "essentially equivalent" to a "constructive" dividend in *Joseph R. Holsey*, 28 T.C. 962 (1958), it can be anticipated that this field of tax law will become even more extensive. While the Tax Court in the *Holsey* case was reversed by the Court of Appeals, Third Circuit, in *Holsey v. Commissioner*, 258 F.2d 865 (3d Cir., 1958), that result was not accomplished without a dissenting opinion.

The provision in Section 201(c) of the Revenue Act of 1918 that a stock dividend was income and taxable as such was declared unconstitutional by the Supreme Court in *Eisner v. Macomber*, 252 U.S. 189 (1920). The statutory change required by that decision was embodied in Section 201(d) of the 1921 Revenue Act which provided that a stock dividend was not income and went on to provide "but if after" distributing a stock dividend the corporation cancelled or redeemed its stock "at such time and in such manner as to make the distribution and cancellation or redemption essentially equivalent to the distribution of a taxable dividend, the amount received in redemption or cancellation" should be treated as a dividend to the extent of earnings and profits accumulated by the corporation after February 28, 1913.

The "after" redemption clause in the 1921 Revenue Act became "before or after" redemption in Section 201(f) of the 1924 Revenue Act, but this "essentially equivalent to a dividend" provision remained tied to a stock dividend.

The cord was severed and the scope of the "essentially equivalent to a dividend" provision greatly widened by Section 201(g) of the Revenue Act of 1926. Under this section the "essentially equivalent" provision was extended to embrace a cancellation or redemption of "stock (whether or not such stock was issued as a stock dividend)."

The more familiar Section 115(g) was the number of the "essentially equivalent to a dividend" section in the Revenue Act of 1928, which was the same as its counterpart in the 1926 Revenue Act except that it contained a clause preventing it from being retroactively applied prior to January 1, 1926. Section 115(g), without the clause as to retroactivity, but embodying the concept contained in the 1926 Revenue Act, was incorporated in the Revenue Acts of 1932, 1934, 1936, and 1938 and became Section 115(g) of the Internal Revenue Code of 1939.

Section 115(g) of the Internal Revenue Code of 1939 remained unchanged until the Revenue Act of 1950, when it became Section 115(g)(1); and by that Act, what had started as a provision limiting nontaxability became a provision which itself was limited by other provisions to prevent taxability. Thus Section 115(g)(3) provided that a stock redemption to pay death taxes was not to be treated as a dividend.

The provisions of Section 115(g) of the Internal Revenue Code of 1939 were incorporated in the Internal Revenue Code of 1954 in Sections 302, 303, and 304, which also contain provisions, new to the taxing statute, which were not to be found in the old Section 115(g). In the 1954 Code, "essentially equivalent to . . . a taxable dividend" became "essentially equivalent to a dividend."

The "essentially equivalent to a dividend" provision was also embodied in Section 346(a)(2) of the 1954 Code. This section of the 1954 Code, which pertains to partial liquidations, was new to the taxing statutes, but not new in the field of law, as it was preceded by cases which applied the "essentially equivalent to a dividend" theory to partial liquidations, e.g., *Flanagan v. Helvering*, 116 F.2d 937 (D.C. Cir., 1940).

Court decisions require that recognition be given to the fact that the "essentially equivalent to a dividend" theory is applicable, not only in the case of the "essentially equivalent" provision, Section 302, *et seq.*, but also the "effect of the distribution of a dividend" provision, Section 356(a)(2), and the "device for the distribution of the earnings and profits" provision, Section 355(a)(1)(B).

The Revenue Act of 1924, Section 203(d)(2), provided that where a distribution made in pursuance of a plan of reorganization "has the effect of the distribution of a taxable dividend," it shall be taxed as a dividend. Hence, it will be seen that it did not take long after 1921 for the "essentially equivalent to a dividend" theory to become embodied in other sections of the taxing statute. The same provision under the same section number was contained in the 1926 Revenue Act.

The more familiar Section 112(c)(2) number was given to the "effect of a dividend" section by the Revenue Act of 1928, which did not change its substance. And Section 112(c)(2) was embodied, without change, in the Revenue Acts of 1932, 1934, 1936, and 1938 and in the Internal Revenue Code of 1939. In the Internal Revenue Code of 1954 it became Section 356 (a)(2).

The "device for the distribution" provision is of more recent vintage. It was legislated into existence by the Revenue Act of 1951 as Section 112(b)(11) of the Internal Revenue Code of 1939, and became Section 355(a)(1)(B) of the 1954 Code. This Section provides that a distribution by a corporation of stock or securities of a corporation which it controls, as a device for distribution of earnings and profits of either corporation, is a transaction with respect to which gain or loss shall be recognized.

Although "essentially equivalent," or "effect of" or "device for," is not mentioned in Section 306 of the 1954 Code, the result apparently sought to be accomplished by enactment of Section 201(d) of the Revenue Act of 1921 can be seen to be the reason underlying the new "Section 306 stock" concept in the 1954 Code.

The case law which has developed around the "essentially equivalent to a dividend" principle is very extensive and has given rise to still more like theories, including the "net effect" theory, set forth in *Commissioner v. Bedford's Estate,* 325 U.S. 283 (1945).

Thus, the decision in *Eisner v. Macomber, supra,* which benefited the taxpayer, may have been the initiator of the vast body of law dealing with the concept of "essentially equivalent to a dividend" which necessitates very careful planning if the taxpayer is not to be taxed upon a dividend as a result of his receipt of cash, or other property of value, from his corporation in a transaction which he expected to produce a tax result less costly to him.

Changes Made by the 1954 Code. The 1954 Code, as amended by the Technical Amendments Act of 1958, contains a number of provisions new to the statute, some of which have so changed the law that reliance upon a case considered to control the tax result of a particular transfer prior to 1954 cannot safely be relied upon until the present legislation is checked for a possible overruling statutory provision.

For example, Sections 302(c) and 318, both of which are new to the tax statute, set forth rules with respect to constructive ownership of stock, the existence of which may disqualify a transfer from capital gain treatment for which it would otherwise have qualified under prior law or under one of the specific provisions of Section 302(b).

Under prior law, the court held, in the case of a taxpayer who owned all of the shares of both Corporation A and Corporation B, that a sale of some of the shares of Corporation A to Corporation B was a genuine sale and gave rise to a capital gain and that the amount received from Corporation B was not to be treated as a distribution essentially equivalent to a dividend, thereby sustaining the taxpayer's position and affirming the decision of the Tax Court. *Commissioner v. Pope*, 239 F.2d 881 (1st Cir., 1957), *aff'g* T.C. Memo., Docket #53344, Feb. 23, 1956. Under Section 304 of the 1954 Code such a transaction would, however, be deemed to be a redemption by Corporation B which might constitute a distribution taxable as a dividend under Section 302.

Similarly, the law established by *Chamberlin v. Commissioner*, 207 F.2d 462 (6th Cir., 1953), was changed by Section 306 of the 1954 Code, which creates a wholly new concept in the taxing statute. Under the *Chamberlin* rule, a sale of preferred stock received as a tax-free dividend on common stock was treated as a sale of a capital asset. Under Section 306, the amount realized from such a transaction may be deemed to be gain from the sale of property which is not a capital asset (and, hence, the full amount of such proceeds be taxable as ordinary income) ; or, if the stock is redeemed by the company instead of being sold to a third party, the amount received may be treated as a taxable dividend. In the case of every disposition of stock originally issued by a corporation as a dividend, it is necessary. to refer to Section 306 to ascertain whether it is "Section 306 stock" and in what circumstances the disposition thereof can qualify as the sale or exchange of a capital asset. Absent such qualification, a redemption of such shares may result in the proceeds being taxable as a dividend, Section 306(a)(2), and a disposition not in connection with a redemption may result in the proceeds being taxable as ordinary income, at a still higher tax cost, Section 306(a)(1).[2]

Portions of Section 312 are new, and must be taken into consideration in determining the amount of earnings and profits of a corporation; e.g., the special rule as to what shall *not* be treated as a distribution of earnings and profits in a partial liquidation or in certain redemptions, Section 312(e), and the special rule where a corporation distributes property at a time when the corporation is indebted on a loan made, guaranteed, or insured by the United States or an instrumentality thereof, Section 312(j).

[2] See heading "Dividends vs. Ordinary Income," p. 10.

Any different treatment which might have resulted where a corporation, upon acquisition of its own shares, held them in its treasury instead of cancelling them, has, for the purposes of Part I of Subchapter C, been eliminated by Section 317(b).

New in the 1954 Code is Section 346, which deals with partial liquidations and is discussed in Chapters 2 and 4.

Receipt of consideration in addition to stock of a controlled corporation is specifically dealt with in Section 356(b) of the Code and may result in income taxable as a dividend. And in the case of the receipt of "other property" in exchange for "Section 306 stock," Section 356(e) specifically provides how the "other property" so received shall be taxed.

It is worth noting at this point that despite the fact that there are some entirely new Code provisions as of 1954, the small number of rulings, the lack of court decisions, and the still incomplete Regulations under the 1954 Code, make it essential to turn to decisions under prior law for guidance. Furthermore, there will be occasion, for some time to come, to resolve problems arising under prior law, so that the latter are almost as likely to confront us at this time as those arising under the 1954 Code. Moreover, to the extent that the 1954 Code did not change prior law, decisions under prior law will continue to be authoritative.

Dividends vs. Ordinary Income. Although the taxation of an individual's income as a dividend is not nearly so desirable as long-term capital gain treatment, it is more desirable than taxation as ordinary income, as the latter does not receive the benefit of the exclusion and tax credit accorded to dividend income, Sections 116(a) and 34. Hence, when planning any particular transfer to an individual, care must be exercised to guard against falling within the "essentially equivalent to a dividend" theory or, even worse, subjecting the resulting income to tax as ordinary income. For example, whenever a transfer by a corporation to its stockholders is being contemplated, consideration must be given to the collapsible corporations provisions of the Code Section 341 as amended by Section 20 of the Technical Amendments Act of 1958, under which any resulting gain on a capital asset held more than six months is deemed to be gain from the sale or exchange of property which is not a capital asset and, in consequence, is taxable as ordinary income.

In *Henry T. Roberts,* T.C. Memo., Docket #9807, Aug. 24, 1948, the stockholder occupied rent-free a dwelling owned by the corporation. The value of the use of the property was held to be "income received from any source," Section 22(a) of the 1939 Code, and, hence, taxable to him as ordinary income rather than as dividend income. A like holding was reached by the Board of Tax Appeals in *Charles A. Frueauff,* 30 B.T.A. 449 (1934).

If the stockholder using the corporation's property rent-free or at a rental below the fair rental value of the property happens to be another corporation instead of an individual, the importance of the foregoing problem assumes far greater proportions because of the potential loss of the 85 per cent dividend received deduction allowed to corporations, Section 243.

Although Section 341 of the 1954 Code and cases such as *Roberts* and *Frueauff, supra,* do not come within the purview of the "essentially equivalent to a dividend" theory, they do come within the purview of the planner who must be concerned with that theory.

Almost any transaction in which a stockholder receives, directly or indirectly, a benefit from a corporation may present the problem of "essentially equivalent to a dividend," in view of the broad terms of the basic rule that every "distribution of property ... made by a corporation to a shareholder with respect to its stock," except as otherwise provided in the Code, is taxable to such shareholder as a dividend, Section 301 of the 1954 Code and Sections 22(e) and 115(a) of the 1939 Code.

Such a distribution may be:

1. In the form of and intended to be a dividend, or
2. An exchange or other transfer in which a stockholder receives property in what would, under the "reorganization" provisions of "Subchapter C" of the Code, be a "tax-free" transaction if such transaction did not, in some manner, fail to meet the requirements for such "tax-free" status, or
3. Some other transfer of property to or for the benefit of

a stockholder, not in the form of a dividend, but having, in whole or in part, all the essential characteristics of a dividend.

Principles applicable in determining whether a transaction is "essentially equivalent to" or "has the effect of" a dividend are discussed in the next chapter and in Chapter 4.

Chapter 2

PRINCIPLES EVOLVED BY COURTS

Any transfer of property which comes within the definition of a dividend *is* a dividend, as defined in Section 316, and is taxable as such, despite the outward form of such transfer. This chapter presents a discussion of various forms of transfers, and the principles applicable in determining whether they constitute distributions "essentially equivalent to a dividend," amplified by quotations from decisions dealing specifically with each type of such transaction.

As yet, there are only a few court decisions dealing with the many new and different rules embodied in the 1954 Code which must be considered in determining whether any "distribution" which may be within the scope of these new provisions is taxable as a dividend.[1] However, many still pending cases are subject to the 1939 Code and many of the decisions under prior law are still significant in applying the provisions of the 1954 Code to determine to what extent a transaction may be deemed to be a distribution taxable as a dividend. Hence, the digest of the arguments advanced by taxpayers in the decided cases involving this issue and the holdings of the courts thereon, tabulated

[1] In regard to Section 302(b), the Report of the Senate Finance Committee on the Internal Revenue Code of 1954 stated at page 233: ". . . In general, under this subsection your committee intends to incorporate into the bill existing law as to whether or not a reduction is essentially equivalent to a dividend under section 115(g)(1) of the 1939 Code, and in addition to provide three definite standards in order to provide certainty in specific instances. . . ."; and further at page 234: "The test intended to be incorporated in the interpretation of paragraph (1) is in general that currently employed under Section 115(g)(1) of the 1939 Code."

in Chapter 3, will be found useful in every instance where this issue is involved.

The general principles applicable to the determination of this issue in various circumstances, as well as certain of the entirely new provisions of the 1954 Code, such as those relating to redemptions of stock, are discussed below.

Part I. Taxability to Stockholder

Distributions in Partial or Complete Liquidation. Under prior law [2] as well as under the present Code, redemptions of a corporation's stock, Section 302, including redemptions in the form of distributions in partial liquidation, Sections 331 and 346, may be treated as sales, and any resulting gain be taxable as a capital gain. The problem was, and still is, to determine when a redemption is to be treated as a sale of the shares redeemed and what is deemed, for this purpose, to be a partial liquidation. In Subchapter C, particularly Sections 302, 318, and 346, the 1954 Code lays down, for the first time, an elaborate set of rules, including rules for the attribution of ownership of stock, Section 318, for determining when a distribution shall be treated as a redemption of stock giving rise to capital gain or loss, rather than as a dividend.

Section 302(b) specifies certain distributions in redemption of stock which are to be treated as exchanges and, hence, not as dividends, such as those in which the redemption is substantially disproportionate or there is a termination of a stockholder's interest in the corporation or the stock redeemed was issued by a railroad company in a plan of reorganization under the Bankruptcy Act. But in determining whether there is a substantially disproportionate redemption or a termination of interest, reference must be made to the rules of attribution in Section 318, under which a shareholder is deemed to be the owner of shares owned by certain members of his family or by his partners or by certain specified trusts, estates, and corporations.

Nevertheless the first of these rules, Section 302(b)(1), is

[2] Section 115(c) of the 1939 Code and corresponding provisions of earlier Revenue Acts.

that a distribution by a corporation in redemption of its stock shall be treated as a payment for such stock (generally afforded capital gain treatment) and not as a dividend, *provided* such distribution "is not essentially equivalent to a dividend," and the Code contains no definition of the latter term. Hence, despite these elaborate rules in the 1954 Code, it may be necessary, in any case involving a redemption of stock, to determine on the basis of court decisions under prior law whether it is or is not a distribution "essentially equivalent to a dividend," that is, a "dividend," as defined in Section 316 of the Code.

Principles established in decisions under the revenue statutes in force prior to 1954, for determining when a transaction not in the form of a dividend is "essentially equivalent to a dividend," are classified and summarized below. Under each heading appropriate quotations from these decisions are given, thus supporting the statements made. It is to be remembered, however, that the 1954 Code contains provisions establishing rules as to the tax effect of transactions not dealt with specifically in prior revenue statutes. Hence, the general principles set forth below are applicable to current transactions only where not in conflict with any specific provision of the 1954 Code.

ALLEGED CONTRACTION OF BUSINESS. Under prior law, where the court found that the redemption of stock resulted from a contraction of the corporation's business, the distribution was held to be a partial liquidation and not taxable as a dividend. ". . . Petitioner has proved conclusively that the need for cash capital had declined by reason of the cancellation of the caterpillar franchise. . . .

"In the premises, the corporation acted prudently and with a real business purpose in redeeming a part of its capital stock. . . . The distribution in question was a distribution in partial liquidation and was not essentially equivalent to a taxable dividend." *Clarence R. O'Brion, et ux.*, T.C. Memo., Docket #24050, Nov. 30, 1951.

Some of the earlier court decisions which dealt with the question whether a distribution was one in partial liquidation, turned upon the so-called "net-effect" test, e.g., *Flanagan v.*

Helvering, 116 F.2d 937 (D.C. Cir., 1940), which, if carried to its logical extreme, would make it impossible to avoid taxable dividend treatment of every distribution in partial liquidation (at least to the extent of earnings and profits accumulated subsequent to February 28, 1913, and of current earnings). Fortunately, that so-called "test" under prior law is not included in Section 346 of the 1954 Code and has been discredited in a recent case under prior law, in which the court, after demonstrating its fallacy, said: "The so-called net-effect test is not a weighted formula by which to solve the issue before the court. The net effect of the transaction is not evidence or testimony to be considered; it is an inference to be drawn or a conclusion to be reached. It is not a solvent but a residuum; it is not a process but a product; it is not a means but an end; it is not a solution but a restatement of the statutory provision; it is the gist of the governing law of the case; it is not a balance for weighing the law against the facts; it is the law itself. 'Net effect' is a paraphrase for 'essentially equivalent.' It is just as if the statute read: 'If a corporation redeems its stock in whole or in part, so that the net effect of the transaction is the same as the payment of a taxable dividend, the amount so distributed shall be treated as a taxable dividend.' The net-effect test is not a test but an attractive abbreviation of the statute, as to which we shall be on safer ground if we stick to the words of the statute: essentially equivalent." *Commissioner v. Sullivan,* 210 F.2d 607 (5th Cir., 1954).

Certain transfers may satisfy the requirements of a redemption [3] and of a partial liquidation [4] as to a particular stockholder. For example, in the partial liquidation of a corporation, all of the shares of stock owned by one stockholder may be redeemed and his interest in the corporation terminated. In such circumstances Section 346(c) of the Code provides that, as to such stockholder, the redemption shall be treated as in a partial liquidation rather than as the termination of a shareholder's interest, thus eliminating the necessity of satisfying the requirements of

[3] Termination of shareholder's interest in the corporation under Section 302(b)(3).
[4] Termination of a business of the corporation under Section 346(b)(1).

Section 302(c), which must be met where there is only a Section 302 redemption, in which case the shareholder's interest in the corporation is terminated.

This rule is significant in two respects. In the first place, the rules embodied in Section 346, and the Regulations §1.346 thereunder, afford a guide which, if followed, will assure that a *partial liquidation* has been accomplished. In the second place, and of even greater significance, the complicated rules with respect to constructive ownership of stock, Section 318, and what constitutes a termination of interest, Section 302(c)(2), which apply to a Section 302 *redemption,* are not applicable to a Section 346 *partial liquidation.*

Regardless whether the transfer is a redemption or in a partial liquidation, we are still left with the problem: *what is "essentially equivalent to a dividend?"* It is with this problem that this entire book deals, and it recurs in many different circumstances. Suffice it to say at this point: if the transaction involves any payment by a corporation to or for the benefit of a stockholder and is subject to the 1954 Code, the relevant provision of "Subchapter C" must be carefully analyzed and applied to the facts and the conclusion reached then checked against the relevant provisions of the Regulations, §1.301, *et seq.,* and whatever court decisions and Internal Revenue Rulings on the subject may have been published to the date when the study is made.

If, however, the conclusion reached on the foregoing basis is not satisfactory, it may be appropriate to consider the effect of the above-mentioned catch-all provision of Section 302(b)(1) as to the capital gain treatment afforded a redemption of stock if it "is not essentially equivalent to a dividend." For this purpose, and in all cases under statutes prior to the 1954 Code, the digests in Chapter 3 of arguments and court holdings will be found to be of great assistance in assaying the probable strength of arguments based upon the facts upon which the case under consideration must rest.

STOCK RETIREMENT—NON PRO RATA. Where the distribution is not pro rata, this may be given weight in determining that, as stated in the opinion of the court quoted below, it is not the *"substantial* [italics supplied] equivalent of" a dividend. "While it is true that it is not an indispensable prerequisite that a distribution to stockholders be pro rata in order to qualify as a taxable dividend, the fact that the payments for stock herein were so out of proportion to the total stockholdings raises a serious question whether the payments were actually intended or had the effect of being the substantial equivalent of a distribution of corporate earnings." *Trust for Rosemary Case Weir,* T.C. Memo., Docket #31579, *et al.,* June 25, 1952.

If a distribution subject to the 1954 Code is in a partial liquidation as defined in Section 346, it is immaterial whether it is or is not pro rata, Section 346(b).

Stock Retirement Alleged To Be for Benefit of Corporation. In other cases the facts have been held to justify the conclusion that a redemption was for the benefit of the corporation and hence not taxable as a dividend. "... It [the evidence] shows equally clearly that the motive was to provide a means of avoiding a forced complete liquidation of a successful business and yet to conform to the fiduciary's demand for safety and the requirements of the Pennsylvania law of apportionment.

"... There is ... an absence of such manner of distribution as to be essentially equivalent to a dividend." *Clara Louise Flinn, et al.,* 37 B.T.A. 1085, 1094 (1938).

Step in an Alleged Complete Liquidation. Where the distribution is in complete redemption of all the stock of a corporation, or one of a series of such distributions, it has been held not to be taxable as a dividend. "A bona fide distribution in complete cancellation or redemption of all of the stock of a corporation, or one of a series of bona fide distributions in complete cancellation or redemption of all of the stock of a corporation, is not essentially equivalent to the distribution of a taxable dividend." *Commissioner v. Roberts,* 203 F.2d 304, 305 (4th Cir., 1953).

Buy-out of One or More of Several Stockholders. Similarly, where the distributee retains no beneficial interest in the corporation, the redemption is not taxable to him as a dividend.[5] "Thus, after the sale of December 13, 1943, petitioner no longer retained any beneficial stock interest whatever . . . He sold all of his stock. The transaction was not the equivalent of the distribution of a taxable dividend as to him." *Carter Tiffany,* 16 T.C. 1443, 1450 (1951).

STOCK PURCHASED BY CORPORATION AS TREASURY STOCK OR FOR RESALE. The defense that shares are repurchased by a corporation to be held in its treasury, rather than redeemed, has been held to be of no avail as evidence that the transaction is "not essentially equivalent to a dividend." "The object of the statute was to avoid the distribution of corporate earnings to stockholders by means of distributing stock dividends or the issuance of stock and taking surplus from the corporation to replace those stock dividends or such stock issued. If an actual physical cancellation or retirement of stock were contemplated, the real object of the legislation would not be accomplished. In our opinion the redemption of stock declared as a stock dividend is accomplished by the repurchase of such stock by the corporation, and the purpose of the statute can not be avoided by placing the stock in the corporation's treasury." *James D. Robinson,* 27 B.T.A. 1018, 1021 (1933).

The 1954 Code, Section 317(b), now specifically so provides with respect to the absence of any distinction, for the purposes of Part I of Subchapter C, between a corporation holding in its treasury purchased shares and the retirement of such shares.

There have, however, been cases under prior law in which the circumstances were held to justify a holding that the corporation's purchase of shares for resale did not constitute a taxable dividend. "The issue . . . is whether or not the payment of $50,000 . . . to the petitioner for his 500 shares of that company's stock was essentially equivalent to the distribution of a taxable dividend . . . the uncontroverted purpose was to set aside certain stock . . . which was to be devoted to . . . sale to . . . key men in the enterprise . . .

[5] However, see Sections 302 and 318 in the case of distributions coming under the 1954 Code, especially as to the effect of reacquisitions of stock of the same corporation.

"We see in the record no deviation from the original intent to reward faithful and valued employees by giving them a share in the business—a wholly legitimate business purpose. No intention to liquidate was evident. No action or intent to redeem or cancel the stock bought from the petitioner was apparent. The stock was merely lodged in the treasury until such time as it would be used to assign and transfer it to the new employee-owners. . . . The company paid out large sums as dividends.

"The sale of the stock in question did not constitute a distribution essentially equivalent to a taxable dividend." *Bernard R. Armour*, B.T.A. Memo., Docket #106256, Aug. 6, 1942.

REDEMPTIONS OR SALES TO OTHERS OF "SECTION 306 STOCK." No longer is it possible to obtain capital gain treatment where a stockholder receives a tax-free preferred stock dividend on common stock and sells or exchanges such preferred stock.[6]

STOCK RETIREMENTS—OTHER. The circumstances and reasons which prompted the issuance, in the first place, of the retired stock and its subsequent retirement may vary considerably from one situation to another and will often be determinative as to whether or not the distribution in redemption is to be treated as essentially equivalent to a dividend. ". . . The distribution did not constitute a taxable dividend . . . because the stock was originally issued for a bona fide corporate purpose—. . . an improvement of the Corporation's credit position with banks by the elimination from its balance sheet of the notes payable . . . when the Corporation eventually redeemed the stock, it was merely completing the initial transaction of repaying the notes and thereby making a cash payment . . . of . . . salary for which the notes had originally been issued. He [the taxpayer] . . . reported the full amount of his salary, including the notes, as taxable income, and to tax the distribution received upon the redemption of the preferred shares . . . would have the effect of taxing twice what was, in reality, the payment of his salary." *Estate of Henry A. Golwynne*, 26 T.C. 1209 (1956).

[6] See Chapter 1.

SIGNIFICANCE OF PRIOR DIVIDEND PAYMENTS. Where the corporation's record is one of distributing profits as dividends, that is taken as a significant factor indicating that a subsequent distribution in redemption of shares of its stock is not essentially equivalent to a dividend. "In this case we have found . . . that the transaction . . . was a sale and not a corporate distribution. . . . We find no indication that the transaction . . . was an effort, plan or scheme, to distribute corporate earnings in such manner that corporate earnings would be freed from tax as ordinary dividends. It must be . . . remembered that the corporation paid dividends in 1940 of $475,000 and that its average annual dividend from 1931 to 1940, inclusive, was $354,750. In our opinion the . . . facts indicate a corporate policy of distributing a large part of its earnings and plowing the remainder thereof back . . ." *Estate of Henry Vernon Foster,* T.C. Memo., Docket #110891, Mar. 22, 1944.

Alleged Loans to Stockholders. Whether a purported loan to a stockholder is to be recognized as such or be treated as a distribution taxable as a dividend is a question which has been litigated in a great number of cases. In a typical case decided against the stockholder, the court said: "We are of opinion that the evidence indicates dividends rather than loans. While true that the absence of notes, the failure to pay interest and the lack of a written agreement are not of themselves conclusive of this view, it is equally true that the recording of withdrawals in accounts receivable and the credits entered in such accounts are likewise inadequate to establish loans. The issue must be decided upon an examination of all the pertinent facts found, and when they are examined, the emerging picture is that of two brothers, always closely associated in business, who own and completely control a corporation to which they jointly contributed over a million dollars in cash as paid-in surplus and from which they drew money at will, making occasional returns of lesser amounts credited to their accounts. The ceiling for such withdrawals and the obligation to repay them on call, being unevidenced by written agreement or corporate resolution, could have been changed by an oral understanding between the

brothers as easily and as informally as it was made. Such a
vague arrangement is not determinative for tax purposes; and,
as the corporation had earnings and profits in 1939 and 1940,
we hold that the withdrawals were dividend distributions to the
extent thereof." *W. T. Wilson,* 10 T.C. 251, 256 (1948).

Applying the same criteria, the courts have, however, frequently found in favor of the stockholder. ". . . The important
fact is . . . whether the withdrawals were in fact loans at the
time they were paid out. . . . The character of the withdrawals
depends upon petitioner's intent and whether he took the company's money for permanent use in lieu of dividends or whether
he was then only borrowing. . . . In this case . . . petitioner's
withdrawals were intended to be loans. There was no agreement, tacit or otherwise, among the company's stockholders
authorizing petitioner's withdrawals. . . . Nor do we have a situation where withdrawals during prior years were cancelled
out by corporate resolution in the taxable year . . .

"In view of the foregoing, . . . petitioner's excessive withdrawals during the taxable year were loans and were not dividends." *Carl L. White,* 17 T.C. 1562, 1568-69 (1952).

Other Payments or Transfers of Property to Stockholders.
NOT IN FORM OF DIVIDEND. The mere fact that a payment to a
stockholder is not in the form of a dividend is not enough to
prevent its being taxed as such. "Furthermore, it is not material that there was no formal declaration of the dividend made
by the corporation in 1934. A declaration of a dividend is not
essential to a taxable dividend distribution." *Emil Stein, et al.,*
46 B.T.A. 135, 140 (1942).

DISTRIBUTIONS DISPROPORTIONATE TO STOCKHOLDINGS. Neither is the fact that a payment to a stockholder is disproportionate to his stockholdings sufficient to prevent it being taxed
as a dividend. "Petitioners argue that the withdrawals did not
constitute a dividend distribution since they received the entire
amount in controversy for their own personal use, whereas they
each owned only one share out of the total 200 shares issued by
Baird & Company, and no distribution was made to the other
stockholders. The law is well settled that the disbursement of

corporate earnings serving the ends of some shareholders may constitute a dividend in such stockholders notwithstanding ... that it is not in proportion to stockholdings; or that some of the stockholders do not participate in its benefits." *William C. Baird, et al.,* 25 T.C. 387 (1955).

ALLEGED PAYMENT OF DEBT OF CORPORATION. Whether a payment to a stockholder is a repayment of a debt due to him from the corporation or a distribution to a stockholder as such rather than as a creditor was once a question of fact, as indicated by the court's opinion quoted below: "The agreement of the stockholders with one another was in legal effect an agreement to loan $100,000 to the corporation for working capital, each shareholder contributing his pro rata share. By accepting the benefit of this agreement the corporation was bound by the corresponding burden to return the money to the contributors. When it did so it repaid the loan in accordance with that agreement. We see no basis here for taxation of this money on the theory that it is income.... [A]s between the government and the stockholders the actual transactions controlled in determining whether or not the money thus advanced and repaid is income..." *Weaver v. Commissioner,* 58 F.2d 755, 756 (9th Cir., 1932).

Today life is no longer so simple! Whether a debt is a debt is no longer a question of fact, but one of feelings, intentions, and economic second-guessing, since the theory of "Thin Incorporation" was evolved. Under this theory, a stockholder's loan to a corporation has been treated by the Internal Revenue Service and the courts, in many instances, as if it were a contribution to the corporation's capital, and its repayment taxed as a dividend! This theory is exemplified by the following statement by the court in a case of alleged "Thin Incorporation": "The question ... is whether the ... $17,960.49, distributed by the Wood Company to its stockholders in 1946, constituted a dividend or repayment of a loan....

. . . . . .

"Another of the factors indicating that the transfer in 1937 was a contribution to capital is the obviously inadequate capitalization that would have existed if the transfer constituted a loan. The corporation's only capital in that event would have been the $2,000 contributed for capital stock. The ... Company purchased 5 to 20 carloads . . . a month at . . . $1,600 and up per carload. Even after taking into account the fact that some . . . purchases were on credit and all . . . sales were for cash, . . . the corporation could not have operated with capital of only $2,000. . . . [T]he stockholders had every reason to believe that the $2,000 contributed for capital stock was only a fraction of the minimum requirement for operating. . . . [W]hen there is an obviously inadequate capitalization, a strong inference arises that a sum transferred to a corporation by its stockholders and called a loan is really risk capital. . . .

". . . the distribution was out of . . . earnings and profits and therefore a taxable dividend . . ." *R. E. Nelson, et al.*, 19 T.C. 575, 578, 579, 580, 581 (1952).

The tax effects of "thin incorporation" are dealt with fully in another book in this series.[7]

PAYMENTS TO STOCKHOLDERS, ALLEGEDLY FOR PROPERTY PURCHASED BY CORPORATION. Whether a payment to a stockholder is, as alleged, for property purchased by the corporation is a question of fact. To the extent, if any, that the payment is in excess of the fair market value of the property purchased,[8] it is taxable as a dividend. "The deficiency is founded essentially in respondent's contention that the partnership had . . . no good will or other intangible assets and that . . . the payment of $100,000 by the corporation to the partners for good will and other intangible assets was . . . a disguised dividend to shareholders . . .

". . . the partnership did own and transfer good will of substantial value . . . had assembled and trained a group of highly skilled employees . . . specially designed equipment had been developed . . . pattern of growth had been established . . .

". . . the corporation would not have been willing to pay an

[7] See Martin M. Lore, *Thin Capitalization* (New York: The Ronald Press Co., 1958).

[8] See Robert S. Holzman, *Arm's Length Transactions* (New York: The Ronald Press Co., 1958), chap. i.

unrelated third party [as much] . . . and, for that reason, . . .
good will valuation . . . is distorted. . . . We have . . . taken into
consideration the various factors . . . and . . . have concluded that
[the partnership] owned and transferred to [the corporation]
intangibles of the value of $45,000." *Sidney V. LeVine,* 24
T.C. 147, 155 (1955).

OTHER PAYMENTS TO OR WITHDRAWALS BY STOCKHOLDERS.
In addition to the transactions described in the foregoing para-
graphs, numerous other transactions, listed in Chapter 3 under
the heading "Other Payments to or Withdrawals by Stockholders," have been alleged to be taxable as dividends. The digests
in that chapter of the arguments and holdings in these cases
make clear the principles involved in each of them.

**Alleged Receipt of "Boot" in "Reorganization Transac-
tions.** Where individual stockholders have reported capital
gain upon the receipt of property in complete liquidation of a
corporation, but have retained only a portion of the property so
received, usually cash and other liquid assets, and have exchanged the remainder of the property for stock of another corporation, the Internal Revenue Service has taken the position
that the receipt of the property is only a step in a reorganization
and that whatever property is retained by the stockholders of
the liquidated corporation constitutes "boot," taxable as a dividend.[9]

The principles upon which the IRS has been sustained are
exemplified in the following quotation from the court's opinion
in such a case: "The controlling factor which we have concluded
brings this case within the statute is that a basic element of the
plan was the continuance of the chemical manufacturing business in the corporate shell of the new company, with the gain
(were it not for the 'boot') not having sufficiently crystallized
for recognition, because the collective interests of the shareholders still remained in solution. . . .

"If the shareholders of the old company had received only
stock in the new company in cancellation of their old shares, . . .

---

[9] *Love v. Commissioner,* 113 F.2d 236 (3d Cir., 1940), decided under the
provisions of Section 112(c)(1) and (2) of the 1939 Code corresponding to
Section 356(a)(1) and (2) of the 1954 Code.

no gain would have been recognized. Because of the 'boot' also distributed, . . . the gain is recognized here." *Lewis, et al. v. Commissioner,* 176 F.2d 646, 650 (1st Cir., 1949).

To the extent that the sole issue in a "boot" case is whether or not there has been a reorganization, the problem does not directly come within the scope of this work. However, digests of some such cases are given in Chapter 3.

Other cases involving the receipt of "boot" in what admittedly are "reorganization" transactions present the issue as to the extent, if any, that such "boot" is taxable as a dividend rather than as a capital gain, e.g., *Commissioner v. Bedford's Estate,* 325 U.S. 283 (1945).

The 1954 Code throws no light on the principles to be applied in resolving this question. Section 356(a)(2), identical with Section 112(c)(2) of the 1939 Code, states that: "If an exchange is described in paragraph (1) but *has the effect of the distribution* of a dividend, then there shall be treated as a dividend . . . [the distributee's] ratable share of the undistributed earnings and profits of the corporation accumulated after February 28, 1913" [italics supplied].

In such case it is, therefore, necessary to turn to the decisions under corresponding provisions of prior law to determine what factors may be given weight in determining whether such a distribution "has the effect" of a taxable dividend. Because of the difference of this language from the phrase "essentially equivalent to a dividend" used in Section 302(b)(1), the decisions under prior law invoking the so-called "net effect test" (digested in Chapter 3) may have great weight. It may be difficult to prove that the receipt of a distribution which includes the distributee's ratable share of profits, does not "have the effect" of the receipt of a dividend. Nevertheless, the cases decided under Section 112(c) of the 1939 Code and corresponding provision of prior law afford some support for the taxpayer's position, e.g., *Commissioner v. Sullivan,* 210 F.2d 607 (5th Cir., 1954), quoted on p. 16.

Cancellation of Stockholders' Indebtedness to Corporation.
The cancellation by a corporation of the indebtedness of a stock-

holder may be equivalent to the distribution of property to such a stockholder and hence taxable as a dividend. "It is also well settled that the cancellation of indebtedness of stockholders of a corporation is sufficient to constitute payment of a dividend . . .

". . . There is no question that on the accounts of the corporation, the stockholders were relieved of liability. Surplus was reduced by the amount of the debit balances and the stockholders were relieved of the charges therefor by credits to their accounts from surplus. This was regular and in order. The corporation had a distributable surplus and the directors had authority to order distribution. If the stockholders desired that surplus be used to relieve themselves of the charge for balances owing by them to the corporation, they were within their rights and there was no one to complain." *Kate Hudson,* 34 B.T.A. 155, 161 (1936).

Payments by Corporation for Benefit of Stockholders. When a corporation makes a payment for the benefit of a stockholder, it may be the equivalent of a dividend.

LIFE INSURANCE PREMIUMS. This situation has come before the courts in a number of cases involving the payment of life insurance premiums. In one such case, the court said: ". . . Permitting the light to shine through, we have an agreement by two stockholders who owned the legal title to all the stock in a corporation providing for a policy of life insurance on one of the stockholders, the proceeds of which are to be used to adjust the purchase price of stock between the parties in the event certain options to purchase are exercised. The stockholders thus appropriated corporate funds to their joint benefit by the premium payments. These payments fall far short of the ordinary and necessary expenses of a corporation engaged in the motion picture theatre business. . . .

"We are of opinion that the premium payments represented dividend distribution, not corporate business expenses, and that the insurance purchased with these premiums was to inure to the benefit of both stockholders." *Paramount-Richards Thea-*

tres, Inc., et al. v. Commissioner, 153 F.2d 602, 604 (5th Cir., 1946).

OTHER PAYMENTS FOR STOCKHOLDERS' BENEFIT. Another typical situation is one in which payments made by the corporation of what are in fact expenses of a stockholder are held to constitute distributions taxable as dividends to such stockholder. "Did Blackwell receive income . . . in the form of automobile expenses . . . which the Commissioner determined represented taxable income . . . ?

"Petitioner did use to some extent, for his personal use, the automobiles which were owned by the corporation . . .

"This issue is largely one of fact. We think the determination of the Commissioner as to these automobile expenses which should be added to petitioner's income is excessive. We think the amounts which petitioner concedes should be allocated to him and added to [his] income . . . are reasonable . . ." *Marvin T. Blackwell, et al.,* T.C. Memo., Docket #52701, Aug. 9, 1956.

Stockholder's Bargain Purchase of Corporate Property. The excess of the fair market value of property sold to a stockholder, over the price paid therefor, may constitute a taxable dividend. "If property is transferred by a corporation to a shareholder for an amount substantially less than its fair market value, regardless of whether the transfer is in the guise of a sale or exchange, the difference between the fair market value of the property and the amount paid for it is considered as a distribution of earnings or profits taxable as a dividend." *Shunk v. Commissioner,* 173 F.2d 747, 750 (6th Cir., 1949).

See discussion in Chapter 4 (p. 289) of principles applied by the courts in holding stockholders taxable on bargain purchases of shares of their corporations' treasury stock.

Corporate Property Used by Stockholders. The Internal Revenue Service has not been successful, so far, in taxing to a stockholder (as a dividend or otherwise) the value of the use of property (other than real property) used by the stockholder but owned by the corporation. In one of the few decisions in which this issue was present, the court said: "The respondent has determined that the farm expenses charged to the corporations and the cost of the farm machinery and equipment which were owned by Louis Greenspon, Inc., but used exclusively on the farm, were corporate distributions to Louis Greenspon. We agree insofar as the farm expenses are concerned, but disagree as to the cost of the machinery and equipment which were owned by the corporation. However, while it is appropriate for the respondent to disallow depreciation taken on the farm machinery and equipment owned by Louis Greenspon, Inc., we do not think that the cost of these items should be added to Greenspon's personal income. It is not disputed that the title to these items remained with the corporation and, while they may have been used on the farm, Greenspon did not own them, and their cost should not be included in his income. We do not decide the question whether under similar facts a stockholder making use of property owned by a corporation should be charged with receiving income to the extent of the value of the use of such property . . ." *Louis Greenspon, et al.,* 23 T.C. 138, 151, 152 (1954); cf. *Security First National Bank of Los Angeles, Executor, et al.,* 28 B.T.A. 289 (1933).

Where the stockholder uses real property belonging to the corporation and pays no rental or an inadequate rental, the value of the *use* of the property may be held to be a dividend to the stockholder-user or, even worse, it may be held to be "other income," [10] and thus denied the benefit of the dividend exclusion, Section 34, and dividends received credit, Section 116(a), provisions of the Code.

Income of Corporation Diverted to Stockholder. The courts have consistently held that the receipt by a stockholder of cash or other property representing income belonging to the corporation constitutes a taxable dividend to such stockholder. "There is little to add to what the Tax Court has said. That Court found, on ample evidence, that a family held corporation entered into a sub-lease to one of the stockholders at a rental very substantially less than the profits which, absent the sub-lease, there was every reason to believe the corporation would

[10] See *Roberts* and *Frueauff, supra,* this chapter and Chapter 1.

earn. The sub-lease involved no legitimate business purpose, for in this context, avoidance of taxes is not included in that category. . . . The income . . . received via the sub-lease was taxable as dividends from the corporation, despite the fact that proportionate dividends were not paid to the other stockholders." *58th Street Plaza Theatre, Inc. v. Commissioner,* 195 F.2d 724, 725 (2d Cir., 1952).

Limitation of Taxability of Distribution on Basis of Amount of Available Earnings and Profits. No distribution is taxable unless paid out of earnings and profits accumulated subsequent to February 28, 1913, or out of earnings and profits of the year in which the distribution is made, Section 316. "It is well settled that 'there can be no accumulated earnings or profits until an operating deficit is made good,' if incurred after March 1, 1913. . . . A distribution under such circumstances is not a 'dividend' within the definition. For that reason it is not taxable to the shareholders." *Foley Securities Corp.,* 38 B.T.A. 1036, 1037 (1938).

Summary of the Problems. A summary of the many problems which may confront the stockholder faced with the "essentially equivalent to a dividend" issue is contained in *Flanagan v. Helvering,* 116 F.2d 937 (D.C. Cir., 1940), wherein the court said at page 939: "Most of the judicial criteria that have been determinative in placing a transaction within §115(g) are presented in the instant case. The major part of the capitalization represented former earnings; only two relatively small cash dividends were paid; the proportional ownership of the shareholders was not changed; the corporation did not manifest any policy of contraction; the initiative for the corporate distribution came from a stockholder who needed cash; it has continued to operate at a profit. Absent here is the maintenance of the same capital liability, and there is no finding of a scheme of tax evasion (bad faith), factors sometimes significant. But the net effect of the distribution rather than the motives and plans of the taxpayer or his corporation, is the fundamental question in administering §115(g)."

Part II. Deductibility by Corporation of Payments to Stockholders

The principles found applicable in cases where the issue is whether the receipt of cash or other property constitutes income taxable as a dividend have been dealt with above.

On the other hand, there have been many instances where the issue was whether a payment, made by a corporation and claimed by it as a deductible expense, was in fact a distribution of profits, i.e., a dividend, and, hence, not allowable as a deduction.

Payments Claimed by Corporation To Be Interest. Of these cases, the greater number involve payments claimed by the paying corporation to be deductible as interest on various forms of indebtedness.

INTEREST ON PROMISSORY NOTES. The question is always one of fact: Is the alleged indebtedness such in fact? [11] "Whether the $8,400 payment made by petitioner to the Ryans in 1948 was a deductible interest expense as it claimed or was essentially a taxable dividend as respondent determined is a question of fact which must be decided from all the relevant circumstances . . .

"In the instant case, petitioner corporation and the Ryans, who controlled it, consistently observed the formal indicia of indebtedness in handling the advances made by them to the corporation. Demand notes payable with a fixed interest rate were issued and petitioner recorded the advances as notes payable on its books. But the form of the transactions does not fix them to be, in fact, what they purport; when an examination of all of the surrounding circumstances indicates that something else was the real intent of the parties, as here we believe it was . . .

"We think that the significant aspects of the Ryans' advances are the complete identity of interest among the Ryan family and their control of the petitioner; that there was no

[11] Cf. Martin M. Lore, *Thin Capitalization* (New York: The Ronald Press Co., 1958).

intention evident on their part to ever demand any repayment of the amounts advanced; and the fact, as Ryan freely admitted, that it would have been impossible for petitioner to have operated to the extent that it did without the funds in question. We are satisfied that the sums advanced by the Ryans were advanced by them as risk capital in the petitioner's business." *Ryan Contracting Corp.*, T.C. Memo., Docket #54335, Aug. 17, 1956.

INTEREST ON "DEBENTURES." Instruments designated as "debentures" have resulted in the greatest number of litigated cases. Many have been held to evidence only a stock interest in the corporation. In one of the cases in which the taxpayer was successful in overcoming the Commissioner's assertion that there was no indebtedness, the court said: "Unlike any of the cases in this field to which we have been referred these debentures have none of the attributes of preferred stock. They fulfilled all the formal requirements of a short-term bond; they had a maturity date fixed 'in the reasonable future,' 10 years after the date of issue; they afforded no basis for participation in management; and they imposed on petitioner a fixed liability to pay interest 4 times annually irrespective of earnings or emergencies, and at a modest rate of $3\frac{1}{2}$ per cent.

". . . No unusual unbalance in petitioner's ratio of equity capital to indebtedness resulted from their issue. . . . As we have found, new property did not flow to petitioner upon their issuance.... In these circumstances, that Walter and petitioner subordinated the debentures to all other creditor claims approximately 2 years after their issue date in order to obtain a favorable credit rating from Dun and Bradstreet would not be significant." *John W. Walter, Inc.*, 23 T.C. 550, 557 (1954).

INTEREST ON "PREFERRED STOCK." In only a very few unusual cases, payments made by a corporation to holders of what are actually designated as shares of its capital stock have been found by the courts to be deductible as interest expense. "Although every case turns on its own facts, the courts have pointed out some of the indicia which mark the distinction between the debtor and creditor and stockholder relationship, such as the name given to the obligation; whether the holders have voting powers, and whether there is a fixed rate of interest. All of the courts agree that the most important, if not the controlling factor, is whether the obligation provides for certainty of payment of a fixed sum on definitely fixed dates. . . .

"When the whole transaction is viewed in the light of actualities, it is clear that the preferred stockholders remained creditors of the corporation, and that the payment on the obligation was deductible as interest." *Bowersock Mills & Power Co. v. Commissioner*, 172 F.2d 904 (10th Cir., 1949).

In the majority of those cases involving payments claimed to be deductible as interest on capital stock which have reached the courts, however, the claims of the taxpayer have been brushed aside with very little discussion. "The question of whether a certain obligation is in reality capital stock or indebtedness and whether the increment therefrom is therefore a dividend or interest has often been the subject of tax litigation . . .

"After considering all of the criteria, we are convinced that the preferred stock, first issue, was clearly capital stock rather than indebtedness. It follows that the respondent was correct in refusing to allow petitioner any deduction for interest . . ." *Verifine Dairy Products Corporation of Sheboygan, Inc.*, 3 T.C. 269, 274-78 (1944). The court reached the same conclusion as to the preferred stock, second issue.

INTEREST ON OTHER FORMS OF INDEBTEDNESS. Where there is a true corporate indebtedness, it will be recognized as such regardless of the form it takes, and interest paid with respect thereto will be allowed as a deduction. "The payments . . . were not made to Taylor under the terms of the preferred stock certificates, but under the terms of the resolution of petitioner's board of directors adopted coincidentally with the issuance of the shares to him. From the wording of the resolution it is apparent that the corporation had to guarantee Taylor against the possibility that he might lose either principal or interest by reason of his surrender of the notes for second preferred stock.

If the corporation had sufficient earnings, Taylor was to get nothing under the terms of the collateral agreement. If the corporation did not have sufficient earnings, as in the taxable years before us, Taylor became entitled to payments which, when added to any earnings available for distribution to second preferred stockholders, would give him a 7 per cent return on $400,000. But any payments made to Taylor in years when the corporation did not have sufficient earnings to pay dividends to all of its second preferred stockholders were to be taken into consideration in later years when the earnings of the corporation justified the payment of back dividends due on its second preferred stock, and were to be charged against the dividends he would then be entitled to receive but for the prior payments. Taylor thus became entitled to certain benefits which were not enjoyed by other holders of petitioner's second preferred stock." *The Brush-Moore Newspapers, Inc.*, 37 B.T.A. 787, 791-92 (1938).

INTEREST ON INDEBTEDNESS NOT EVIDENCED BY INSTRUMENT. Even where the corporate debt is not evidenced by any instrument at all, it may still be recognized as a debt and interest thereon allowed as a deduction. "In determining the character of advances made by a stockholder to his corporation, it is proper to consider, among other things, the form of the transaction, the expressions of intent of the parties, the manner in which the advances were treated for bookkeeping purposes, the expectation or fact of repayment, and the adequacy of the capital previously invested in the corporation . . .

"After considering all of the relevant factors, we conclude that the advances . . . made . . . by or on behalf of its sole stockholder were intended as and were in fact loans.

"The evidence shows that when each of the advances was made . . . , the petitioner acknowledged receipt of the money as a loan. It also entered the amount of each advance in its books as a loan payable. The conduct of the parties at all times has been consistent with the petitioner's characterization of the advances as loans.

"It has been stipulated that, in each of the years 1944

through 1949, petitioner accrued on its books and deducted in its tax returns interest attributable to the loans payable.

"The petitioner repaid the advances in full in September 1949. . . .   .

"In our opinion, the fair and reasonable inference to be drawn from all of the facts is that the advances were loans." *Pier Management Corp.*, T.C. Memo., Docket ##50756, 50820, June 20, 1955.

Usually, though, the corporate taxpayer finds it far more difficult to obtain the benefit of the interest deduction where no instrument evidencing an indebtedness is in existence. "We are not convinced . . . that the disputed item should be considered as interest on an indebtedness. Among the criteria considered in reaching this conclusion are the following: O'Sullivan turned over to petitioner upon its incorporation the assets of a sole proprietorship having a net value a little in excess of $100,000 for $650 par value of common stock plus a so-called debt of $100,000; petitioner's total outstanding common stock amounted to only $971; even though O'Sullivan's associates subscribed to a little over $10,000 of preferred stock, it was obvious that petitioner . . . would require . . . more capital than that represented by its formal capital account . . . ; O'Sullivan's testimony that he intended to leave the . . . $100,000 in the corporation 'for the time being' as 'a set debt' indicates his recognition of petitioner's need for . . . this sum as capital; despite the entries on petitioner's books and tax returns, no note was ever issued . . . to evidence any 'debt'; no maturity date or method of repayment of the 'debt' was established . . . ; although . . . prior to . . . incorporation it was agreed that the rate of 'interest' . . . was 6 per cent, the amounts paid . . . were variable and were accrued and paid irregularly indicating that payments were made . . . when the corporate earnings and other circumstances would justify them; on at least two occasions O'Sullivan formally subordinated this 'debt' to all other creditors of petitioner in order not to affect the credit rating; and, finally, there was never any corporate action by petitioner's directors or stockholders . . . which confirmed the terms of any understanding . . .

that it would be indebted ... in the amount of $100,000." *Artistic Venetian Blind Corp.*, T.C. Memo., Docket #50420, Feb. 24, 1956.

Payments Claimed by Corporation as Other Expenses. Other types of payments to or for the benefit of stockholders, claimed by the corporation as deductible expenses but alleged by the Internal Revenue Service to be nondeductible dividends, have included compensation for services, rents, and royalties; the question is always one of fact, to be decided in the light of all the circumstances.

How such claims have, in many instances, been dealt with by the courts is exemplified in the following quotations:

COMPENSATION FOR SERVICES. "The petitioner claims that the distribution of surplus for the taxable years was a payment of commissions for work sent to the petitioner by its stockholders, and that such payments are deductible from gross income.

"We think the facts do not substantiate this contention. . . . [W]hen, at the end of the year, the balance of surplus was divided among all stockholders equally, regardless of the amount of business each had brought to the petitioner, there was no relation between such payments and 'personal services actually rendered.'" *United Tailors & Cleaners Co.*, 10 B.T.A. 172, 173-74 (1928).

RENTS. "After giving consideration to all of the testimony and the evidence in this case, it is our conclusion that all payments in excess of $700 per month made by petitioner corporation to G. L. Limerick, its chief stockholder, under the designation of rent were in truth and in fact distributions of dividends to Limerick and, therefore, are not deductible." *Limericks, Inc., et al.*, 7 T.C. 1129, 1136 (1946).

ROYALTIES. "No authority is needed for the statement that the mere designation of the payments as royalties does not legally characterize them as such. Nor does the fact that the written obligation of the petitioner might, at least under some circumstances, have compelled their payment by the petitioner.

... The question is whether, in fact, the payment was a deductible expense, as a royalty or otherwise, under the controlling statute. The answer to this question is, of course, purely factual.

"In our opinion, the contested payments were neither royalties nor ordinary and necessary expenses, and therefore, they are not deductible.

"The series of transactions between the two corporations and the stockholders . . . were obviously not at arm's length. . . . The series of transactions constituted integrated steps in a single plan and must be so considered for tax purposes, which resulted in an unnecessary 'obligation' upon the part of petitioner to pay the so-called overriding 'royalty.' . . . We think under the circumstances, the payment of this . . . 'royalty' was a distribution of corporate profits to the stockholders receiving the same and therefore was not a deductible expense, either as a 'royalty' or otherwise." *Ingle Coal Corp.*, 10 T.C. 1199, 1204, 1205 (1948).

OTHER EXPENSES. ". . . the corporation issued to Joel H. Anderson two checks in the amount of $1,250 each. Anderson, an attorney, represented petitioner and the corporation in the . . . Chancery suit.

". . . the corporation reimbursed petitioner . . . to cover court stenographic fees he advanced in connection with the Chancery suit. Since both petitioner and the corporation were parties to such suit, the expense incurred was for the benefit of both.

"While the record does not furnish any satisfactory basis upon which a precise allocation of these expenses can be made, we think that an allocation of an equal basis would be fair and just and have so found as a fact. Therefore, we hold that one half of the amount . . . paid out of corporate funds, constitute distributions essentially equivalent to a taxable dividend . . ." *Frank P. Holloway*, T.C. Memo., Docket #21532, Dec. 12, 1951.

Conclusion

As the foregoing has shown, the "essentially equivalent to a dividend" theory embraces a multitude of factual situations and may cause a stockholder to be subjected to a tax liability other than was contemplated and, in certain circumstances, may deprive the corporation distributor of anticipated tax benefits by reason of the disallowance of claimed deductions from income. Hence, the basic problem and its many facets demand minute consideration whenever a corporation makes a payment or transfer of property to or for the benefit of one or more of its stockholders.

Chapter 3

THE CASES

The question whether a particular payment (or transfer of property) is "essentially equivalent to a dividend" or "has the effect of a dividend" has been before the courts in a great number of different circumstances. The arguments considered in all significant cases involving this question, and the courts' holdings as to all such arguments, have been digested and are presented in this chapter, classified under the headings and subheadings listed below:

Part II. DEDUCTIBILITY BY CORPORATION

A. PAYMENTS CLAIMED AS INTEREST

Use of the Digests. After scanning the foregoing classification of court decisions dealing with the question of what constitutes a distribution "essentially equivalent to a dividend," the digests of those decisions dealing most directly with the issue under consideration should be read. This will make it possible to select for reading and study all those cases which may be in point.

Taxpayer's Position   *Court's Holding*

Part I. TAXABILITY TO STOCKHOLDER

A. Distributions in Partial or Complete Liquidation
   1. Alleged Contraction of Business

Proceeds were from the sale of stock to the corporation.

Corporate ownership and control remained substantially unchanged; no contraction of the business was contemplated; the shareholder needed money to pay his taxes; there was an immense amount of earnings and profits which were available for distribution; hence, it was found that the proceeds were essentially dividends.

Taxpayer's Position	*Court's Holding*

A, 1. ALLEGED CONTRACTION OF BUSINESS—*Continued*

	Wilson v. United States, 257 F.2d 534 (2d Cir., 1958).
Payment was in partial liquidation of the corporation.	There was no contraction of the business; capitalization was immediately restored to its former amount by the capitalization of earnings; distribution was pro rata; there was no business purpose for the redemption; hence, distribution was essentially a dividend. *E. H. Stolz,* 30 T.C. 530 (1958), *app. (T) pending,* 5th Cir.
Distribution in redemption was made to distribute capital no longer required in the business.	Distribution was pro rata and did not effect or coincide with any contraction of the business or of the capital structure; hence, distribution was a dividend. *Kessner v. Commissioner,* 248 F.2d 943 (3d Cir., 1957).
The original purpose for which the stock was issued had been satisfied.	Not shown to be a fact. *Towers, et al. v. Commissioner,* 247 F.2d 233 (2d Cir., 1957).
The capital represented by the stock redeemed was no longer needed by the company in its operation.	This is a sound reason, but in the instant case not supported by the facts. *Towers, et al. v. Commissioner, supra.*
Distributions to the sole taxpayer-stockholder upon purchase and retirement of one half of his shares were of capital assets; a legitimate business purpose existed for such distributions, which were made pur-	Although some of the corporation's properties were sold, about 90% were retained in the active business, and no plan of contraction was shown; the corporation had paid practically no dividends; accumulated

Taxpayer's Position

suant to a plan of contraction of the business; therefore, the payments constituted a partial liquidation and were not essentially equivalent to a dividend.

Payment was a return of capital pursuant to a corporate resolution to reduce the corporation's stated capital.

A distribution of stock of other corporations with contemporaneous reduction in par value of stock of distributor was a partial liquidation.

Distribution in redemption of preferred stock was a partial liquidation.

Distribution was in partial liquidation of the corporation.

Court's Holding

earnings were sufficient to cover the payment made; whether or not the action of the board of directors was in good faith is not an important factor; the net effect of the distribution was a taxable dividend. *Earl v. Woodlaw*, 245 F.2d 119 (9th Cir., 1957).

The distribution was a dividend. *Joseph H. Miller*, 26 T.C. 115 (1956).

Distribution was a dividend. A mere recapitalization or reduction in par value of capital stock, does not, in itself, constitute a partial liquidation. *Avco Manufacturing Corp.*, 25 T.C. 975 (1956), *remanded only to recompute overpayment*, — F.2d — (2d Cir., 1957).

There was no contraction or restriction in the scope of activities, initiative for the distribution came from the stockholder, who was in need of cash; there was no change in ownership; corporation had a poor dividend record; hence, distribution was essentially a dividend. *Rockwell Spring & Axle Co. v. Granger*, 140 F. Supp. 390 (D.C.Pa., 1956).

Distribution was not part of a planned series of distributions to be made in the process of liquidation, and no partial liq-

Taxpayer's Position	*Court's Holding*

A, 1. ALLEGED CONTRACTION OF BUSINESS—*Continued*

	uidation was effected by the distribution; no stock was cancelled or redeemed; hence, distribution was a dividend. *Ronning v. United States,* — F. Supp.—(D.C.Minn., 1956).
Distribution was made in redemption of stock at par, in a partial liquidation resulting from a contraction of the corporation's business.	Corporation had sold one of its divisions for cash, thereby decreasing its working capital needs; number of employees had been reduced; building space required for operations was reduced substantially; there was a contraction of the business and the distribution credited against advances received by taxpayers from corporation was not a dividend. *Sam Rosania, et ano.,* T.C. Memo., Docket #56511, May 14, 1956.
Distribution was in partial liquidation.	Corporation had manifest a continuing intention to liquidate, had ceased business activity, and was liquidating its assets; therefore, each distribution was a partial liquidation, not a dividend. *Maguire v. Commissioner,* 222 F.2d 472 (7th Cir., 1955).
Distribution in redemption of stock was made in partial liquidation.	Corporation had undergone a consistent pattern of declining business accompanied by a gradual disposal of assets; hence, not a dividend. *Paul J. McDaniel,* 25 T.C. 276 (1955).

Taxpayer's Position

Partial redemption of stock was authorized because of a contraction in the business of the corporation.

Distribution was in partial liquidation.

Distribution in kind in redemption of stock resulted in a contraction of the corporation's business.

Pro rata redemption was occasioned by a contraction in the business.

There was a bona fide partial liquidation of the corporation, where operating assets were distributed pro rata in partial redemption of stock and the corporation retained the real estate and the contracts

Court's Holding

On the facts, the payments for the stock constituted a partial liquidation, not a dividend. *Atlantic National Bank of Jacksonville v. Fahs,* — F. Supp. — (D.C.Fla., 1955).

Redemption substantially altered proportionate ownership of corporation; bank loan could be obtained only if preferred stock was retired; payments for redemption were charged to preferred stock account; hence, distribution was in partial liquidation and not a dividend. *Jones v. Griffin,* 216 F.2d 885 (10th Cir., 1954).

This is a sound reason; hence, distribution was not a dividend. *Commissioner v. Sullivan,* 210 F.2d 607 (5th Cir., 1954).

Nominal diminution in the size of the business is not a contraction of the business; hence, redemption was essentially equivalent to a dividend. *Estate of Chandler, et al. v. Commissioner,* 228 F.2d 909 (6th Cir., 1956).

The distribution was not essentially equivalent to a dividend. *Estate of Vannie E. Cook,* T.C. Memo., Docket ##35815, *et al.,* Aug. 23, 1954.

Taxpayer's Position   *Court's Holding*

A, 1. ALLEGED CONTRACTION OF BUSINESS—*Continued*

with respect to the operating assets.

Distribution in redemption of stock inherited from only other shareholder was a distribution in partial liquidation, as stock redeemed must be regarded as that of deceased stockholder.

Not substantiated, as stock redeemed was inherited prior to the redemption, after which the relationship of the sole stockholder to the corporation remained unchanged. Corporation had large surplus; no plan of liquidation or contraction of business; and redemption had no business purpose. *Commissioner v. Roberts*, 203 F.2d 304 (4th Cir., 1953).

Distribution was in partial liquidation resulting from a contraction of the business.

Corporation had a liberal dividend record; partial liquidation was caused by a contraction of the business which subsequently led to a cessation of business; hence, distribution was not a dividend. *Favrot v. Scofield*, — F. Supp. — (D.C. Tex., 1953).

Pro rata distribution in redemption of part of original issue stock was made soon after incorporation, as the need for cash capital had declined because of abandonment of original purpose underlying formation of the corporation.

This is a real business purpose for the redemption, as it represents a contraction of the purpose underlying the formation of the corporation; hence, not a dividend. *Stanley Sagner*, T.C. Memo., Docket #37089, Nov. 30, 1953.

A change in the business of the corporation resulted in a decrease in the need for cash capital; hence, a redemption of

Corporation's need for cash had declined as a result of the cancellation of its franchise, and it acted prudently and with

Taxpayer's Position	*Court's Holding*
part of its stock was made for a business purpose.	a business purpose in redeeming part of its capital stock; hence, distribution was not essentially equivalent to a dividend. *Clarence R. O'Brion, et ux.,* T.C. Memo., Docket #24050, Nov. 30, 1951.
Distribution was occasioned by reduction in operations (a) because of war conditions and shortage of necessary materials, making such operations unprofitable, and (b) because principal building owned by the corporation was damaged by fire, making facilities inadequate to carry on certain operations, thereby reducing the amount of capital required by the corporation.	This was a bona fide contraction of business operations and consequent reduction in capital used. Company had a real and legitimate purpose for reducing its outstanding capital stock, and redemption was not made at such time and in such manner as to be essentially equivalent to the distribution of a taxable dividend. *J. W. Imler,* 11 T.C. 836 (1948).
Distribution was made in partial liquidation solely for the purpose of utilizing the corporate assets more efficiently.	A sound reason for a partial liquidation; hence, distribution was not essentially equivalent to a dividend. *L. M. Lockhart,* 8 T.C. 436 (1947).
Redemption by subsidiary was dictated by reasonable business needs and was a partial liquidation.	No liquidation of any part of business; events indicated business would increase; prior decline in business was accompanied by increase in cash and liquid assets; parent wanted cash; earnings were three times the amount paid; price was not fair market value; hence, essentially equivalent to a dividend. *Pullman, Inc.,* 8 T.C. 292 (1947).

Taxpayer's Position   *Court's Holding*

A, 1. ALLEGED CONTRACTION OF BUSINESS—*Continued*

Distributions upon retirement of one half of corporation's preferred stock were not in partial liquidation as there was no contraction of business, corporation was in fact expanding and statute is inapplicable where transaction is not in effect liquidating. (Under pre-1942 Act, gain on partial liquidation was treated as short term.)

Business purpose and corporate intent are irrelevant as statute applies, not to a distribution in liquidation of a corporation or its business, but to a distribution in cancellation of a part of its stock; held a partial liquidation. *Stern v. Harrison,* 152 F.2d 321 (7th Cir., 1945).

Distributions were not in partial liquidation as corporation did not intend to curtail its normal operations. (Under pre-1942 Act, gain on partial liquidation was treated as short term.)

Motives of corporation are immaterial as the effect of the transactions must be determined by their substance; held a partial liquidation. *Yankey, et al. v. Commissioner,* 151 F.2d 650 (10th Cir., 1945).

Amounts were distributed in partial liquidation of the corporation and were not taxable as dividends because they were not paid from earnings and surplus.

The stockholder failed to show that the capital of the corporation was in any way contracted or impaired by the distributions made to him pursuant to a plan of liquidation which was never completed; therefore, taxpayer did not overcome the presumption that the distributions were made from earnings rather than from capital. *Jones v. Dawson,* 148 F.2d 87 (10th Cir., 1945).

Distribution was occasioned by an abandonment of plans to expand plant facilities in view of a contraction of the corporation's business and a plan of

In the circumstances, a sound reason for the redemption; hence, distribution was not a dividend. *Samuel A. Upham,* 4 T.C. 1120 (1945).

Taxpayer's Position	*Court's Holding*
ultimate liquidation, thereby leaving the company with excess capital.	
Distribution was in partial liquidation as there was a contraction of the business.	Stock was retired for sound business reasons—abandonment of unprofitable activities —and was not a cloak for the distribution of earnings. Long record of substantial cash dividends is impressive. *Heber Scowcroft Investment Co., et al.*, T.C. Memo., Docket ##5393, *et al.*, June 28, 1945.
Distributions were in partial liquidation.	Not substantiated; there was no business reason for the distribution as there was no decrease in business as a result of the redemption; hence, a dividend. *United National Corp. v. Commissioner*, 143 F.2d 580 (9th Cir., 1944).
The redemptions at par of that part of two issues of preferred stock originally issued at par for cash were necessitated by a contraction of business and were not a dividend.	The shares were originally issued for a business purpose, and the redemption thereof was not equivalent to a dividend. *De Nobili Cigar Co. v. Commissioner*, 143 F.2d 436 (2d Cir., 1944).
Distributions made after a reduction in par value constituted a liquidating dividend.	There was no intent to liquidate or to curtail activities; there were sufficient earnings; hence, a dividend. *Wilcox, et al. v. Commissioner*, 137 F.2d 136 (9th Cir., 1943).
Payment was received as a distribution in partial liquidation.	The corporation continued to operate profitably and there was no policy to contract; there

Taxpayer's Position   *Court's Holding*

A, 1. ALLEGED CONTRACTION OF BUSINESS—*Continued*

was a large surplus, earnings and profits accumulated since 1913 exceeded the amount distributed; there was no decline in corporate business and no proof that capital was excessive; no prudent business reason to reduce capital appeared; there was nothing to indicate that a winding up of business was contemplated; hence, distribution of a dividend was effected. *Rheinstrom v. Conner,* 125 F.2d 790 (6th Cir., 1942).

Redemption of stock by banking corporation was occasioned by decrease in capital requirements due to decrease in demand for loans.

A sound business reason for a redemption; hence, distribution was not essentially equivalent to a dividend. *John P. Elton,* 47 B.T.A. 111 (1942).

Redemption was accomplished to distribute idle funds originally set aside for expansion plans which had subsequently been dropped.

On the basis of the facts, distribution was a dividend. *E. M. Peet, et ano.,* 43 B.T.A. 852 (1941).

Distribution was partial liquidation as there was a contraction of business.

Major part of capitalization represented prior earnings; only two prior cash dividends; proportional ownership unchanged; no policy of contraction; initiated by stockholder needing cash; continued operation at a profit; therefore, distribution was essentially equivalent to a dividend. *Flanagan v. Helvering,* 116 F.2d 937 (D.C. Cir., 1940).

Taxpayer's Position	*Court's Holding*
Distribution was made in connection with the reduction of capital of a bank and was a partial liquidation.	On the facts the distribution was not essentially equivalent to a dividend. *Kelly v. Commissioner*, 97 F.2d 915 (2d Cir., 1938).
Pro rata redemption of preferred stock due to decrease in corporation's working capital requirements for the future.	On the facts redemption was a distribution in partial liquidation. *Rockwood v. Commissioner*, 82 F.2d 359 (7th Cir., 1936).
Redemption of preferred shares for cash immediately after receipt of stock dividend was merely a return of capital, as capital was not needed in business.	Sufficient to justify treating redemption as mere device for distribution of earnings and therefore a dividend. *Arthur M. Godwin*, 34 B.T.A. 485 (1936).
Redemption of a portion of stock previously issued as a stock dividend was occasioned by a decline in business of the corporation.	Redemption was not essentially equivalent to a dividend. *Cordingley v. Commissioner*, 78 F.2d 118 (1st Cir., 1935).
Redemption was occasioned by a substantial shrinkage in the business.	Not essentially equivalent to a dividend. *Commissioner v. Champion*, 78 F.2d 513 (6th Cir., 1935).
Redemption of stock previously issued as a stock dividend was occasioned by a decline in corporate earnings.	A legitimate business purpose and, therefore, not a dividend. *Commissioner v. Quackenbos*, 78 F.2d 156 (2d Cir., 1935).
Redemption of stock previously issued as a stock dividend was to effect partial liquidation of the business because of unfavorable conditions affecting it.	Not proved; other evidence showed a unified plan to distribute surplus. *Adler v. Commissioner*, 77 F.2d 733 (5th Cir., 1935).

Taxpayer's Position	*Court's Holding*

A, 1. ALLEGED CONTRACTION OF BUSINESS—*Continued*

Distribution in redemption of stock previously issued as a stock dividend was made after it was determined not to enter an affiliated field, thereby releasing capital for distribution in a partial liquidation.	Distribution was in partial liquidation, as there was no plan to distribute earnings; hence, not a dividend. *Alfred E. Fuhlage,* 32 B.T.A. 222 (1935).
Distribution in exchange for part of outstanding stock was one in partial liquidation and, hence, not essentially equivalent to a dividend.	The corporation was sharply contracting its business; the redeemed stock was not originally issued with a view toward ultimate redemption; hence, the distribution was not essentially equivalent to a dividend. *Babson v. Commissioner,* 70 F.2d 304 (7th Cir., 1934).
There was a genuine contraction of the business.	Sufficient and compelling reason for redemption. *Babson v. Commissioner, supra.*
Distribution in redemption of stock was a partial liquidation accomplished for the purpose of disposing of certain assets not necessary in the business.	Not controlling in the circumstances. *Hyman v. Commissioner,* 71 F.2d 342 (D.C. Cir., 1934).
Distributions were in partial liquidation.	Distribution was intended to be in partial liquidation, consequent upon the sale of the principal asset; hence, distribution was in partial liquidation; not essentially equivalent to a dividend. *Tyson, et al. v. White,* — F. Supp. — (D.C. Mass., 1933).

Taxpayer's Position	*Court's Holding*
Payment was of an ordinary dividend declared by the Board of Directors, capital was not impaired, and it was a dividend under the applicable statute.	Payment was of a liquidating dividend as all assets, except cash, were previously sold and Directors intended a distribution in partial liquidation. *Tootle v. Commissioner,* 58 F.2d 576 (8th Cir., 1932).

A. DISTRIBUTIONS IN PARTIAL OR COMPLETE LIQUIDATION—*Continued*
   2. STOCK RETIREMENT—NON PRO RATA

Distributions in redemption of preferred stock were disproportionate and changed the interests of the stockholders.	This is a sound reason. Here the stockholders received different payments than would have been received as dividends, and their interest in the corporation was substantially changed; hence, the distribution was not essentially equivalent to a dividend. *Northup v. United States,* 240 F.2d 304 (2d Cir., 1957).
The stockholder surrendered a portion of his stock for redemption, and thus reduced his interest in the corporation; therefore, the distribution was not pro rata and not taxable as a dividend.	The surrender of a portion of the taxpayer's stock for redemption whereby his holding of voting stock was reduced to less than half, thus depriving him of control of the corporation, constituted a capital transaction. *George F. Ferris v. United States,* 135 F. Supp. 286 (Ct. Cl., 1955).
The payment made was in redemption of preferred stock.	Based upon the holding of a prior case, *Jones v. Griffin,* and the amount received by the stockholder being vastly different from what it would have been had a dividend been paid; and the resulting proportionate

Taxpayer's Position   *Court's Holding*

A, 2. STOCK RETIREMENT—NON PRO RATA—*Continued*

	ownership of stock being drastically changed; the payment was in redemption and not essentially equivalent to a taxable dividend. *Leake v. Jones,* — F. Supp. — (D.C.Okla., 1955).
Distribution was highly disproportionate to the stockholdings.	A significant factor; held, no dividend. *Rosemary Case Weir, Trust for,* T.C. Memo., Docket ##31579, *et al.,* June 25, 1952.
Stock redemption was not pro rata.	Might be a cogent reason, but facts not proved. *Boyle v. Commissioner,* 187 F.2d 557 (3d Cir., 1951).
The payment was out of what had been capital and was not a dividend.	Surplus had been transferred to capital and later retransferred to surplus, and the distribution thereof was equivalent to a dividend, the stockholder's proportionate interest in the corporation remaining unchanged. *Sheehan v. Dana,* 163 F.2d 316 (8th Cir., 1947).
The redemption was not pro rata.	Not determinative. *A. C. Monk,* T.C. Memo., Docket #9511, Aug. 28, 1947.
There was a considerable reduction of stockholder's proportionate stock interest as a result of the redemption.	Good reason but not conclusive in itself that redemption was not a dividend. *A. C. Monk, supra.*
Proportionate ownership of shares was changed, albeit fractionally.	A significant factor. *Estate of Henry Vernon Foster,* T.C. Memo., Docket #110891, Mar. 22, 1944.

Taxpayer's Position	*Court's Holding*
Distribution was not pro rata and the company acquired no stock from other stockholders.	A significant factor. *Estate of Henry Vernon Foster, supra.*
The reduction in common stock gave the preferred stockholders a larger share of the corporation on liquidation.	A circumstance to be considered, but not conclusive; reduction of stock was proportionate. *Rheinstrom v. Conner,* 125 F.2d 790 (6th Cir., 1942).
The corporation did not purchase stock from its shareholders pro rata.	Absence of pro rata redemption does not remove the transaction from being essentially equivalent to a dividend if other facts and circumstances show that it was. *R. W. Creech,* 46 B.T.A. 93 (1942).
Distribution was not a dividend as it was not in proportion to stockholdings.	Distribution of profits on a basis other than stockholdings can still be a dividend. *Juneau Dairies, Inc.,* 44 B.T.A. 759 (1941).
Redemption was not made pro rata among the preferred stockholders.	Not a controlling factor. *William Swindells, et ux.,* 44 B.T.A. 336 (1941).
Redemption was not pro rata.	Not controlling. Immaterial. *Hirsch v. Commissioner,* 124 F.2d 24 (9th Cir., 1941).
Absence of plan to avoid tax; non pro rata redemption; small percentage of stock redeemed; payment of substantial cash dividends; lack of complete control by stockholders; no debts due from stockholder.	Evidence that transaction did not constitute dividend payment. *H. F. Asmussen,* 36 B.T.A. 878 (1937).

Taxpayer's Position	*Court's Holding*

A, 2. STOCK RETIREMENT—NON PRO RATA—*Continued*

Redemption was not pro rata and affected only taxpayer.	Not determinative. *J. Natwick*, 36 B.T.A. 866 (1937).
Redemptions not pro rata among all stockholders.	Not determinative of whether distribution was a dividend. *Adler v. Commissioner*, 77 F.2d 733 (5th Cir., 1935).

A. DISTRIBUTIONS IN PARTIAL OR COMPLETE LIQUIDATION—*Continued*

   3. STOCK RETIREMENT ALLEGED TO BE FOR BENEFIT OF CORPORATION

Cancellation of stockholder's indebtedness to corporation by redeeming part of his stockholdings was accomplished for the purpose of improving the appearance of the corporation's balance sheet for credit purposes.	The mere existence of a single bona fide corporate purpose will not, standing alone, conclusively determine that the transaction is not essentially equivalent to the distribution of a taxable dividend. Other factors must be considered. *Fewell v. United States*, 255 F.2d 496 (5th Cir., 1958).
It was to the advantage of the company to terminate the charge for dividends accruing on this stock.	Not shown that any such advantage was substantial or material. *Towers, et al. v. Commissioner*, 247 F.2d 233 (2d Cir., 1957).
There was no dividend distribution as the shares were redeemed because the franchise grantor required that a trust not own shares and that the remaining shareholders retain their same proportionate interests.	The evidence did not sustain that the franchise grantor specified the requirements; aside from eliminating the trust, identical interests of the shareholders were retained, a strong circumstance to be considered; no dividends had been declared and accumulated earnings were distributed; no corporate purpose was present and stockholders were benefited, which

Taxpayer's Position

Court's Holding

is highly persuasive; there was no contraction of corporate business, nor was one contemplated; hence, the distribution was essentially equivalent to a dividend. *Phelps v. Commissioner*, 247 F.2d 156 (9th Cir., 1957).

Distribution was made in redemption of stock for the purpose of eliminating one stockholder, a trust, so as to comply with a franchise agreement.

Redemption of the trust's shares reduced the interest of the trust in the corporation and represented a step in a plan to eliminate the trust as a stockholder; hence, as to the trust the distribution was not a dividend; as to the other stockholders, they retained their same interest and redemption of their stock did not result in a curtailment of the business; hence, as to them the distribution was essentially a dividend. *Jackson Howell, et al.*, 26 T.C. 846 (1956), *aff'd sub nom.*, *Phelps v. Commissioner, supra.*

Distributions out of profits made to a former stockholder as part consideration for the sale of his stock to the manager of the corporations were not dividends to the manager, as they were made part of an agreement, the main purpose of which was to protect the corporation's main asset, an automobile franchise.

In the circumstances the payments were not dividends. *Tucker v. Commissioner*, 226 F.2d 177 (8th Cir., 1955).

Payments were made in redemption of preferred stock;

The transaction was for the purpose of permitting the cor-

Taxpayer's Position   *Court's Holding*

A, 3. STOCK RETIREMENT ALLEGED TO BE FOR BENEFIT OF CORPORATION—*Continued*

redemption of the stock was necessary to further the business of the corporation.

poration to obtain bank loans, the amounts paid were charged to the preferred stock account and not to accumulated earnings and profits; it bore a marked relation to the business of the corporation, and it resulted in changes of stockholder's proportionate interests; hence, it was a redemption and not essentially equivalent to a dividend. *Jones v. Griffin,* 216 F.2d 885 (10th Cir., 1954).

Distribution was in redemption of stock which was issued to stockholder in settlement of a note and subsequently redeemed, all for the purpose of improving the corporation's credit position.

Distribution was not actually pro rata, and the net effect test does not preclude the consideration of a legitimate corporate purpose for a redemption in determining whether or not the distribution was essentially equivalent to a dividend; here, it was not. *Keefe v. Cote,* 213 F.2d 651 (1st Cir., 1954).

Distribution in kind in redemption of stock relieved the corporation of properties which it did not need in its business and some of which it did not use.

This is a sound reason; hence, distribution was not a dividend. *Commissioner v. Sullivan,* 210 F.2d 607 (5th Cir., 1954).

Distribution in kind of certain oil properties and equipment in redemption of stock was made to protect remaining oil leases.

This is a sound reason; hence, distribution was not a dividend. *Commissioner v. Sullivan, supra.*

Transfer of stock to corporation in settlement of an in-

The desired improvement in credit was effected; taxpayer

Taxpayer's Position

Court's Holding

debtedness was a sale of stock made solely for the purpose of improving the corporation's credit position.

received no cash; there was no general corporate distribution; hence, transaction was not essentially equivalent to the distribution of a dividend. *Ada Murphy McFarlane,* T.C. Memo., Docket #37563, May 14, 1954.

Corporation had a consistent policy in the past to buy its stock where the purchase could be made for a price considerably below book value.

A significant factor; purchase held not to be essentially equivalent to a dividend. *Trust for Rosemary Case Weir,* T.C. Memo., Docket ##31579, *et al.,* June 15, 1952.

Redemption of part of the outstanding preferred stock was for the purpose of reducing the corporation's annual liability thereon.

This is a sound reason for the redemption in view of the fact that taxpayer owned no common stock. *Marie W. F. Nugent-Head Trust,* 17 T.C. 817 (1951).

Redemption of part of majority stockholder's stock to cancel his indebtedness to corporation was solely to improve corporation's credit rating.

Definite and valid business purpose for redemption. *Isaac C. Eberly,* T.C. Memo., Docket #26459, Dec. 13, 1951.

Purchase and retirement of all the stock of a stockholder at a price in excess of the fair market of stock were accomplished to avoid a threatened receivership action by stockholder and therefore was not a dividend to the remaining stockholders.

In the circumstances there was a good business reason for the purchase and no part of the purchase price was a dividend. *Fred F. Fischer,* T.C. Memo., Docket #8737, May 8, 1947.

Redemption was accomplished for financial reasons as the corporation's ability to bor-

This is a sound reason. *A. C. Monk,* T.C. Memo., Docket #9511, Aug. 28, 1947.

Taxpayer's Position	*Court's Holding*

A, 3. STOCK RETIREMENT ALLEGED TO BE FOR BENEFIT OF CORPORATION—*Continued*

row from banks was being threatened.	
Distribution was in redemption of stock which was originally issued for a bona fide corporate purpose and not with the intent to evade tax.	The fact that stock was originally issued for bona fide reasons does not affect a distribution of earnings to redeem such stock; hence, distribution was a dividend. *Kirschenbaum v. Commissioner,* 155 F.2d 23 (2d Cir., 1946).
Distributions upon retirement of preferred stock were not in partial liquidation, since funds were derived from bank loans as part of a plan to reduce interest rate on corporation's outstanding obligations. (Under pre-1942 Act, gain on partial liquidation was treated as short term.)	Statute makes no distinction between such distributions whether from borrowed funds or corporate surplus; held a partial liquidation. *Stern v. Harrison,* 152 F.2d 321 (7th Cir., 1945).
Funds received from sale of stocks to corporation, where taxpayer borrowed money and temporarily purchased stock to prevent liquidation by majority stockholder (principal debtor) when corporation financially unable to purchase, were not dividends.	In substance, acquisition of stock was on behalf of corporation for expediency and transaction was not "essentially equivalent to a dividend." *Fox v. Harrison,* 145 F.2d 521 (7th Cir., 1944).
Redemption was for the purpose of improving the financial standing of the company.	Not substantiated; the net effect of the transaction was the distribution of a dividend. *Hirsch v. Commissioner,* 124 F.2d 24 (9th Cir., 1941).

Taxpayer's Position	*Court's Holding*
Redemption was for the purpose of improving the corporation's financial and business standing.	Not substantiated. *William Swindells, et ux.*, 44 B.T.A. 336 (1941).
The pro rata redemption of a portion of the preferred stock was for the reasonable needs of the business in that it enabled the corporation to collect debts from the stockholders.	The primary purpose of such a redemption is for the benefit of the stockholders; hence, essentially equivalent to a dividend. *A. E. Levit, et al.*, 43 B.T.A. 1077 (1941).
Redemption of stock was made to obtain better credit rating because of elimination of indebtedness from stockholders and officers.	Legitimate business reason for redemption. *Bona Allen, Jr.*, 41 B.T.A. 206 (1940).
Corporation's purchase of its own shares was to avoid a forced liquidation by trustee unwilling to accept risks of the particular business.	The distribution was not made at such time and in such manner as to be essentially equivalent to a dividend. *Clara Louise Flinn, et al.*, 37 B.T.A. 1085 (1938).
Distribution in redemption was motivated by pressure from creditor banks.	Evidence does not show how company's financial position would be improved. Large withdrawals against substantial earnings, sparsity of cash dividends, expansion of business, and fact that taxpayer's position as majority stockholder was unchanged support finding of a dividend. *J. Natwick*, 36 B.T.A. 866 (1937).
Distribution in redemption of stock was made only after plans for expansion were abandoned, leaving surplus capital in the corporation.	Notwithstanding the fact that profits were accumulated for expansion, it does not follow that the transaction was not a distribution essentially equiv-

Taxpayer's Position   *Court's Holding*

A, 3. STOCK RETIREMENT ALLEGED TO BE FOR BENEFIT OF CORPORATION—*Continued*

alent to a dividend. *McGuire v. Commissioner*, 84 F.2d 431 (7th Cir., 1936).

Issue of preferred stock was in payment of dividends due; its subsequent redemption was only to conserve cash for immediate corporate needs.

The stock was held for more than two years before it was redeemed; the redemption effected a reduction in capital; hence, redemption was not made at such time or in such manner as to be essentially equivalent to a dividend. *Louis Rorimer*, 27 B.T.A. 871 (1933).

Distribution was made in redemption of stock for the purpose of adjusting the corporation's capital structure so as to satisfy bank requirement for a loan.

The redemption was not pro rata; there was a valid business reason for the redemption; hence, distribution was not a dividend. *Harry A. Koch*, 26 B.T.A. 1025 (1932).

Distribution was in redemption made to satisfy a creditor bank's request for an improved financial statement.

The corporation adjusted its capital structure to comply with the demand of the bank and enabled the corporation to continue its line of credit; hence, distribution was not a dividend. *Harry A. Koch, supra.*

A. DISTRIBUTIONS IN PARTIAL OR COMPLETE LIQUIDATION—*Continued*
    4. STEP IN AN ALLEGED COMPLETE LIQUIDATION

Distribution in redemption of preferred stock was a step in carrying out an intent to liquidate.

While the evidence appears undisputed that there was an intent to liquidate, subjective motives cannot overcome objective facts which establish that the net effect of the distribution was essentially equivalent to a dividend. *Rockwell*

Taxpayer's Position	*Court's Holding*
	Spring & Axle Co. v. Granger, 140 F. Supp. 390 (D.C.Pa., 1956).
Distribution was in partial liquidation as one of several distributions in a complete liquidation.	Corporation had manifest a continuing intention to liquidate, had ceased business activity, and was liquidating its assets; therefore, each distribution was a partial liquidation, not a dividend. *Maguire v. Commissioner,* 222 F.2d 472 (7th Cir., 1955).
Payments were distributions in liquidation.	The account of the corporation corroborates the taxpayer's contention; hence, there was no taxable dividend distribution. *Rota-Cone Oil Field Operating Co.,* T.C. Memo., Docket ##6808–9, July 29, 1947, *aff'd on other issues,* 171 F.2d 219 (10th Cir., 1948).
Payment was made as one of a series in complete liquidation of the corporation in accordance with a bona fide plan.	The final plan of liquidation was never agreed upon, and none of stock was cancelled or redeemed in accordance with a bona fide plan; hence, the distribution was taxable as a dividend. *Jones v. Dawson,* 148 F.2d 87 (10th Cir., 1945).
Distribution was one of a series in complete cancellation and redemption of all the stock of the corporation.	Distribution was as alleged; hence, not a dividend. *R. D. Merrill Co.,* 4 T.C. 955 (1945).
Corporate distribution made after reduction in the capital stock of the corporation was a capital distribution made in	There must be a manifest intention to liquidate and a continuing purpose to terminate and dissolve the corporation in

Taxpayer's Position   *Court's Holding*

A, 4. STEP IN AN ALLEGED COMPLETE LIQUIDATION—*Continued*

partial liquidation of the corporation.

order that a corporate distribution be determined nontaxable. In this instance the distribution was a taxable dividend. *Beretta v. Commissioner,* 141 F.2d 452 (5th Cir., 1944).

The distribution was in partial liquidation under a plan of complete liquidation, certain assets being retained by the corporation only to obtain a better price.

The distribution was not essentially equivalent to a dividend. *Bynum v. Commissioner,* 113 F.2d 1 (5th Cir., 1940).

Distribution in redemption of 40% of the stock on a pro rata basis was the first of a series of distributions in liquidation of the corporation.

Distribution was not made in the ordinary course of business and was not coupled with an intent to maintain the company as a going concern; hence, not essentially equivalent to a dividend. *Albert E. Perkins, et al.,* 36 B.T.A. 791 (1937).

Two distributions were made in the ordinary course of business and hence were taxable as dividends; the third distribution was in liquidation and constituted full payment for taxpayer's stock. (1926 Act, Section 216, provided that dividends were credited for the purpose of normal tax and, therefore, measured only the surtax; amounts distributed in liquidation were subject to both the normal and surtax.)

The fact that the distributions were called dividends by the directors of the corporation, and were made in part from earnings, and that some were made before the liquidation proceeding was commenced, is not controlling; all distributions were in liquidation. *Holmby v. Commissioner,* 83 F.2d 548 (9th Cir., 1936).

Taxpayer's Position	*Court's Holding*
There was a complete liquidation of the business and only the corporate shell was retained.	Corporation had disposed of all its assets and limited its activities to the conversion of some securities into cash; hence, distribution was not essentially equivalent to a dividend. *Ward M. Canaday, Inc. v. Commissioner*, 76 F.2d 278 (3d Cir., 1935).
Distribution was in partial liquidation and a step toward a complete liquidation of the corporation.	The business of the corporation had declined; key employees had died; its scope steadily narrowed; all activities were directed toward winding up with a minimum loss; hence, distribution was in partial liquidation and not a dividend. *Straub v. Commissioner*, 76 F.2d 388 (3d Cir., 1935).
Distributions were in complete liquidation of the corporation and not part of a reorganization which occurred prior to the liquidation.	On the facts the distribution was made in complete liquidation of the corporation, which occurred after the reorganization and which was not part of the reorganization; hence, distribution was not a dividend. *Rudolph Boehringer*, 29 B.T.A. 8 (1933).
Distribution of cash after sale by corporation of all its assets was one of a series of distributions in complete redemption of stock rather than the distribution of a dividend in the ordinary course of business (Commissioner).	The distribution was one of a series of distributions in complete cancellation of the corporation's stock; hence, not a dividend. *William H. Monk, Jr., et al.*, 29 B.T.A. 556 (1933).

Taxpayer's Position	*Court's Holding*

A, 4. STEP IN AN ALLEGED COMPLETE LIQUIDATION—*Continued*

Although payments to stockholders were made just prior to payment of a liquidating dividend, they were paid from earnings and were thus ordinary dividends. (1926 Act, Section 216, provided that dividends were credited for the purpose of normal tax and, therefore, measured only the surtax; amounts distributed in liquidation were subject both to the normal tax and to the surtax.)

What the directors may call a distribution does not alter its character; at the time of the distribution the corporation was not a going concern and dissolution was already under way; the distribution was very unusual and entirely outside the due course of the business of the corporation; it was, therefore, a liquidating dividend. *Gossett v. Commissioner,* 59 F.2d 365 (4th Cir., 1932).

Payment was not a distribution in liquidation, as the applicable section refers to distributions of capital while here there was a distribution of surplus.

"It must be clear that this dividend was never intended nor understood to be nor could be other than 'one of a series of distributions' in complete cancellation or redemption of all . . . of its stock." Hence, the distribution was in partial liquidation. *Tootle v. Commissioner,* 58 F.2d 576 (8th Cir., 1932).

Since the corporation was in the process of completely winding up, the distributions were in partial liquidation of the corporation.

Facts showed distribution to be one in partial liquidation, not essentially equivalent to a dividend. *Fred T. Wood,* 27 B.T.A. 162 (1932).

There was a distribution out of earnings and profits which constituted dividends not subject to normal tax.

Payment was made in the liquidation of the corporation; hence, it was not a distribution essentially equivalent to a dividend. *Hellwick v. Hellman,* 276 U.S. 233 (1928).

Taxpayer's Position   *Court's Holding*

A. DISTRIBUTIONS IN PARTIAL OR COMPLETE LIQUIDATION—*Continued*

    5. BUY-OUT OF ONE OR MORE OF SEVERAL STOCKHOLDERS

Distribution of debentures was in redemption of all the stock owned by taxpayer.

Securities received in exchange for the preferred stock more closely resembled preferred stock than debentures; payment was to be made solely out of earnings; hence, distribution was essentially a dividend. *Mary Duerr*, 30 T.C. 944 (1958).

Where a husband and wife owned all the shares of a corporation and the wife's shares were redeemed by the corporation, there was a partial liquidation giving rise to capital gain.

All of the shares of one stockholder were redeemed, and whether the shares were acquired by gift or otherwise, the complete redemption of one stockholder's shares is not a distribution essentially equivalent to a dividend. Even though the shares may have had a value greater than redemption price, that was immaterial, although it may have created a gift tax issue not before the court. *United States v. Summerfield*, 249 F.2d 446 (6th Cir., 1957).

Distribution was in redemption of part of taxpayer's stockholdings and was a step toward his complete withdrawal from the corporation.

The redemption resulted in a normal reduction of taxpayer's ownership position and rights in the corporation and was merely an attempt by the taxpayer to recoup his capital; it was a significant step in his withdrawal from the company; hence, distribution was not a dividend. *Estate of Lukens, et*

Taxpayer's Position   *Court's Holding*

A, 5. Buy-out of One or More of Several Stockholders—
Continued

                                      al. v. Commissioner, 246 F.2d
403 (3d Cir., 1957).

There was a complete liquidation of the old corporation, giving rise to capital gain, as a former 20% stockholder retained no interest in the new corporation.

It is not unusual in a reorganization for minority shareholders to liquidate their interests and withdraw; hence, there was a reorganization and the old corporation's distribution of its earnings and profits had the effect of a dividend distribution to the remaining 80% stockholders. *Liddon v. Commissioner*, 230 F.2d 304 (6th Cir., 1956).

Redemption in part and sale in part of preferred stock and a sale of all the common stock on the same day.

An over-all plan of the corporate stockholder to divest itself of all the stock it owned had the effect of a sale and not a distribution of a dividend. *Auto Finance Co. v. Commissioner*, 229 F.2d 318 (4th Cir., 1956).

Distribution was intended to redeem one stockholder's shares and not as a dividend distribution.

Amounts distributed were proportionate to stockholdings; corporation had funds available; hence, a dividend. *Edward Stevens*, T.C. Memo., Docket #53934, Dec. 28, 1955.

Payment was in redemption of all the shares of one stockholder and constitutes a partial liquidation giving rise to capital gain.

Although the stockholder sold one half of her shares three weeks before the other half was redeemed, the redemption was of all the shares of stockholders; hence, it was not essentially equivalent to a dividend,

Taxpayer's Position	*Court's Holding*
	as the taxpayer has a right to decrease taxes by adopting a particular method of transaction where another alternative method would increase tax liability. *Zenz v. Quinlivan*, 213 F.2d 914 (6th Cir., 1954).
Payments by corporation were made to the estate of a former stockholder to retire all the stock held by the estate and were not made to satisfy an obligation of the taxpayer.	Payments were in satisfaction of corporation's indebtedness and not that of taxpayer; hence, payments were not essentially equivalent to a dividend to taxpayer. *Ray Edenfield*, 19 T.C. 13 (1952).
Amounts were set aside in escrow to buy out stockholder per agreement.	Stockholder had no control of funds in escrow, and facts showed that amounts placed in escrow were to be used only for purchase of stock; hence, such funds were not essentially dividend distributions. *Frank E. Elliott*, T.C. Memo., Docket #29696, Oct. 28, 1952.
Distribution was a redemption as taxpayer did not retain any beneficial interest whatever in any stock of the corporation.	A decisive factor; hence, not a dividend. *Carter Tiffany*, 16 T.C. 1443 (1951).
Transfer of stock to corporation was a sale to the corporation for the purpose of paying stockholder's debt to the corporation and was not a redemption of the stock.	Transfers of stock in discharge of stockholder's debt to corporation were bona fide sales. Sales were not made pro rata but were the sale of all the shares of one stockholder. *Estate of Ira F. Searle, et al.*, T.C. Memo., Docket #24804, Oct. 31, 1950.

Taxpayer's Position   *Court's Holding*

A, 5. BUY-OUT OF ONE OR MORE OF SEVERAL STOCKHOLDERS—
Continued

Amounts received from corporation to which taxpayer-stockholder had sold all of its shares owned by him were instalments of sales price and not dividends, even though designated as "dividends" and paid at dates and in amounts corresponding to dividends.

Beneficial interest in prospective dividends was in corporation buying its own stock, and amounts received by selling stockholder were part of selling price and not dividends. *Levy v. United States,* 67 F. Supp. 958 (Ct. Cl., 1946).

Dividends were accounted for in reduction of sales price, under a contract providing for buy-out, over a period of time, of some stockholders by remain-stockholders and are not dividends to selling stockholders.

Fact that corporate distribution affected buyer's contractual obligations does not affect its character. As distribution was received by sellers as shareholders, it is a dividend. *Max Viault, et al.,* 36 B.T.A. 430 (1937).

Petitioner received a dividend to the extent of earnings and profits when he received liquid assets and not proceeds from the sale of his stock.

Evidence indicates that the several distributions were all part of the sale transaction; there is no indication that the liquid assets were received before the taxpayer ceased to be a stockholder or that the corporation ever declared or paid a dividend to him. *Philip D. C. Ball,* 27 B.T.A. 388 (1932), *aff'd on another issue sub nom., Von Weise v. Commissioner,* 69 F.2d 439 (8th Cir., 1934).

The company's payment for purchase of its shares from a stockholder was not dividends to the remaining stockholders.

The selling stockholder and not the remaining stockholders benefited from the payment, and hence, the payment was

Taxpayer's Position	*Court's Holding*
	not a dividend to the remaining stockholders. *J. S. Hatcher*, 18 B.T.A. 632 (1930); *George Youell*, 18 B.T.A. 599 (1929).

A. DISTRIBUTIONS IN PARTIAL OR COMPLETE LIQUIDATION—*Continued*
  6. STOCK PURCHASED BY CORPORATION AS TREASURY STOCK OR FOR RESALE

Stock was not cancelled but held as treasury stock.	Not controlling. *Wilson v. United States*, 257 F.2d 534 (2d Cir., 1958).
Redeemed stock held as treasury stock.	Of no particular significance, as taxpayers retained identical proportionate interests in corporation. *Thomas J. French, et al.*, 26 T.C. 263 (1956).
The corporation's purpose in purchasing some of the stockholder's shares was not to distribute earnings but to acquire stock which the corporation could use for resale to an employee.	The shares were purchased by the corporation for resale to an employee as an inducement to his continued employment; the proportionate interests of the shareholders were substantially altered; hence, there was no dividend distribution. *Smith v. United States*, 130 F. Supp. 586 (Ct. Cl., 1955).
No redemption inasmuch as stock redeemed was held by corporation in its treasury.	Does not prevent taxing as a dividend amount received for stock. *Boyle v. Commissioner*, 187 F.2d 557 (3d Cir., 1951).
Distribution represented proceeds from a bona fide sale of stock to the corporation, which needed it for a business purpose.	Corporation purchased stock so that it would be available for sale to employees; sale resulted in a substantial change in ownership; corporation had

Taxpayer's Position   *Court's Holding*

A, 6. STOCK PURCHASED BY CORPORATION AS TREASURY STOCK OR FOR
RESALE—*Continued*

	a liberal dividend record; hence, distribution was not a dividend. *Commissioner v. Snite,* 177 F.2d 819 (7th Cir., 1949).
The stock transferred to the corporation was not cancelled or redeemed but held as treasury stock.	Immaterial. *Wall v. United States,* 164 F.2d 462 (4th Cir., 1947).
Redeemed stock was, not cancelled but held as treasury stock.	Not conclusive. *A. C. Monk,* T.C. Memo., Docket #9511, Aug. 28, 1947.
Company purchased stock from sole stockholder for sale to key employees of its wholly owned subsidiary.	Sound business reason for the purchase. *Bernard R. Armour,* B.T.A. Memo., Docket #106256, Aug. 6, 1942.
The shares purchased by the corporation were not cancelled and retired but were retained in the treasury and subsequently used to collateralize a bank loan to the corporation.	A factor evidencing a purchase of stock by the corporation and not a dividend distribution. *R. W. Creech,* 46 B.T.A. 93 (1942).
Payments were proceeds from the sale of stock to the corporation and retained by it as treasury shares.	The stock was not retired but was retained as treasury stock; the reacquisition was not pro rata from the stockholders. There was a purchase and sale; hence, payments were not dividends. *Rollin C. Reynolds,* 44 B.T.A. 342 (1941).
The purpose of the preferred stock dividend was to make that stock available to younger executives; subsequent purchase of a portion thereof by	Valid business purpose present; hence, not a dividend. *H. F. Asmussen,* 36 B.T.A. 878 (1937).

Taxpayer's Position	*Court's Holding*

the corporation was to make such stock available for investment by employee associations.

Redeemed stock was held as treasury stock.	Not determinative. *J. Natwick*, 36 B.T.A. 866 (1937).

A. DISTRIBUTIONS IN PARTIAL OR COMPLETE LIQUIDATION—*Continued*

   7. REDEMPTION OF PREFERRED SHARES

Distribution was in redemption of all the outstanding preferred stock made pursuant to the provision of the stock which provided for annual redemption of such stock.	The repurchase of the long issued and outstanding preferred stock, originally issued for value, the terms of which specifically direct its retirement at a fixed price slightly above par upon the happening of certain events which actually occurred, is a factor which points to the existence of a business motive for the redemption; hence, distribution was not a dividend. *Bullock v. Commissioner*, 253 F.2d 715 (2d Cir., 1958).
Plan of reorganization called for issuance of bonds to taxpayer, but plan was changed and preferred stock was substituted for the bonds pursuant to a later agreement; payments were received in redemption of the preferred stock, and hence gave rise to gains taxable as capital gains.	Preferred shares were received from the successor corporation in lieu of bonds as provided in the original plan of reorganization; distributions made in redemption of preferred stock were partial liquidating distributions, and thus taxable as capital gain. *Callan Court Co., et al. v. Cobb*, — F. Supp. — (D.C.Ga., 1958).
Preferred stock redeemed was originally issued for notes which were accepted in lieu of a cash payment for salary, re-	On the facts, a tax on the distribution as a dividend would have the effect of taxing the salary twice, a result to be

Taxpayer's Position   *Court's Holding*

A, 7. REDEMPTION OF PREFERRED SHARES—*Continued*

ported as income upon receipt; therefore, to tax the redemption would have the effect of taxing twice what was in reality the payment of a salary.

avoided unless required by the express mandate of the taxing act. *Estate of Henry A. Golwynne,* 26 T.C. 1209 (1956).

The payment made was in redemption of preferred stock.

Based upon the holding of a prior case, *Jones v. Griffin,* 216 F.2d 885 (10th Cir., 1954), and the amount received by the stockholder being vastly different from what it would have been had a dividend been paid, and the resulting proportionate ownership of stock being drastically changed, the payment was in redemption and not essentially equivalent to a taxable dividend. *Leake v. Jones,* — F. Supp. — (D.C.Okla., 1955).

Payment received was for sale of preferred stock to the corporation by one of two brothers who were stockholders.

Corporation never declared or distributed cash dividends; redemption was solely for the purpose of providing stockholder with funds for personal use; hence, redemption was essentially equivalent to a dividend distribution. *Koepke v. Commissioner,* 230 F.2d 950 (6th Cir., 1956).

Payments were made in redemption of preferred stock; redemption of the stock was necessary to further the business of the corporation.

The transaction was for the purpose of permitting the corporation to obtain bank loans; the amounts paid were charged to the preferred stock account and not to accumulated earning and profits; it bore a

Taxpayer's Position

Court's Holding

marked relation to the business of the corporation; and it resulted in changes of stockholder's proportionate interests; hence, it was a redemption and not essentially equivalent to a dividend. *Jones v. Griffin*, 216 F.2d 885 (10th Cir., 1954).

Distribution in redemption of preferred stock consisted of contingent rights to possible future income.

Contingent rights had no ascertainable fair market value; hence, not a dividend. *Eleanor A. Bradford*, 22 T.C. 1057 (1954), *rev'd on another issue*, 233 F.2d 935 (6th Cir., 1956).

Preferred stock retired was originally issued in cancellation of stockholder loans with the understanding at that time that stock would eventually be redeemed.

This is indicative of the fact that the redemption was not a disguised dividend. *Marjory K. Hatch*, T.C. Memo., Docket #44563, April 14, 1954.

Distribution in redemption of preferred stock was made to meet cash requirements of sole stockholder.

Distribution in redemption took place at such time and such manner as to make it essentially equivalent to a dividend. *Frenette v. Brodrick,—* F. Supp. — (D.C.Kan., 1954).

Controlling stockholder's desire to retain voting control after his retirement led to plan for redeeming preferred stock.

This is indicative of the fact that the redemption was not a disguised dividend. *Marjory K. Hatch*, T.C. Memo., Docket #44563, April 14, 1954.

Distribution in redemption of preferred stock was a partial liquidation.

Distribution was not pro rata; there was a valid business reason for the issuance and redemption of preferred stock; hence, distribution was a partial liquidation and not a dividend.

Taxpayer's Position   *Court's Holding*

A, 7. REDEMPTION OF PREFERRED SHARES—*Continued*

Georgia P. Johnson, et al., T.C. Memo., Docket ##7589, *et al.,* June 5, 1947.

Preferred stock redeemed was part of a bona fide original issue.

Immaterial in determining whether a distribution is essentially a dividend. *Bertram Meyer,* 7 T.C. 1381 (1946).

Distribution upon retirement of preferred stock was not in partial liquidation as there was no change in corporate structure or capitalization. (Under pre-1942 Act gain on partial liquidation was treated as short term.)

Facts are clearly to the contrary; held, a partial liquidation. *Stern v. Harrison,* 152 F.2d 321 (7th Cir., 1945).

Distributions were not in partial liquidation as preferred stock was issued in payment of debt of predecessor corporation and was required to be retired out of earnings with no reduction of invested capital. [sic] (Under pre-1942 Act gain on partial liquidation was treated as short term.)

By command of the statue, a distribution of funds of a corporation in complete retirement of a part of its stock, or one of a series of distributions in complete retirement of all or part of its stock, constitutes a partial liquidation. *Yankey, et al. v. Commissioner,* 151 F.2d 650 (10th Cir., 1945).

Redemption of preferred stock was an honest business transaction and therefore not taxable.

The distribution was pro rata; the corporation had large earnings; and there was no view of curtailing the business; hence, distribution was essentially equivalent to a dividend. *Stein v. United States,* 62 F. Supp. 568 (Ct. Cl., 1945).

Preferred stock redeemed

Immaterial. *Bertram Meyer,*

Taxpayer's Position

was part of a bona fide original issue.

Preferred stock declared as dividends because of business necessity was redeemed because of a business contraction, and there was no connection between the stock dividends and the redemptions; hence, the redemptions were not essentially equivalent to a dividend.

Reacquisition of preferred stock previously issued as a stock dividend was not a dividend distribution. (Commissioner's position.)

Purchase of preferred stock by corporation whose common stock was purchased by taxpayer resulted in no distribution of earnings to taxpayer.

Redemption of preferred stock previously issued as a stock dividend was made to ex-

Court's Holding

5 T.C. 165 (1945), *remanded for additional facts,* 154 F.2d 55 (3d Cir., 1946).

The stock dividends were distributed for stockholder purposes; one reason was to accomplish a division of earnings among the stockholders and the other was in lieu of a dividend in kind; hence, both redemptions were essentially equivalent to a dividend. *De Nobili Cigar Co. v. Commissioner,* 143 F.2d 436 (2d Cir., 1944).

There was no contraction of business; capital structure was undiminished; no sound business reason for the redemption; cash dividends were not commensurate with earnings; corporation possessed more cash than was adequate to meeting operating requirements; hence, distribution was a dividend. *Fostoria Glass Co. v. Yoke,* 45 F. Supp. 962 (D.C.W.Va., 1942).

Purchase of preferred stock by corporation was not a constructive dividend to taxpayer, who was under no obligation to purchase the stock from the seller. *S. K. Ames, Inc.,* 46 B.T.A. 1020 (1942).

Good reason for treating the redemption as a distribution essentially equivalent to a divi-

Taxpayer's Position   *Court's Holding*

A, 7. REDEMPTION OF PREFERRED SHARES—*Continued*

tend financial assistance to stockholders.

dend. *William Swindells, et ux.*, 44 B.T.A. 336 (1941).

Distribution from sinking fund to retire part of the outstanding preferred stock was a partial liquidation. (Commissioner's position.)

The distribution was a partial liquidation and was not essentially equivalent to a dividend. *Haffenreffer Brewing Co. v. Commissioner*, 116 F.2d 465 (1st Cir., 1940).

Redemption of all outstanding preferred stock was a partial liquidation.

The preferred stock was issued shortly before its redemption; corporation had a large earned surplus and a poor dividend record and had no business reason for the redemption; hence, a taxable dividend. *Goldstein v. Commissioner*, 113 F.2d 363 (7th Cir., 1940).

Redemptions of preferred stock were part of a plan to diminish gradually the interests of the older stockholders and increase the interests of the younger men.

Not controlling. A business plan wholly legitimate in its inception may so operate as to effect a distribution essentially equivalent to a taxable dividend. *William H. Grimditch*, 37 B.T.A. 402 (1938).

At the time the preferred stock was redeemed, the holders thereof were not owners of common stock, and the redemption was pursuant to a plan to give the younger executives a greater share in the company.

The redemptions of the preferred stock twice in the same year amounted to the distribution of a dividend. *William H. Grimditch, supra.*

Distribution was in retirement of preferred shares and was in partial liquidation.

Transaction is clearly within the statutory definition of partial liquidation. *Max Viault, et al.*, 36 B.T.A. 430 (1937).

Taxpayer's Position

Redemption of preferred stock issued as a dividend was not part of any unified plan of distributing corporate earnings.

Preferred stock, which had been issued to holders of common stock, was redeemed, in many instances, from persons who had purchased it from the original holders; therefore the amount received in the redemption by an original holder was not essentially equivalent to a dividend.

Redemption of preferred stock previously issued as a dividend was not originally issued to disguise later cash distributions but issued to satisfy request of stockholder anticipating retirement from business that the larger portion of the stockholders' investments be in preferred stock.

No plan or design to evade taxation in the issuance of preferred stock as a dividend or in its subsequent redemption.

Distribution was in partial liquidation.

Court's Holding

Redemption was a consistent practice; hence, equivalent to the distribution of a dividend. *C. A. Goding, et ano.,* 34 B.T.A. 201 (1936).

Amount paid in redemption of the preferred stock is taxable as a dividend, although many stockholders, not including taxpayer, had sold their stock to third persons; what the character of the payments to other holders of preferred stock may have been is not determinative of the tax consequence to the taxpayer. *Randolph v. Commissioner,* 76 F.2d 472 (8th Cir., 1935).

This is indicative of a legitimate business reason for the stock dividend and the absence of a plan to disguise the future distribution of a cash dividend; hence, distribution was not a dividend. *George A. Lembcke,* 33 B.T.A. 700 (1935).

No circumstances of time and manner of redemption showed the redemption to be essentially equivalent to a dividend. *Brown v. Commissioner,* 69 F.2d 602 (7th Cir., 1934).

Corporation had large accumulated undivided earnings; preferred stock was redeemed at a time when it was sup-

Taxpayer's Position   *Court's Holding*

A, 7. REDEMPTION OF PREFERRED SHARES—*Continued*

planted by an issue of common stock in like amount, and therefore its outstanding capital stock was unchanged in amount; hence, distribution was a dividend. *Hill v. Commissioner,* 66 F.2d 45 (4th Cir., 1933).

The preferred stock had not been issued as a stock dividend, had been actively traded, and was redeemed in accordance with its terms.

There was no premeditated plan or artifice to avoid taxation; hence, such a redemption is not equivalent to a dividend. *James A. Connelly, et al.,* 30 B.T.A. 331 (1933).

In order to keep surplus cash available for growth of the business, preferred stock was distributed as a dividend in lieu of cash; it was fully intended to retire the preferred stock when the corporation's cash account justified such action; therefore, payments received, even though by corporation, in redemption of preferred stock were essentially equivalent to a dividend.

Redemption of corporate stockholder's preferred stock was not equivalent to the distribution of a taxable dividend because, under the Revenue Act of 1926, dividends received by a corporation were not taxable; hence, the payments were made in partial liquidation. *Salt Lake Hardware Co.,* 27 B.T.A. 482 (1932).

Redemption of preferred stock received as a stock dividend did not amount to the distribution of a dividend.

In the circumstances the redemption was not essentially equivalent to the distribution of a dividend. *Robert R. Meyer,* 27 B.T.A. 44 (1932).

Purchase by the corporation of preferred stock previously issued as a stock dividend was a sale by taxpayer.

The transaction was a sale and not a distribution essentially equivalent to a dividend. *Alfred A. Laun, et al.,* 26 B.T.A. 764 (1932).

Taxpayer's Position	*Court's Holding*
The amounts withdrawn were in a liquidation and were not dividends.	The record does not sustain the claim that there was a liquidation. *Christopher v. Burnet*, 55 F.2d 527 (D.C. Cir., 1931).

A. DISTRIBUTIONS IN PARTIAL OR COMPLETE LIQUIDATION—*Continued*
   8. STOCK RETIREMENT—OTHER

The cancellation of the debt was after the stockholder contracted to sell his stock and constituted part of the sales price.	Although it took place after the stockholder contracted to sell his shares, cancellation of his debt resulted in a taxable dividend to him and was not a prepayment of part of the purchase price for his shares. *Wilson v. Commissioner*, 255 F.2d 702 (5th Cir., 1958).
Distribution was in redemption of stock owned by stockholder who was not active in the management or conduct of corporation's business.	On the facts, the redemption was not essentially equivalent to the distribution of a dividend. *Rainwater v. United States*, — F. Supp. — (D.C. S.C., 1958).
Distribution was in partial liquidation. (Commissioner's position.)	Corporation did not adopt any plan or policy of contraction of its business; there was no change in the proportionate ownership of stock; corporation had a poor history of dividend payments in years of high earnings; all distributions were charged to earned surplus, with no accompanying capital reduction; distribution accomplished the same result as the declaration of a dividend; hence, distribution was essentially a dividend. *Pacific*

Taxpayer's Position   *Court's Holding*

A, 8. STOCK RETIREMENT—OTHER—*Continued*

Vegetable Oil Corp. v. Commissioner, 251 F.2d 682 (9th Cir., 1957).

Taxpayer borrowed money from the corporation, gave it his promissory note, and purchased its stock from the original holder of the stock; surrender of part of his stock in cancellation of the notes was in redemption of the stock.

The shares were purchased with money borrowed from the corporation, and the surrender of shares in cancellation of the indebtedness was a dividend distribution, the stockholder retaining undiminished fractional interest in the corporation. *Bell v. Commissioner*, 248 F.2d 947 (6th Cir., 1957).

Distribution in redemption was exactly the same amount as was paid in for the stock.

This does not conclusively establish a partial liquidation. *Rockwell Spring & Axle Co. v. Granger*, 140 F. Supp. 390 (D.C.Pa., 1956).

Dividends previously credited to instalment shares are capital gains on redemption at maturity.

Distribution was from earnings and profits and, even though accumulated until maturity rather than paid at intervals, was substantially equivalent to a dividend. *Friedman v. Smith*, 144 F. Supp. 349 (D.C.Pa., 1956).

Redemption of stock to cancel stockholders' notes which were originally given in payment of stock was merely a revision of an agreement to purchase stock.

Redemption did not diminish the fractional interests in the corporation, and the manner in which transaction was accomplished was in effect equivalent to a distribution of a dividend. *Woodworth, et al. v. Commissioner*, 218 F.2d 719 (6th Cir., 1955).

Taxpayer's Position	*Court's Holding*

Withdrawals were return of capital investment and repayment of advances.

No evidence of partial liquidation or repayment of advances; hence, taxable as a dividend. *William B. Benjamin,* T.C. Memo., Docket #22748, Oct. 26, 1955).

The redemption did not represent an artifice to disguise the payment of a dividend.

Absence of a plan to avoid taxation is not controlling. *Estate of Chandler, et al.,* 22 T.C. 1158 (1954), *aff'd,* 228 F.2d 909 (6th Cir., 1955).

Amounts received from surrender of shares represented proceeds of a sale, the purchase price being measured by future dividends for a specified period.

The ten-year certificates received in consideration of the sale had no ascertainable market value when received; hence, the vendor received only an instalment on the purchase price and not a dividend. *Estate of Raymond T. Marshall,* 20 T.C. 979 (1953).

The amount received was out of capital and in a partial liquidation of the corporation.

No part of the corporation's outstanding shares was redeemed or cancelled, there being a mere reduction in par value; hence, the distribution was essentially equivalent to a dividend. *Albert G. Rooks, et al.,* T.C. Memo., Docket ##29716–7, Feb. 9, 1953.

Redemption was made for the purpose of eliminating balances in drawing accounts of stockholders.

Redemption was pro rata, and its only purpose was to extinguish loans made by the corporation to stockholders; hence, essentially equivalent to the distribution of a dividend. *Lowenthal, et al. v. Commissioner,* 169 F.2d 694 (7th Cir., 1948).

Taxpayer's Position	*Court's Holding*

A, 8. STOCK RETIREMENT—OTHER—*Continued*

Retirement of stock was not essentially equivalent to a dividend when two related steps are considered as part of one transaction.	The lapse of time and other circumstances show that no step transaction was intended or existed; hence, a dividend. *Wall v. United States,* 164 F.2d 462 (4th Cir., 1947).
Distribution, if handled in another manner, would clearly have given rise to no assertion that it was a dividend.	Where two methods are available, the one which is used and its tax consequences are determinative. *Wall v. United States, supra.*
Distribution resulted in reducing the value of stockholder's interest and no gain was realized.	This is entirely beside the point. *Wall v. United States, supra.*
The transfer of shares to the corporation was adequate consideration for the distribution.	Not controlling. *Wall v. United States, supra.*
Distributions were not in partial liquidation as no stock was surrendered and company intended to stay in business. (Under pre-1942 Act gain on partial liquidation was treated as short term.)	There was no complete cancellation or redemption of all or a portion of the stock. Without it there was no liquidation, partial or complete. *Thornton v. Commissioner,* 159 F.2d 578 (7th Cir., 1947).
Distribution in redemption was made because of the desire to separate one business of the corporation from another.	This is a sound business reason for distribution; hence, distribution was not essentially equivalent to a dividend. *L. M. Lockhart,* 8 T.C. 436 (1947).
Stock, not issued as a dividend, was redeemed at its book value.	Evidentiary, but not conclusive, that redemption was not a dividend. *A. C. Monk,*

Taxpayer's Position	*Court's Holding*
	T.C. Memo., Docket #9511, Aug. 28, 1947.

There was a sound business reason for the distribution in reduction of capital, as it was pursuant to a recapitalization, and the corporation did not declare a dividend.	There were earnings and profits, and hence the transaction had the effect of a distribution of a dividend. *Dunton v. Clauson*, 67 F. Supp. 839 (D.C.Me., 1946).
Shares redeemed were purchased from widow of deceased stockholder and could not be sold to third party.	Not a valid business purpose of the corporation for the redemption; hence, distribution taxable as a dividend. *Kirschenbaum v. Commissioner*, 155 F.2d 23 (2d Cir., 1946), *aff'g Harry Banner, et al.*, T.C. Memo., Docket ##3655–6, Mar. 27, 1945.
Preferred stock declared as dividends because of business necessity was redeemed because of a business contraction, and there was no connection between the stock dividends and the redemptions; hence, the redemptions were not essentially equivalent to a dividend.	The stock dividends were distributed for stockholder purposes; one reason was to accomplish a division of earnings among the stockholders and the other was in lieu of a dividend in kind; hence, both redemptions were essentially equivalent to a dividend. *De Nobili Cigar Co. v. Commissioner*, 143 F.2d 436 (2d Cir., 1944).
The exchange of common stock for preferred stock resulted in no change of the capital stock and surplus accounts.	To come within the scope of a distribution essentially equivalent to a dividend, the distribution must result in a reduction of the corporation's capital. Here there was no distribution out of earnings and profits and the surplus and capital stock accounts both remained un-

Taxpayer's Position   *Court's Holding*

A, 8. STOCK RETIREMENT—OTHER—*Continued*

Taxpayer's Position	Court's Holding
	changed in amount; hence, distribution was not essentially a dividend. *Louis Wellhouse, Jr., et ano.,* 3 T.C. 363 (1944).
Amount received in exchange for stock was nominal and evidenced no plan to distribute earnings.	A significant factor. *Estate of Henry Vernon Foster,* T.C. Memo., Docket #110891, Mar. 22, 1944.
Transaction was an isolated one solely to raise money to pay estate taxes and debts.	It purported to be, and was, a sale; hence, not a dividend. *Estate of Henry Vernon Foster, supra.*
Distributions were in partial liquidation, as the par value of the stock was reduced.	There was no redemption or cancellation of all or a part of the corporation's stock, as no shares were actually cancelled; distribution was a dividend. *Oscar R. Micklethwait,* T.C. Memo., Docket #111351, June 8, 1943.
Stock redeemed was issued bona fide and not merely for the purpose of distributing earnings.	Not controlling. *Vesper Co. v. Commissioner,* 131 F.2d 200 (8th Cir., 1942).
Distribution was made out of current earnings and not accumulated earnings and therefore could not be essentially equivalent to the distribution of a dividend.	Not controlling. *Vesper Co. v. Commissioner, supra.*
Distribution was in partial liquidation of the corporation.	Distribution was approximately equal to year's earnings, and purpose was to effect distribution of current earnings which would otherwise be ille-

Taxpayer's Position	*Court's Holding*
	gal under state law because of a deficit; distribution was essentially equivalent to a dividend. *Vesper Co. v. Commissioner, supra.*
Redemption price was approximately equivalent to the fair market value of the shares redeemed.	This is indicative of a valid partial liquidation. *John P. Elton,* 47 B.T.A. 111 (1942).
Redemption was part of a refinancing plan.	There was a partial liquidation, and the gain was taxable as a dividend (under the 1936 Revenue Act). *James Irvine,* 46 B.T.A. 246 (1942).
Redemption was made when the corporation's credit improved and it was enabled to borrow all the funds that it required, which it was unable to do at the time the redeemed stock was originally issued.	Stock was retired for a good business reason; hence, distribution was not a dividend. *Edwin L. Jones,* B.T.A. Memo., Docket #106135, Oct. 15, 1942.
There was no bad faith, artifice, or subterfuge between the issuance of the stock and its redemption.	Not determinative. *E. M. Peet, et ano.,* 43 B.T.A. 852 (1941).
Distribution in redemption of stock issued as a dividend was a partial liquidation.	There was no business purpose for the issuance and redemption of the stock; the redemption was accomplished for personal advantage of principal stockholder and resulted in no change of ownership; hence, distribution was a dividend. *Smith v. United States,* 121 F.2d 692 (3d Cir., 1941).
Distribution in redemption of stock previously issued as	Stock redeemed had been issued bona fide, and in such

Taxpayer's Position   *Court's Holding*

A, 8. STOCK RETIREMENT—OTHER—*Continued*

stock dividends was a partial liquidation, and not a dividend, as redeemed shares were issued bona fide.

cases Section 115(g), under which redemptions essentially equivalent to a dividend are made taxable as dividends, never applies. *Patty v. Helvering,* **98** F.2d **717** (2d Cir., 1938).

There was no direct relationship between the issuance of the stock and its subsequent redemption.

Not determinative. *William H. Grimditch,* 37 B.T.A. 402 (1938).

There was no bad faith, artifice, or subterfuge in redeeming the preferred stock.

Not determinative. *William H. Grimditch, supra.*

Payments represented the proceeds of a sale of stock to the corporation.

Corporation had an extraordinarily large profit it desired to distribute; there was no intent to liquidate the corporation; the relative stock interests of the principal stockholders were not materially changed; hence, payments were dividends. *W. & K. Holding Corp., et al.,* 38 B.T.A. 830 (1938).

Payments were proceeds from the sale of stock and were not received in a tax-free reorganization which was a transaction separate from the sale.

Two separate transactions occurred: a reorganization and a sale of stock; hence, payments were not dividends. *Harris v. Commissioner,* 92 F.2d 374 (3d Cir., 1937).

Amount received on redemption of stock purchased from third party was not a dividend.

Facts do not show that redemption was essentially equivalent to distribution of a dividend. *Parker v. United States,* 88 F.2d 907 (7th Cir., 1937).

Taxpayer's Position	*Court's Holding*
There was no causal relation between issuance and redemption of stock.	Not determinative. *J. Natwick*, 36 B.T.A. 866 (1937).
Distributions were dividends as they were payable only because of shareholdings (opposing Commissioner's instalment sale-interest theory).	Distributions were made with respect to shareholdings, and their character as dividends must be recognized by both Government and taxpayer. *Max Viault, et al.*, 36 B.T.A. 430 (1937).
There was no intent to distribute profits or bad faith in redeeming the stock.	Not controlling. *McGuire v. Commissioner*, 84 F.2d 431 (7th Cir., 1936).
A partial, pro rata redemption was to accommodate a minority stockholder who desired to, but did not, sell all his stock.	This is not a dividend. (Dissenting opinion to the contrary.) *Commissioner v. Ahlborn*, 77 F.2d 700 (3d Cir., 1935).
The redemptions took place two to four years after the stock dividend.	Strong evidence of dividend. *Adler v. Commissioner*, 77 F.2d 733 (5th Cir., 1935).
Shares redeemed had been purchased by stockholder from son of a deceased stockholder.	No change in the stockholder's ownership and control of the corporation; hence, distribution taxable as a dividend. *Wm. T. Brown v. Commissioner*, 79 F.2d 73 (3d Cir., 1935).
Distribution in redemption of stock held by an estate was accomplished for the purpose of avoiding any conflict between the life tenants and the remaindermen of the estate.	The transaction was free from artifice and the element of tax avoidance was not present; distribution was not intended to be, and did not essentially result in, a division of profits. *Girard Trust Co., et al.*, 32 B.T.A. 926 (1935).

Taxpayer's Position	*Court's Holding*

A, 8. STOCK RETIREMENT—OTHER—*Continued*

Distribution in redemption of stock was made at the same price that was originally paid for the stock.	Not controlling. *Hyman v. Commissioner*, 71 F.2d 342 (D.C. Cir., 1934).
No corporate action for dissolution was taken under state law.	The corporation was, in fact, in process of liquidation and dissolution, and the distribution was in connection therewith. *Tootle v. Commissioner*, 58 F.2d 576 (8th Cir., 1932).

A. DISTRIBUTIONS IN PARTIAL OR COMPLETE LIQUIDATION—*Continued*
   9. SIGNIFICANCE OF PRIOR DIVIDEND PAYMENTS

Corporation's policy was to distribute a large part of its earnings as dividends.	A significant factor. *Estate of Henry Vernon Foster*, T.C. Memo., Docket #110891, Mar. 22, 1944.
Corporate earnings were distributed as dividends.	A significant factor. *R. W. Creech*, 46 B.T.A. 93 (1942).
Substantial dividends were paid for many years prior to the redemption of stock.	Evidence of lack of purpose to avoid tax by means of redemption. *Commissioner v. Champion*, 78 F.2d 513 (6th Cir., 1935).
Distribution of substantial dividends during years prior to redemption negated any intent to distribute earnings by a redemption.	Evidentiary but not controlling. *Alfred E. Fuhlage*, 32 B.T.A. 222 (1935).
Substantial ordinary cash dividends paid.	Evidence that redemptions were not dividends. *Babson v. Commissioner*, 70 F.2d 304 (7th Cir., 1934).

Taxpayer's Position   *Court's Holding*

B. ALLEGED LOANS TO STOCKHOLDERS

Payments were loans.

There were no notes or other evidence of indebtedness, no agreements for repayment, no interest paid, and no security given for the loan; hence, distributions were dividends to extent of corporation's earnings and profits. *Lou Levy,* 30 T.C. 1315 (1958).

Withdrawals constituted bona fide loans which were made on open account; were not made in proportion to stock holdings; and substantial repayments had been made on these loans.

Withdrawals were not represented by notes, no security was given for repayment, there was no agreement to pay interest or any understanding with regard to repayment; hence, withdrawals were dividends. *Elliott J. Roschuni,* 29 T.C. 1193 (1958).

Amount received was a loan from the corporation.

Stockholder intended to make repayment, had given the corporation a note, the corporation's books reflected it as a loan, and reason existed for nonpayment; hence, there was no dividend distribution. *Callan Court Co., et al. v. Cobb,* — F.Supp. — (D.C.Ga., 1958).

The amounts withdrawn were loans to the stockholders.

The amounts withdrawn were obtained by the corporation's borrowing money; the stockholders gave notes for the withdrawals and were financially able to pay them; the amounts were carried on the corporation's books as loans receivable, and repayment was made after the corporation was

Taxpayer's Position   *Court's Holding*

B. ALLEGED LOANS TO STOCKHOLDERS—*Continued*

dissolved and liquidated, which was not contemplated when the loans were made and which served a good business purpose; hence, the withdrawals were loans and not dividends. *Estate of I. Benjamin,* 28 T.C. 101 (1957).

The amounts withdrawn were loans by the corporation to the stockholder and not dividends.

There were both an intent and obligation to repay; the amounts were repaid before any notice that the transaction was questioned; that there were no notes given or interest paid weaken the stockholder's case but are not controlling; hence, there was no dividend distribution received by the stockholder. *A. J. Dalton,* T.C. Memo., Docket #50393, Jan. 31, 1957.

The amount withdrawn from the corporation by each of the 50% stockholders was a loan.

The loan was authorized by the stockholders and the Board of Directors; promissory notes were delivered, payable in 36 months with interest at 4½%; the notes were carried as accounts receivable by the company; although the taxpayer did not pay interest, which is indicative that there was no loan, the other stockholder did; all the facts indicate a loan, and not a dividend distribution. *J. H. Perkins,* T.C. Memo., Docket #56782, July 12, 1957.

Taxpayer's Position	*Court's Holding*
Withdrawals were loans which had been repaid.	Alleged repayments were capital contributions; hence, withdrawals were essentially dividends. *Republic National Bank of Dallas v. United States,* — F. Supp. — (D.C.Tex., 1957).
Withdrawals were loans which taxpayer intended to repay.	Loan was evidenced by a note; it was carried on the corporate books as a note receivable; partial repayments were made; hence, withdrawals were loans, not dividends. *William D. Bryan,* T.C. Memo., Docket ##49533–4, Sept. 24, 1957.
Withdrawals were loans.	Withdrawals were loans, as there existed the intent to repay; in fact, some repayments were made; hence, withdrawals were not dividends. *Walter Freeman,* T.C. Memo., Docket ##54900–1, Jan. 28, 1957.
Indebtedness was valid even though the corporation was inadequately capitalized because the capitalization reflected the business judgment of unrelated persons.	Not controlling. *The Colony, Inc. v. Commissioner,* 244 F.2d 75 (6th Cir., 1956), *rev'd on other grounds,* 357 U.S. 28 (1958).
Indebtedness was valid because the transaction was carried out in the form proper to create an indebtedness, rather than a contribution to capital.	Of no significance. *The Colony, Inc. v. Commissioner, supra.*
Indebtedness was valid because the notes were issued to the stockholders in amounts that were disproportionate to their stockholdings.	In the circumstances this factor is not controlling. *The Colony, Inc. v. Commissioner, supra.*

Taxpayer's Position	*Court's Holding*

B. ALLEGED LOANS TO STOCKHOLDERS—*Continued*

Distributions were loans and not dividends.	Intent at time of withdrawal is controlling, and intent that loans were made is supported by subsequent giving of interest-bearing demand notes and repayments or attempts to repay the sums involved; hence, not dividends. *Estate of Helene Simmons*, 26 T.C. 409 (1956).
Withdrawals were not shared in by all stockholders and therefore were not dividends but loans.	Not determinative. *B. F. Crabbe, et al.*, T.C. Memo., Docket ##44359–60, Mar. 5, 1956.
Withdrawals were loans, and insurance policies on lives of the stockholders in favor of the corporation were given as security for repayment.	Withdrawals were dividends and there was no evidence that policies were intended as security for the withdrawals. *William C. Baird, et al.*, 25 T.C. 387 (1955).
The stockholders intended the withdrawals to be loans and intended to repay.	Evidence indicates withdrawal of earnings. No evidence of intention to repay. *William C. Baird, et al., supra.*
The stockholders gave demand notes for balance due on withdrawals.	Notes given only after revenue agent claimed withdrawals were dividends are not evidence that amounts withdrawn were loans. *William C. Baird, et al., supra.*
Withdrawals were recorded as notes receivable on the books of the corporation.	Not sufficient by itself to support contention that withdrawals were loans. *William C. Baird, et al., supra.*
The amounts withdrawn	That the money was bor-

Taxpayer's Position	*Court's Holding*
were corporate loans to the stockholders.	rowed to finance the purchase of the stock is not too significant; the loans were a prudent business arrangement; interest was paid to the company whereas otherwise the funds would have been idle; the loans were repaid; hence, the transaction was a loan and not a dividend distribution. *Smith v. United States*, 130 F. Supp. 586 (Ct. Cl., 1955).
Withdrawals were loans intended to be repaid, part of which had been repaid.	In the circumstances the withdrawals were not dividend distributions. *In re Ward*, 131 F. Supp. 387 (D.C.Colo., 1955).
Withdrawal was a loan.	There was no note or mortgage to evidence the loan nor was the withdrawal carried as an account receivable; hence, withdrawal constituted taxable income. *Leroy B. Williams*, T.C. Memo., Docket #46516, Dec. 14, 1955.
Repayments of withdrawals were made consistently.	Conduct indicates that parties regarded the withdrawals as loans, not dividends. *Al Goodman, Inc., et al.*, 23 T.C. 288 (1954).
Loan to stockholder was for an unusual emergency; evidenced by an interest-bearing note; secured by a pledge having a value in excess of twice the amount of the loan; treated as an asset on the books of the corporation; major portions of	On the facts, the corporation and the stockholders treated the advance as a loan which was to be repaid; consequently, it was not taxable as a dividend. *Al Goodman, Inc., et al.*, *supra*.

Taxpayer's Position   *Court's Holding*

B. ALLEGED LOANS TO STOCKHOLDERS—*Continued*

repayment were derived from dividends received.

Stockholder at all times had ample resources to satisfy any withdrawals.

Indicates that parties regarded the withdrawals as loans and intended repayment. *Al Goodman, Inc., et al., supra.*

Running loan accounts maintained by sole stockholder and his wife reflected loans; they were carried on the books as such; were paid off occasionally; and were in part evidenced by notes.

In the circumstances the loans were not essentially equivalent to the distributions of dividends. *Victor Shaken,* 21 T.C. 785 (1954).

The transfer of some of its assets by the corporation to a partnership, the partners of which were also principal stockholders of the corporation, was made for a bona fide business purpose and was a loan to the partnership, not a distribution to the stockholders.

The stockholders intended to repay the debt and the transaction resulted in a debt; hence, there was not a dividend. *Jacksonville Paper Co.,* T.C. Memo., Docket ##14884, *et al.,* July 30, 1954.

Proceeds retained from sales of corporate property were loans rather than dividends.

Facts showed that a debtor-creditor relationship existed; hence, the retained proceeds were loans, not dividends. *H. C. Thorman,* T.C. Memo., Docket ##31431–3, Aug. 27, 1953.

Withdrawals were loans, not dividends.

Facts showed withdrawals were loans. Taxpayer always had the means to make repayment, and the withdrawals were represented as loans by the corporation in credit state-

Taxpayer's Position	*Court's Holding*
	ments to banks; hence, not dividends. *Frank W. Sharp,* T.C. Memo., Docket #33405, July 20, 1953.
Amount paid in for preferred stock redeemed was intended to be a loan.	No evidence of loan; hence, redemption essentially equivalent to a dividend. *Samuel L. Cantor,* T.C. Memo., Docket #40043, May 26, 1953.
Withdrawals were loans intended to be repaid and carried on the books in the same manner as advances to customers.	Taxpayer had sufficient assets to repay the advances and both parties treated them as loans; hence, not a dividend. *Courtemanche, Jr. v. Earle,* — F. Supp. — (D.C.Ore., 1953).
Interest was received or charged on the loans in question.	Evidence of loan. *Adams v. Glenn,* — F. Supp. — (D.C. Ky., 1950).
Withdrawals regarded as indebtedness by both the stockholders and the corporation.	Evidence of loan. *Adams v. Glenn, supra.*
Stockholder's intention was to make repayment.	Evidence of loan. *Adams v. Glenn, supra.*
Payments secured by stockholders' notes or otherwise.	Evidence of loan. *Adams v. Glenn, supra.*
Payments by corporation to stockholders reported on books as accounts receivable.	Evidence of loan. *Adams v. Glenn, supra.*
Withdrawals were loans, not dividends.	Repayments were made on the withdrawals; the remaining stockholders objected to the excessive loans and forced the excessive withdrawals to be secured by a pledge of the company's stock to the company; hence, the withdrawals were

Taxpayer's Position   *Court's Holding*

B. Alleged Loans to Stockholders—*Continued*

	loans, not dividends. *Carl L. White*, 17 T.C. 1562 (1952).
Withdrawals from corporation by two brothers, sole stockholder officers, each limited to $150,000 maximum recorded in corporation's accounts receivable with oral agreement to repay on call, created a loan.	Vagueness of oral agreement created possibility of changing obligation at will; therefore, in absence of corporate resolutions and notes establishing loans, withdrawals were dividends. *W. T. Wilson*, 10 T.C. 251 (1948).
Withdrawals were loans, not dividend distributions.	Debts were reflected in corporate accounts and despite absence of notes, interest, and repayment, there was no proof that payment was not intended. *Wilson v. Commissioner*, 163 F.2d 680 (9th Cir., 1947).
Distributions were loans and not dividends.	Not substantiated, corporation made no effort to collect; there was no evidence of indebtedness or requirement of interest payments; hence, a dividend. *H. L. Gumbiner*, T.C. Memo., Docket #5312, Dec. 31, 1946.
Withdrawals were loans recorded on the books as debts of taxpayers.	There was no evidence of indebtedness, no accrued interest, and only negligible repayments over a period of years; hence, withdrawals were essentially equivalent to a dividend. *Regensburg v. Commissioner*, 144 F.2d 41 (2d Cir., 1944).
Withdrawals were loans, not dividend distributions.	Stockholder was always solvent, paid interest on debt, and repaid amounts on principal

Taxpayer's Position

Court's Holding

annually; hence, not a dividend. *Alvin H. Phillips*, T.C. Memo., Docket #109395, May 1, 1943.

Parent corporation borrowed money from its subsidiaries and did not receive dividends from them, and payment by parent to its stockholders was not out of profits.

The separate corporate entities are to be respected, and the parent did borrow from its subsidiaries in absence of a contrary showing; hence, such loans were not dividends and what the parent's shareholders received were not profits. *Page, et al. v. Haverty*, 129 F.2d 512 (5th Cir., 1942).

Amounts withdrawn by sole-stockholder were recorded on books as loans, all interested parties intended amounts to be loans; and amounts were repaid.

On the basis of all the facts, the withdrawals were not dividends. *Irving T. Bush*, 45 B.T.A. 609 (1941), *remanded on the issue*, 133 F.2d 1005 (2d Cir., 1943).

Repayments as well as interest payments were made with respect to the withdrawals.

Not persuasive here, as the withdrawals always exceeded any repayments. *Ben R. Meyer, et al.*, 45 B.T.A. 228 (1941).

Withdrawals were loans, not dividends.

Not substantiated; withdrawals were used for personal and living expenses and the recipients could not have made repayment. *Ben R. Meyer, et al., supra.*

Withdrawals were carried on the books as loans.

Not controlling. *Ben R. Meyer, et al., supra.*

Demand notes were given to the corporation in the face amount of the withdrawals.

Not persuasive; collection of notes was under control of person making the withdrawals. *Ben R. Meyer, et al., supra.*

Taxpayer's Position	*Court's Holding*

B. Alleged Loans to Stockholders—*Continued*

Execution of trust deed whereby taxpayers conveyed all their property to guarantee corporation's indebtedness to others evidenced that withdrawals were loans.	Trust deeds bore no relation to the withdrawals in question. *Ben R. Meyer, et al., supra.*
Withdrawals in excess of salary were loans which were not forgiven upon liquidation of the corporation but were treated as assets with all the other assets transferred to the partnership.	On the facts, the transfer to the partnership of amount withdrawn constituted a liquidating dividend. *Jas. J. Gravley,* 44 B.T.A. 722 (1941).
Withdrawals were loans which were intended to be repaid.	The withdrawals bore interest which was paid; the taxpayer had the means of repaying them; they bore no relation to earnings or surplus; there were no comparable withdrawals by certain other stockholders. They were loans and not dividend distributions. *Rollin C. Reynolds,* 44 B.T.A. 342 (1941).
Distributions were loans, not dividends.	Not substantiated; there was no evidence of any intent to repay, and a payment after a revenue audit was not conclusive of intent to make repayment. *Jesse B. Hawley,* B.T.A. Memo., Docket #83371, April 29, 1939.
Withdrawals by decedent stockholder remained as obligations of the estate as evidenced by corporate resolution reaffirming existence of debt.	Contrary to the resolution, the stockholders account was credited and surplus reduced in the amount of the debt; hence, a dividend. *Hudson v. Com-*

Taxpayer's Position   *Court's Holding*

missioner, **99** F.2d **630** (6th Cir., **1938**).

Stock of par value equal to debt was subsequently surrendered.

No evidence that actual value of stock surrendered had any relation to amount of debt; corporate assets were not increased, and the position of the stockholders was substantially unchanged; hence, a dividend. *Hudson v. Commissioner,* **99** F.2d **630** (6th Cir., **1938**).

Withdrawals were loans, not dividends.

The withdrawals were evidenced by a note, carried interest, and were ultimately repaid. They were not distributions of dividends. *George S. Groves,* **38** B.T.A. **727** (**1938**).

Advances to sole stockholder were loans which were ultimately repaid.

Advances represented *bona fide* loans which were carried on the books as loans and represented a corporate asset; hence, advances were not dividends. *Moses W. Faitoute,* **38** B.T.A. **32** (**1938**).

Distributions made on stockholder's behalf were loans to stockholder.

Not substantiated; taxed as dividend. *A. W. Mellon,* **36** B.T.A. **977** (**1937**).

Withdrawals were carried on the books as loans.

Only evidentiary; not conclusive. *Roy J. Kinnear,* **36** B.T.A. **153** (**1937**).

Withdrawals by stockholder from corporate funds were loans.

Both stockholder and corporation treated withdrawals as loans; shown in balance sheet as receivable; later interest-bearing note was given; interest was paid; stockholder was always solvent; withdrawals

Taxpayer's Position	*Court's Holding*

B. ALLEGED LOANS TO STOCKHOLDERS—*Continued*

	were disproportionate to stock-holding; the loans were repaid in full; hence, not dividends. *Herman M. Rhodes,* 34 B.T.A. 212 (1936), *rev'd on other issue,* 100 F.2d 966 (6th Cir., 1939).
Withdrawals were loans, not dividends.	The withdrawals did not carry interest; taxpayer was sole stockholder and used the funds for living expenses, as he had no outside income and showed no intent to repay the withdrawals. Withdrawals were dividends. *George P. Marshall,* 32 B.T.A. 956 (1935).
Withdrawals were loans, not dividends.	There was no corporate authority to make loans; there were no notes or other evidence of indebtedness; no interest was charged or paid; hence, the withdrawals were not loans but dividend distributions. *M. Jackson Crispin,* 32 B.T.A. 151 (1935).
Net amount of withdrawals were loans carried on books of corporation as assets, were intended to be repaid, and some had been repaid.	Withdrawals were largely personal expenses and there were no notes or agreements to pay interest. Net withdrawals increased from year to year; hence, they must be treated as distributions of net profits, taxable as dividends, where substantially all stock is owned *or* controlled by one stockholder. *C. W. Murchison,* 32 B.T.A. 32 (1935).

Taxpayer's Position	*Court's Holding*
Withdrawals were loans, not dividends. (Commissioner's position.)	Not substantiated; hence, the withdrawals were dividends. *W. A. Graeper,* **27** B.T.A. 632 (1933).
Distributions were loans and not liquidating dividends.	Distributions were dividends. There was no intent to repay nor was any amount ever repaid; the existing indebtedness was offset by omitting cash distribution to stockholder, after which stockholder shared pro rata. *Sam Weisberger,* **29** B.T.A. 83 (1933).
Withdrawals by majority stockholder were loans, recorded as such on the corporation's books.	Mere book entries cannot convert a distribution into an asset, and there is no necessity for the formal declaration of a dividend; hence, the distribution amounted to a dividend. *Christopher v. Burnet,* 55 F.2d 527 (D.C. Cir., 1931).
Withdrawals were loans rather than dividends.	There was no evidence of indebtedness; no repayments were ever made; hence, the withdrawals were dividends. *M. Schulein Co., et al.,* **20** B.T.A. 264 (1930).
Withdrawals were loans, not dividends.	The corporation and the stockholders regarded the withdrawals as loans, and substantial repayments were made on the withdrawals; hence, the withdrawals were loans and not dividends. *D. Bruce Forrester, et al.,* 12 B.T.A. 104 (1928).
Payment was a loan rather than a dividend.	The payment was a loan and not a dividend. *Howard M.*

Taxpayer's Position   *Court's Holding*

B. ALLEGED LOANS TO STOCKHOLDERS—*Continued*

Taylor, et al., 14 B.T.A. 863 (1928).

Amounts withdrawn by stockholder in proportion to stock interest were loans and were recorded on the books as such.

The ratable withdrawals, coupled with a provision in the corporate charter against loans to stockholders, held sufficiently to justify conclusion that amounts were dividends. *Chattanooga Savings Bank v. Brewer*, 17 F.2d 79 (6th Cir., 1927).

Amounts withdrawn but not credited to stockholder are not dividends.

Amounts withdrawn by stockholder and carried on corporation's books as accounts receivable are not dividend distributions. *E. T. Renfro*, 8 B.T.A. 1295 (1927).

Amounts withdrawn were loans, and not dividends to stockholder, and were part of corporation's invested capital.

The stockholder having given a note; recognized his obligation and being financially able to repay; having counterbalanced the sum not only out of future dividends but also out of salary; and having been the only one of several stockholders to make such withdrawals; the amounts withdrawn were loans. *Comey & Johnson Co.*, 8 B.T.A. 52 (1927).

The amounts withdrawn were loans to stockholders.

Amounts were withdrawn by stockholders over a period of years, and the facts show that they never intended to make repayment; hence, such amounts were distributions of profits.

Taxpayer's Position	*Court's Holding*
	Feist & Bachrach, Inc., 2 B.T.A. 1228 (1925).
Withdrawals were loans evidenced by notes.	Not substantiated, as notes were subsequently charged off as worthless when stockholder could have paid them. *Daniel Hunt, Sr.*, 6 B.T.A. 558 (1927).
Withdrawals were loans rather than dividends.	Repayments were made in cash or by crediting dividends against the account; withdrawals were not in proportion to stockholdings and were treated on the books as loans; hence, they were loans and not dividends. *Kate E. Ryan*, 2 B.T.A. 1130 (1925).
Notes were given by stockholders for their withdrawals; amounts were subsequently repaid; amounts were recorded on books as accounts receivable.	On the facts, withdrawals were not dividends. *Albert Bettens, et al.*, 2 B.T.A. 535 (1925).

C. OTHER PAYMENTS OR TRANSFERS OF PROPERTY TO STOCKHOLDERS
   1. NOT IN FORM OF DIVIDEND

There was no intent to distribute a dividend when the corporation's treasury shares were transferred to the stockholder.	The intent of the parties is not controlling in the circumstances. The evidence justifies a finding that a dividend distribution was intended. *Waldheim v. Commissioner*, 244 F.2d 1 (7th Cir., 1957).
There was no formal declaration of a dividend.	Not determinative. *B. F. Crabbe, et al.*, T.C. Memo., Docket ##44359–60, Mar. 5, 1956.

Taxpayer's Position	*Court's Holding*

C, 1. NOT IN FORM OF DIVIDEND—*Continued*

Book entries treated the withdrawals as accounts receivable.	Not determinative. *B. F. Crabbe, et al., supra.*
There was no actual cash distributed.	Important factor in these circumstances. *Ada Murphy McFarlane,* T.C. Memo., Docket #37563, May 14, 1954.
Distribution is not within the definition in Regulations 111, Section 29.115-1, of a dividend as a "distribution in the ordinary course of business."	Not controlling; decision to be based on facts in each case. *L. M. Lockhart,* 8 T.C. 436 (1947).
There was no formal declaration of a dividend.	Not controlling. *Dunton v. Clauson,* 67 F. Supp. 839 (D.C. Me., 1946).
There was no formal declaration of a dividend.	Not conclusive against a finding that withdrawals were dividends. *Regensburg v. Commissioner,* 144 F.2d 41 (2d Cir., 1944).
There was no formal declaration of a dividend.	A declaration of a dividend is not essential to a taxable dividend distribution. *Emil Stein, et al.,* 46 B.T.A. 135 (1942).
There was no formal declaration of a dividend.	Not controlling. *Hudson v. Commissioner,* 99 F.2d 630 (6th Cir., 1938).
There was no formal declaration of a dividend.	The formal declaration of a dividend by a corporation is not essential under the tax laws. *Helvering v. Gordon,* 87 F.2d 663 (8th Cir., 1937).

Taxpayer's Position	*Court's Holding*
There was no formal declaration of a dividend.	Not determinative. *Roy J. Kinnear*, 36 B.T.A. 153 (1937).
The amount received was a return of capital, as the agreement between the parties required the return of capital before profits were distributed.	The amount received was less than earnings and profits and, under the taxing statute, was a dividend distribution. *Bing & Bing, Inc., et al.*, 35 B.T.A. 1170 (1937).
Stockholder purchased from the corporation shares it had purchased from another stockholder, and neither the bonds issued by the company for the shares nor the amount paid on the principal amount of the bonds were dividends.	The stockholder and not the corporation made the purchase and, although the issuance of its bonds by the company were not dividends to the purchasing stockholder, the amount paid on principal of the bonds was such a dividend. *George D. Mann, et al.*, 33 B.T.A. 281 (1935).
There was no formal declaration of a dividend.	Not controlling. *M. Jackson Crispin*, 32 B.T.A. 151 (1935).
There was no formal declaration of a dividend.	Not controlling. *Security First National Bank of Los Angeles, Executor, et al.*, 28 B.T.A. 289 (1933).
There was no formal declaration of a dividend.	Not controlling. *E. T. Schuler*, 29 B.T.A. 415 (1933).
There was no declaration of a dividend.	There was a determination of amount of profits to which shareholders were entitled and crediting of proportionate amounts to certain stockholders on the corporation's books; other stockholders being paid, made it a taxable dividend distribution. *Hadley v. Commis-*

Taxpayer's Position	*Court's Holding*

C, 1. NOT IN FORM OF DIVIDEND—*Continued*

	sioner, 36 F.2d 543 (D.C. Cir., 1929).
Receipt from a corporation of rights to subscribe to stock of a second corporation, which rights were sold, did not give rise to a dividend.	The stockholders received a distribution of corporate assets which were of value, and the income received, as a result of the sale of the rights, constituted taxable income. *Metcalf's Estate v. Commissioner,* 32 F.2d 192 (2d Cir., 1929).
There was no formal declaration of a dividend.	Not controlling. *United Tailors & Cleaners Co.,* 10 B.T.A. 172 (1928).
Distributions made to pay stockholder's tax liability were not dividends, as there was no formal declaration of a dividend.	Not controlling. *F. G. Lamb,* 14 B.T.A. 814 (1928).

C. OTHER PAYMENTS OR TRANSFERS OF PROPERTY TO STOCKHOLDERS
   —*Continued*
   2. DISPROPORTIONATE TO STOCKHOLDINGS

Payments were not disguised dividends, as corporation continued to make similar payments to a former stockholder.	Payments to former stockholder were totally unrelated to stockholdings; and that factor constitutes another reason for determining that the payments were of a royalty, and not disguised dividends. *Finn H. Magnus, et al. v. Commissioner,* 259 F.2d 893 (3d Cir., 1958).
Distribution was not pro rata.	Not conclusive. *Gooding Amusement Co. v. Commissioner,* 236 F.2d 159 (6th Cir., 1956).

Taxpayer's Position	*Court's Holding*
Diversion of corporate funds amounted to embezzlement rather than a dividend, as all the stockholders did not participate in the receipt of funds.	The corporation and its stockholders should not be permitted to escape taxation because the distributions were technically illegal. *Drybrough, et al. v. Commissioner*, 238 F.2d 735 (6th Cir., 1956).
The amount involved was not a dividend distribution, as other stockholders received nothing.	The taxpayer dominated the corporation; it is well settled that dividends, for purposes of Federal income tax, need not be proportional to shares held or be paid to all shareholders. *Hub Cloak & Suit Co., Inc., et al.*, T.C. Memo., Docket ##36937–8, Aug. 28, 1956.
Withdrawals were not in proportion to stockholdings and, therefore, were not dividends but loans.	Not determinative. *B. F. Crabbe, et al.*, T.C. Memo., Docket ##44359–60, Mar. 5, 1956.
Withdrawals were not made in proportion to stockholdings.	Non pro rata distribution may be a dividend. *William C. Baird, et al.*, 25 T.C. 387 (1955).
Distribution was intended to redeem one stockholder's shares and not as a dividend distribution.	Amounts distributed were proportionate to stockholdings; corporation had funds available; hence, a dividend. *Edward Stevens*, T.C. Memo., Docket #53934, Dec. 28, 1955.
Payments were disproportionate among the stockholders.	Not controlling. *58th Street Plaza Theatre, Inc. v. Commissioner*, 195 F.2d 724 (2d Cir., 1952).
Withdrawals were not proportionate to stockholdings nor	Not conclusive against a finding that withdrawals were

Taxpayer's Position	*Court's Holding*

C, 2. DISPROPORTIONATE TO STOCKHOLDERS—*Continued*

participated in by all the shareholders.	dividends. *Regensburg v. Commissioner*, 144 F.2d 41 (2d Cir., 1944).
The mere purchase of the corporation's treasury shares by some, but not all, the stockholders did not give rise to income.	All stockholders consented to the sale; hence, the excess above book value constituted a dividend distribution. *Elizabeth Susan Strake Trust*, 1 T.C. 1131 (1943).
Withdrawals were not in proportion to stockholdings.	Not determinative. *Ben R. Meyer, et al.*, 45 B.T.A. 228 (1941).
Distribution was not in proportion to the stock ownership.	Not controlling. *Hudson v. Commissioner*, 99 F.2d 630 (6th Cir., 1938).
Withdrawals were not in proportion to stockholdings.	Not determinative. *Roy J. Kinnear*, 36 B.T.A. 153 (1937).
The distribution was not pro rata.	Not controlling. *McGuire v. Commissioner*, 84 F.2d 431 (7th Cir., 1936).
Entire amount was received by taxpayer, whereas he actually owned only one half of stock and no distribution was made to other stockholders.	If taxpayer received the money, corporate irregularity as to payment is not a bar to taxability to recipient. *C. W. Murchison*, 32 B.T.A. 32 (1935).
Distribution was not pro rata.	Not determinative. *Lincoln Nat. Bank v. Burnet*, 63 F.2d 131 (D.C. Cir., 1933).
Distribution was not pro rata.	Not controlling. *E. T. Schuler*, 29 B.T.A. 415 (1933).
Withdrawals were not pro rata among all stockholders.	Insufficient to support conclusion that amounts were not

Taxpayer's Position

Distributions were not in proportion to stockholdings.

Distribution was not pro rata.

Distribution was not pro rata and therefore could not be a dividend.

Court's Holding

dividends. *Christopher v. Burnet,* 55 F.2d 527 (D.C. Cir., 1931).

Not controlling. *F. G. Lamb,* 14 B.T.A. 814 (1928).

Not controlling. *Ida L. Dowling, et al.,* 13 B.T.A. 787 (1928).

Not controlling. *Joseph Goodnow & Co.,* 5 B.T.A. 1154 (1927).

C. OTHER PAYMENTS OR TRANSFERS OF PROPERTY TO STOCKHOLDERS
   —*Continued*

   3. ALLEGED PAYMENT OF DEBT OF CORPORATION

Taxpayers transferred stock to a successor corporation in an arms' length transaction in return for corporate notes; the subsequent payments to taxpayer were payments on the notes.

The sale of stock to the successor corporation was not at arm's length and despite the sale of stock the stockholders retained control; payments made by successor corporation were in effect distributions essentially equivalent to dividends. *Kolkey v. Commissioner,* 254 F.2d 51 (7th Cir., 1958).

Repayments to its stockholders of money borrowed from them by a corporation do not result in dividends to stockholders.

Payments to the stockholders are repayments of loans to the extent of funds advanced by the stockholder and are taxable dividends as to the excess of the payment over the loan. *Garden State Developers, Inc.,* 30 T.C. 135 (1958).

The amount received was payment on an instalment sales

"Thin capitalization" standing alone is not sufficient to

Taxpayer's Position   *Court's Holding*

C, 3. ALLEGED PAYMENT OF DEBT OF CORPORATION—*Continued*

contract and not a dividend distribution.

justify treating an instalment sales contract as equity investment; although the debt-stock ratio was 50 to 1, the company was adequately capitalized; hence, the receipt was principal of an instalment sale and not a dividend. *J. I. Morgan, Inc., et al.,* 30 T.C. 881 (1958).

The receipt during the year involved was repayment of a loan, evidenced by notes, to the corporation by the stockholder.

Based upon the facts, the court was justified in concluding that payment made in a prior year, barred by the statute of limitations, was on account of the loan, and that payment made in the year involved, when the notes were surrendered to the corporation, was not repayment of the loan but a dividend distribution to the extent of earnings and profits. *C. H. Wentworth v. Commissioner,* 244 F.2d 874 (9th Cir., 1957).

The amount received was in payment of a note.

The notes issued upon incorporation were in direct proportion to stockholdings and were equity investment rather than indebtedness; hence, payment of the note was essentially equivalent to a dividend. *Gunn v. Commissioner,* 244 F.2d 408 (10th Cir., 1957).

Amounts received were repayments of loans made to the corporation.

The sole stockholder diverted to himself the funds of the corporation; hence, the

Taxpayer's Position	*Court's Holding*
	amounts involved were additional unreported income of the stockholder. *Leo L. Lowy,* T.C. Memo., Docket #11085, May 15, 1957, *remanded for additional facts,* 262 F.2d 809 (2d Cir., 1959).
The amount received was repayment of loan to the corporation and not a dividend.	The intention was to make a loan and not a contribution to capital; hence, repayment of the sum advanced was not a distribution essentially equivalent to a dividend. *J. H. Perkins,* T.C. Memo., Docket #56782, July 12, 1957.
The amount received was repayment of loan to the corporation, not a dividend.	The intention was to make a loan and not a contribution to capital; hence, repayment of the sum advanced was not a distribution essentially equivalent to a dividend. *Joseph Adrey,* T.C. Memo., Docket #56809, May 31, 1957.
Payment in satisfaction of obligation arising out of advances made to corporation.	Advances were erroneously credited to capital surplus; stockholder's personal checkbooks indicated that payments to corporation were loans; hence, payments were not essentially equivalent to a dividend. *Joseph Adrey, supra.*
The receipt by the stockholders was payment of a debt owed to them by the corporation and not a dividend distribution.	When the individuals exchanged assets for securities of the corporation, it was known that the value of the assets exceeded the value of the securities issued, and the excess

Taxpayer's Position   *Court's Holding*

C, 3. ALLEGED PAYMENT OF DEBT OF CORPORATION—*Continued*

constituted a loan to the corporation; hence, payment of such excess by the corporation was payment of a loan and not a distribution essentially equivalent to a dividend. *Moll, et al. v. Carey,* — F. Supp. — (D.C.Ohio, 1957).

Payment was a partial payment of principal of outstanding notes.

Notes represented a genuine indebtedness and were issued for a good business reason; hence, payments were in reduction of principal of the notes. *Miller v. Commissioner,* 239 F.2d 729 (9th Cir., 1956).

Payment received was in the liquidation of the corporation and hence, not taxable as a dividend, but as a capital gain.

Stockholders made cash contribution to new corporation prior to the distribution to them of the liquid assets of the old corporation; and to the extent of the contribution, the distribution was not taxable, as it was, in effect, the repayment of an advance. *Liddon v. Commissioner,* 230 F.2d 304 (6th Cir., 1956).

The amount received was repayment of a loan made to the corporation, and not a dividend.

The money was advanced by the stockholders to improve the realty of the corporation, which was not thinly incorporated, and was intended as a loan; hence, repayment was not a dividend distribution. *L. J. Erickson,* T.C. Memo., Docket #54828, Nov. 19, 1956.

Withdrawals constituted a

There was no evidence to

Taxpayer's Position

repayment of a loan made to
the corporation.

Payment was a repayment
of a loan.

Payment was a payment of
the principal on outstanding
notes of the corporation.

The amount received was
payment of a note giving rise
to capital gain.

Payments were of amounts
loaned to the corporation.

Court's Holding

show that the amounts withdrawn were applied in repayment of the loan. *M. L. Cot-
tingham, et al.*, T.C. Memo.,
Docket ##46721–2, 56880–1,
Aug. 14, 1956.

Repayment of the loan was
in effect made by distributions
in prior years (closed by the
statute of limitations) and,
therefore, the current distribution was essentially equivalent
to the distribution of a dividend. *C. H. Wentworth*, 25
T.C. 1210 (1956).

Notes represented a valid
debt; the corporation was adequately capitalized and the
evidence showed that there was
no intent to place the amount
represented by the notes at the
risk of the business; hence, the
payment did not constitute a
dividend. *Sheldon Tauber, et
al.*, 24 T.C. 179 (1955).

The several steps whereunder partnership assets were
transferred to a corporation for
stock and notes was but one
transaction, and payment of
the note was a distribution of
earnings; hence, there was a
dividend distribution. *Houck
v. Hinds*, 215 F.2d 673 (10th
Cir., 1954).

The distributions were repayments of a loan; hence, not
dividend distributions. *Charles*

Taxpayer's Position	*Court's Holding*

C, 3. ALLEGED PAYMENT OF DEBT OF CORPORATION—*Continued*

	H. Martin, et al., T.C. Memo., Docket #32497, Jan. 8, 1954.
Payment by the corporation was repayment of a loan and inconsistent book entries were erroneous.	A fair preponderance of the evidence shows that the entries were erroneous and the distribution was in repayment of a loan and not a dividend. *William H. Cousins*, T.C. Memo., Docket ##40391–2, June 23, 1953.
Amounts withdrawn were repayments of amounts which stockholders intended to be loans, although there was no written memorandum thereof.	Written instruments are not necessary to support loans, and testimony of stockholders as to their intention is acceptable (in Texas); hence, no dividend. *Bane v. Campbell*, — F. Supp. — (D.C.Tex., 1953).
Distribution constituted repayment of a loan made to the corporation by its organizers upon its incorporation.	The sum was to be repaid to whomever were the stockholders; company was inadequately capitalized; no evidence of indebtedness; carried on books as donated surplus, the contributions were proportionate to the stock issued; the contribution was treated as invested capital in excess profits tax returns. *R. E. Nelson, et al.*, 19 T.C. 575 (1952).
Redemption of preferred stock was in reality the repayment of a loan made by the stockholders to the corporation.	On the facts, the transaction was analogous to the partial recovery of capital loans which were found to be unnecessary, although founded on sound business reasons, and therefore was not the equivalent of a

Taxpayer's Position	*Court's Holding*
	dividend distribution. *G. E. Nicholson,* 17 T.C. 1399 (1952).
Payments were in repayment of corporation's debt to stockholder.	Not substantiated; debt to stockholders had previously been paid; distributions were dividends. *Edward H. Rowekamp,* T.C. Memo., Docket #30035, Aug. 31, 1951.
Advances were made between two valid, unrelated and separate corporations and were intended as loans and recorded on the books of each corporation as such.	Advances were intended as loans which was evidenced by book entries and subsequent repayments. *Washington Institute of Technology, Inc.,* T.C. Memo., Docket #23794, Jan. 9, 1951.
Amounts received by stockholders were payments of indebtedness of corporation which arose as a result of increase in value of assets originally transferred to corporation in exchange for its stock.	No valid obligation existed; payments were essentially equivalent to a dividend. *Joseph T. Coyle,* T.C. Memo., Docket ##19409–10, Jan. 25, 1950.
The credit received on a subscription for stock was a repayment, per agreement, for stock previously donated to the corporation for the purpose of strengthening its financial condition.	There was a valid agreement to return what had been contributed, and not a mere contribution to surplus. *Wm. D. Moorer,* 12 T.C. 270 (1949).
Assumption of liability of corporation was part of consideration for distribution of assets.	This consideration was in addition to mere cancellation of stock, and no ordinary incident of a dividend. *L. M. Lockhart,* 8 T.C. 436 (1947).
Distributions were not in partial liquidation, as preferred	By command of the statute, a distribution of funds of a cor-

Taxpayer's Position   *Court's Holding*

C, 3. ALLEGED PAYMENT OF DEBT OF CORPORATION—*Continued*

stock was issued in payment of debt of predecessor corporation and was required to be retired out of earnings with no reduction of invested capital. (Under pre-1942 Act gain on partial liquidation was treated as short term.)

poration in complete retirement of a part of its stock, or one of a series of distributions in complete retirement of all or part of its stock, constitutes a partial liquidation. *Yankey, et al. v. Commissioner*, 151 F.2d 650 (10th Cir., 1945).

Payment was repayment of funds loaned to corporation rather than a repayment of a capital investment.

Not substantiated; funds were placed at risk of the business; there was no liability on part of corporation with respect to amounts paid in; hence, a dividend. *Bertram Meyer*, 5 T.C. 165 (1945), *remanded for additional facts*, 154 F.2d 55 (3d Cir., 1946).

A mere repayment of a debt due stockholder was effected.

The corporation's bookkeeping entries do not indicate that there was any debt due to the stockholders. *Rheinstrom v. Conner*, 125 F.2d 790 (6th Cir., 1942).

Payments were in repayment of the corporation's debt to the stockholder.

On the facts, the distributions were repayments of a bona fide debt owed to the stockholder; hence, not a dividend. *Frank W. Ross*, 44 B.T.A. 1 (1941).

Payments were of an obligation of the corporation to the stockholder, being the amount of the excess of the value of assets transferred to the corporation over the par value of shares issued to the taxpayer.

The receipt of stock in exchange for the assets transferred was consideration for the transfer, and the transaction did not give rise to an obligation on the part of the corporation; hence, payment had

Taxpayer's Position	*Court's Holding*
	the effect of a dividend distribution. *George P. Dickey,* B.T.A. Memo., Docket #100363, July 22, 1941.
Payments were of an obligation of the corporation, as the value of the assets transferred to the corporation exceeded the par value of shares issued to the taxpayer; and the amount of the excess was a debt due to the stockholder.	In the circumstances the payments were a distribution of a dividend. *Charles C. Tanner,* B.T.A. Memo., Docket #77664, Jan. 26, 1937.
Payments were in repayment of a loan made to the corporation for the purpose of enabling it to carry out a series of transactions to meet the requirements of a local statute in regard to intercorporate holdings of stock.	This was a sound reason; not dividends. *George P. Pitkin,* 31 B.T.A. 403 (1934).
Payments were in repayment of a loan made to the corporation by the stockholders.	Agreement between stockholders in making the advance to the corporation evidenced an intent to make a loan rather than an additional investment; hence, repayment of loan was not a dividend. *Weaver v. Commissioner,* 58 F.2d 755 (9th Cir., 1932).
The stockholders received repayment of a debt owed to them.	The agreement was for a loan to the corporation and, although carried on its books as contributed surplus, the repayment thereof was not a dividend distribution. *Weaver v. Commissioner, supra.*

Taxpayer's Position   *Court's Holding*

C, 3. ALLEGED PAYMENT OF DEBT OF CORPORATION—*Continued*

The amount withdrawn was payment of a sum due to the stockholders.

The amount withdrawn was less than the amount standing to the stockholder's credit on the corporation's books and was not a dividend to him. *Max Feiges,* 13 B.T.A. 1366 (1928).

Withdrawals by sole stockholder were repayments of loans, even though partly paid from earnings.

Carried in company's accounts as separate and distinct from its capital account and regarded by taxpayer as loans; therefore, not dividends. *Carl G. Fisher,* 7 B.T.A. 968 (1927).

Distribution was a repayment of a loan made to the corporation.

Distribution was not essentially equivalent to a dividend. *Benjamin J. Schiff,* 3 B.T.A. 640 (1925).

C. OTHER PAYMENTS OR TRANSFERS OF PROPERTY TO STOCKHOLDERS —*Continued*

4. PAYMENTS TO STOCKHOLDERS, ALLEGEDLY FOR PROPERTY PURCHASED OR USED BY CORPORATION

Payments represented a portion of the consideration for the transfer of patents by taxpayer to corporation.

Taxpayer transferred all substantial rights in the patents, inventions had not been reduced to successful commercial use, royalties were reasonable in amount, and there was no intent to disguise dividends; hence, not a dividend. *Finn H. Magnus, et al. v. Commissioner,* 259 F.2d 893 (3d Cir., 1958).

Payments by corporation to stockholder of settlement proceeds of patent infringement lawsuit constituted part of the

Corporation was under no obligation to pay over proceeds, taxpayer had relinquished all rights in any such suit and was

Taxpayer's Position	*Court's Holding*
consideration for the transfer of patents to the corporation.	also controlling stockholder; hence, payment was a disguised dividend. *Finn H. Magnus, et al. v. Commissioner,* 259 F.2d 893 (3d Cir., 1958).
The payments received were proceeds of an instalment sale giving rise to capital gain.	The newly formed corporation was not "thinly incorporated" and its acquisition from the incorporators was an instalment purchase; hence, the payment was not essentially equivalent to a dividend. *Perrault v. Commissioner,* 244 F.2d 408 (10th Cir., 1957).
What the stockholder received was for equipment sold to the corporation and not a dividend.	Equipment was sold to the corporation by the stockholder, and at a fair price; hence, the transaction did not result in a distribution essentially equivalent to a dividend. *Jolly's Motor Livery Co., et al.,* T.C. Memo., Docket ##36607, 36745, 41269–70, Dec. 16, 1957.
Individual stockholders sold to a corporation, controlled by them, stock in another corporation immediately prior to the declaration of a dividend by the latter corporation.	The stock was sold for a fair and adequate price prior to the declaration of the dividend; hence, no portion of the sales price was essentially equivalent to a dividend. *Charles Dreifus Co. v. United States,* 140 F. Supp. 499 (D.C.Pa., 1956).
Half of the corporate profits distributed to the sole stockholders represented additional consideration for the original transfer of assets to the corporation.	The stock received by the stockholders originally was adequate consideration for the transfer of the assets; and the distribution, although cast in the form of consideration, was a dividend distribution. *Crab-*

Taxpayer's Position   *Court's Holding*

C, 4. PAYMENTS TO STOCKHOLDERS, ALLEGEDLY FOR PROPERTY
    PURCHASED OR USED BY CORPORATION—*Continued*

	tree v. Commissioner, 221 F.2d 807 (2d Cir., 1955).
Payments were for goodwill.	Goodwill was of value and amount paid therefor, to the extent of its true value, was not essentially equivalent to a dividend. *Sidney V. LeVine*, 24 T.C. 147 (1955).
Moneys received by two petitioners and a third party for sale of story to two corporations, in one of which petitioners owned all stock, in excess of assumption of payment of cost by corporation, constituted capital gain, although in similar proportion to stockholdings.	Bona fide sale at arm's length and not a disguised dividend. *Fred MacMurray*, 21 T.C. 15 (1953).
Purchase was from a third party seller who held no stock.	Although not conclusive, fortifies conclusion of bona fide of sale. *Fred MacMurray, supra.*
The portion of price received in excess of the value of the physical assets transferred by the sole stockholders upon the sale to the corporation of a going business constituted payment for goodwill.	The amount paid in excess of the value of the physical assets was not a dividend. *George J. Staab*, 20 T.C. 834 (1953).
Additional payment was for assets transferred to the corporation in exchange for stock after an adjustment was made in the book value of the assets by the Internal Revenue Service.	The adjustment was capital in nature and no income was created thereby. *Hugh Walling, et ux.*, 19 T.C. 838 (1953).

Taxpayer's Position

Property retransferred to sole stockholder by corporation, to which he had previously transferred same property, was owned by stockholder; and corporation's payments for the use thereof were rent, not informal dividends.

Court's Holding

No tax avoidance motive since corporation had rented all such property since before 1913; and, further, the property transferred was only a small part of similar property so used; therefore, the transfer had substance and must be recognized. *Greenspun, et al. v. Commissioner,* 156 F.2d 917 (5th Cir., 1946), *on remand,* T.C. Memo., Docket ##108233, *et al.,* July 22, 1948.

No part of amount received by sole stockholder from corporation for use of his property, pursuant to binding contract, is a dividend.

Amounts paid under a legally binding rental agreement are not to be considered essentially equivalent to a dividend to the extent of corporation's obligation to make payment. *Greenspun, et al. v. Commissioner, supra.*

No part of amounts received by sole stockholder from corporation for use of his property are dividends as contract permitted corporation to increase rental.

Payments by corporation to stockholder in excess of minimum rental required by contract are informal dividends to stockholders. *Greenspun, et al. v. Commissioner, supra.*

Sale by parent of subsidiary stock to subsidiary was a capital transaction.

Fact that subsidiary treated distribution as from capital and showed no change in surplus account is not controlling. *Pullman, Inc.,* 8 T.C. 292 (1947).

Amount received was in payment of property sold to the corporation.

The land was acquired by the corporation and the stockholder did not intend it to be a gift or contribution to the capital of the corporation; hence, the amount received was

Taxpayer's Position   *Court's Holding*

C, 4. PAYMENTS TO STOCKHOLDERS, ALLEGEDLY FOR PROPERTY
PURCHASED OR USED BY CORPORATION—*Continued*

proceeds of sale and not a dividend distribution. *Herff & Dittmar Land Co., et al.,* **32** B.T.A. 349 (1935).

Exchange of property for art objects placed at the complete control of stockholder was made for business purposes to increase the value of adjoining land owned by corporation.

Not substantiated; if transfer affected value of adjoining property, the effect was incidental, unintentional, and not the real purpose of the transaction; hence, transfer amounted to a dividend. *Security First National Bank of Los Angeles, Executor, et al.,* **28** B.T.A. **289** (1933).

Distribution in form of a dividend and credited against stockholders indebtedness to corporation was in reality a payment for assets transferred to corporation.

In the circumstances the distribution was not a dividend but a payment of the purchase price of assets. *Curran v. Commissioner,* 49 F.2d 129 (8th Cir., 1931).

Withdrawals were applied against the purchase price of property for the corporation.

Stockholder received no benefit for that part of withdrawal used to buy property for corporation; hence, to that extent the withdrawals were not dividends, but withdrawals in excess of the purchase price were dividends. *Joseph McReynolds,* 17 B.T.A. 331 (1929).

Amounts paid to a stockholder were not dividends but payments for lumber purchased by the corporation from the stockholders before they became such.

The sellers of the lumber took stock of the corporation in part payment for the lumber, and the current payments to them were to them as stockholders and recorded by the

Taxpayer's Position

Payments were part of the purchase price for merchandise delivered to the corporation by the stockholders and not dividends.

Court's Holding

corporation as dividends; hence, they must be treated as such. *Peavy-Byrnes Lumber Co., et al.*, 14 B.T.A. 625 (1928).

In the circumstances, the payments represented part of the purchase price for merchandise and were not essentially equivalent to a dividend. *Mobile Delivery Co.*, 8 B.T.A. 1224 (1927).

C. OTHER PAYMENTS OR TRANSFERS OF PROPERTY TO STOCKHOLDERS
   —*Continued*
   5. PAYMENTS TO STOCKHOLDERS FOR TRANSACTION ALLEGEDLY ON
   BEHALF OF CORPORATION

Amounts withdrawn were reimbursed sales expenses and loans, and were not dividends.

On the facts shown, the position of the stockholder is sustained. *Carl B. Carter*, T.C. Memo., Docket ##56923–7, Aug. 29, 1958, *app. (T) pending*, 5th Cir.

Payments were for expenses incurred by stockholder on behalf of corporation.

Payments were for the personal expense of the stockholder; hence, they were dividends. *Lash v. Commissioner*, 245 F.2d 20 (1st Cir., 1957).

Assumption of a liability by the corporation of what appeared to be a liability of the stockholders was in fact a liability of the corporation.

Corporation assumed an entire transaction originally entered into by the stockholders; the assumption of the liabilities was part of the transaction and the liabilities not the stockholders'; hence, there was no dividend. *Estate of James F. Suter*, 29 T.C. 244 (1957).

Stockholder was a mere con-

Money loaned was used to

Taxpayer's Position   *Court's Holding*

C, 5. PAYMENTS TO STOCKHOLDERS FOR TRANSACTION ALLEGEDLY ON BEHALF OF CORPORATION—*Continued*

duit for transmittal of cash from corporation to vendor.

discharge taxpayer-stockholder's own obligations, not those of corporation. *Thomas J. French, et al.*, 26 T.C. 263 (1956).

Stock redeemed was a part of the stock purchased by the sole stockholder as agent for the corporation.

Facts showed that stockholder did not act for anyone but himself and distribution was essentially eqiuvalent to a dividend. *Mendle Silverman*, T.C. Memo., Docket #40835, June 11, 1954.

Withdrawal constituted funds held for the corporation and later used for its account.

In the circumstances, the withdrawal was not a loan nor a dividend but funds held for the corporation in safekeeping during the time they were not needed by the corporation. *Arthur Rosencrans, et al.*, T.C. Memo., Docket #38618, Feb. 26, 1954.

Distribution to stockholder was as reimbursement for his purchase of stock on behalf of corporation from a dissident stockholder.

Distribution was essentially equivalent to a dividend, as there was no indication that purchase was made on behalf of corporation. *Holloway v. Commissioner*, 203 F.2d 566 (6th Cir., 1953).

Funds received by stockholder from sale of corporate assets were held by him as agent for the corporation and were reinvested or expended in the interest of the corporation.

Not substantiated. *E. T. Schuler*, 29 B.T.A. 415 (1933).

Taxpayer's Position   *Court's Holding*

C. OTHER PAYMENTS OR TRANSFERS OF PROPERTY TO STOCKHOLDERS
—*Continued*

    6. PAYMENTS TO STOCKHOLDERS FOR SHARES OF A SISTER-
    CORPORATION

Proceeds were from the sale of stock in a corporation controlled by taxpayer to a corporation wholly owned by him.

Sale was motivated by business purposes and did not lack economic reality; hence, proceeds were not dividends. *Busch v. United States,* — F. Supp. — (D.C.Calif., 1958).

The payment received was for the sale at arm's length by taxpayer of shares of A Corp. to B Corp. and could not be considered the receipt of a dividend.

Stockholder of Corp. A was the beneficial owner of the shares of Corp. B, the purported sale was not bona fide, the stockholder continued as the sole stockholder after the sale; hence, stockholder received earnings and profits of the corporation taxable as ordinary income. *Sam Gold,* T.C. Memo., Docket #59591, Jan. 13, 1958.

Sale of stock of one corporation to another by majority stockholder of both was for good business reasons and did not constitute a dividend.

On the facts the transaction was not lacking in economic reality; hence, not a dividend. *Trianon Hotel Co.,* 30 T.C. 156 (1958); *Commissioner v. Pope,* 239 F.2d 881 (1st Cir., 1957).

Payments represented proceeds from the sale of stock of one controlled corporation to another controlled corporation.

Sale did not in effect lack economic reality; hence, payments were not dividends. *Westerhaus Co.,* T.C. Memo., Docket #59557, Nov. 15, 1957.

Amounts received by stockholders from wholly owned corporation represented proceeds from the sale to the corpora-

Sales prices were equal to those which would have been present in an arm's length transaction and did not repre-

Taxpayer's Position   *Court's Holding*

C, 6. Payments to Stockholders for Shares of a Sister-Corporation—*Continued*

tion of stock of three other wholly owned corporations.

sent a diminution of corporate surplus, as assets were increased by property at least as valuable as the cash paid out; hence, payments were not dividends. *Emma Cramer,* 20 T.C. 679 (1953).

Amounts were proceeds from the sale of stock by the stockholders of a corporation to the corporation's subsidiary.

The subsidiary did not cancel or redeem its stock when it purchased the stock of its parent company; hence, proceeds were not dividends. *Commissioner v. Wanamaker, Phila., Trustees Common Stock,* 178 F.2d 10 (3d Cir., 1949).

C. Other Payments or Transfers of Property to Stockholders —*Continued*

7. Alleged Gifts

The receipt by the widow of a stockholder of funds from a closely held corporation was a gift and not a dividend.

The deceased husband-president had been fully compensated and the payment was intended as a gift; hence, the receipt was not a dividend. *United States v. Bankston,* 254 F.2d 641 (6th Cir., 1958).

Payments to deceased employee's widow-stockholder were a gift.

Payments were not made to employee's estate; were intended as gifts; requisite gift tax returns were filed; corporation derived no benefit from payment which was made to taxpayer who performed no services for corporation; hence, payments were not dividends.

Taxpayer's Position	*Court's Holding*
	Friedlander v. United States,— F. Supp. — (D.C.Wis., 1958).
Payments to certain stockholders were gratuities in consideration of past services performed for the corporation by their deceased husbands.	A distribution by a corporation to its stockholders is, by definition, a dividend. *Lengsfield v. Commissioner,* 241 F.2d 508 (5th Cir., 1957).
Payments to deceased president's wife who owned about 13% of the company's shares were gifts and not dividends.	The facts showed that the payments were intended as gifts; hence, payments were not dividends. *Estate of John A. Maycann,* 29 T.C. 81 (1957).
Cancellation of taxpayer's debt by an insolvent corporation which was a subsidiary of a corporation of which taxpayer was the principal stockholder was a gift.	Taxpayer received no benefit, nor were his assets increased; he performed no services and gave no consideration; it was a gift to another debtor as well as to taxpayer and, hence, not a dividend to taxpayer. *Gibson v. Commissioner,* 83 F.2d 869 (3d Cir., 1936).
Cancellation of stockholder's indebtedness to corporation was a gift.	Not substantiated. *Waggaman v. Helvering,* 78 F.2d 721 (D.C. Cir., 1935).
Cancellation of indebtedness was a gift, not a dividend.	Not substantiated; hence, a dividend. *Fitch v. Commissioner,* 70 F.2d 583 (8th Cir., 1934).
Transfer to stockholders of stock of another corporation received as a stock dividend was a gift intended as such by the Board of Directors.	Not determinative of the nature of the distribution as a division of profits not changed by manner in which accomplished; hence, distribution was a dividend. *Lincoln Nat. Bank v. Burnet,* 63 F.2d 131 (D.C. Cir., 1933).

Taxpayer's Position	*Court's Holding*

C, 7. ALLEGED GIFTS—*Continued*

Transfer of property was a gift.	Not substantiated; hence, transfer was a dividend. *Security First National Bank of Los Angeles, Executor, et al.,* 28 B.T.A. 289 (1933).
Cancellation by a corporation of a debt of the largest stockholder, created by withdrawals over a period of years, was a gift.	Taxable as a dividend. *Hugh H. Miller,* 25 B.T.A. 418 (1932).
Cancellation and forgiveness of stockholder's indebtedness to corporation was a gift from the corporation.	Cancellation of indebtedness was a distribution in the nature of a dividend. *Henry D. Muller,* 16 B.T.A. 1015 (1929).
Cancellation of loans made to stockholders was not a distribution of profits but a gift.	Not substantiated; hence, distribution was a dividend. *Ida L. Dowling, et al.,* 13 B.T.A. 787 (1928).

C. OTHER PAYMENTS OR TRANSFERS OF PROPERTY TO STOCKHOLDERS —*Continued*
     8. OTHER PAYMENTS TO OR WITHDRAWALS BY STOCKHOLDERS

Proceeds were from the sale of stock to the corporation.	Corporate ownership and control remained substantially unchanged; no contraction of business was contemplated; shareholder needed money to pay taxes; there was immense amount of earnings and profits available for distribution; hence, proceeds were essentially dividends. *Wilson v. United States,* 257 F.2d 534 (2d Cir., 1958).
Proceeds of insurance policy	Stockholders were not acting

Taxpayer's Position	*Court's Holding*
on life of deceased officer-stockholder were received by stockholders directly and not by corporation.	on behalf of corporation in applying for insurance and in receiving and disbursing the proceeds. The proceeds therefore did not constitute a dividend distribution. *Doran v. Commissioner*, 246 F.2d 934 (9th Cir., 1957).
Payments represented the proceeds of a sale of stock to the corporation.	There was no business purpose of the corporation served by its acquisition of the stock, but rather an obligation of taxpayer was discharged by the payment; hence, payment was a dividend. *Ferro v. Commissioner*, 242 F.2d 838 (3d Cir., 1957).
Distribution of shares of subsidiaries to parent's stockholder's, at which time par value of parent's shares was reduced, was a dividend distribution and not a capital distribution which reduced parent's invested capital.	Reduction of par value of shares did not constitute a redemption or cancellation of shares; hence, the distribution of the shares of the subsidiaries was not in a liquidation but a dividend distribution for invested capital purposes. *Avco Manufacturing Corp.*, 25 T.C. 975 (1956), *remanded only to recompute overpayment*, — F.2d — (2d Cir., 1957).
Corporation had no intention of distributing earnings under the guise of discharging debts.	Not material. *Gooding Amusement Co. v. Commissioner*, 236 F.2d 159 (6th Cir., 1956).
The funds were withdrawn by minority stockholders not in control of corporate affairs.	The stockholders were in control, as wives owned balance of stock and withdrawn funds were for personal use of stock-

Taxpayer's Position   *Court's Holding*

C, 8. OTHER PAYMENTS TO OR WITHDRAWALS BY STOCKHOLDERS—
Continued

holders. *William C. Baird, et al.,* 25 T.C. 387 (1955).

Funds represented proceeds of illegal factoring of nonexistent accounts receivable.

No evidence of which proceeds were legal and which were illegal; distribution taxable as a dividend. *William B. Benjamin,* T.C. Memo., Docket #22748, Oct. 26, 1955.

Distribution to stockholders, made just prior to sale to a third party of all their stock, was part of the purchase price of the stock and was not a dividend distribution.

Taxpayers, as stockholders, authorized the distribution, as directors declared the dividend and as stockholders received it in proportion to their stockholdings; the minutes of the stockholders' and directors' meetings show clearly that this distribution was a dividend. *Albert G. Rooks, et al.,* T.C. Memo., Docket ##29716–7, Feb. 9, 1953.

Distribution was pursuant to an agreement whereby subsidiary was to pay its parent its pro rata share of the consolidated tax liability.

Payment pursuant to a contractual liability does not prevent classifying as a dividend the amount of payment in excess of subsidiary's pro rata share of consolidated tax liability; hence, to such extent distribution was a dividend. *Beneficial Corporation,* 18 T.C. 396 (1952), *aff'd,* 202 F.2d 150 (3d Cir., 1953).

The rights under a contract owned by the corporation which were retained by the stockhold-

The value of such rights assigned to the selling stockholders held essentially equivalent

Taxpayer's Position	*Court's Holding*
ers when they sold their stock were part of the consideration for the stock sold.	to a dividend. *T. J. Coffey, Jr., et al.,* 14 T.C. 1410 (1950).
Distribution was authorized by the comptroller of currency.	Not controlling. *Dunton v. Clauson,* 67 F. Supp. 839 (D.C. Me., 1946).
Amounts were withdrawn from corporation for personal use of stockholder. (Here, taxpayer sought to have withdrawals taxed as a dividend.)	Such withdrawals are essentially dividends. *Estate of Louis F. Buff,* T.C. Memo., Docket #4253, Dec. 20, 1945.
A note was received in connection with a recapitalization; there was no formal declaration of a dividend; nor did the stockholder consider the receipt of the note to be a dividend; nor was bad faith involved.	Taxpayer's contentions are irrelevant because pro rata payments on the corporation's note held by stockholders were out of current earnings and profits and, hence, constituted a dividend. *Emil Stein, et al.,* 46 B.T.A. 135 (1942).
Withdrawals were not dividends, as the borrowers were not stockholders of the corporation making the loan but stockholders of its parent corporation.	Through their control of and their beneficial and real ownership of stock of the subsidiary, the taxpayers were shareholders for dividend purposes. *Ben R. Meyer, et al.,* 45 B.T.A. 228 1941).
Payments were proceeds of a life insurance policy no longer owned by the corporation on the life of the corporation's president.	Not substantiated. Corporation reserved all rights in the policy, paid the premiums, retained title to the policy and carried it on the books as an asset; hence, distribution of insurance proceeds was essentially a dividend. *Golden v. Commissioner,* 113 F.2d 590 (3d Cir., 1940).

Taxpayer's Position   *Court's Holding*

C, 8. OTHER PAYMENTS TO OR WITHDRAWALS BY STOCKHOLDERS—
Continued

Payments were proceeds of an insurance policy on the life of the corporation's president, under which the stockholders were the beneficiaries; the corporation merely acted as trustee for the stockholders in receiving the funds.

Not substantiated, as the corporation was the real beneficiary of the insurance policy; hence, the distribution was a dividend. *Cummings, et al. v. Commissioner*, 73 F.2d 477 (1st Cir., 1934).

Payment was a distribution of capital authorized by state commissioner of corporations.

Where corporation's earnings and surplus were sufficient to cover the distribution, it must be deemed to have been paid therefrom and to be a taxable dividend. Neither the action of the state commissioner nor of the corporation is decisive. *Faris v. Helvering*, 71 F.2d 610 (9th Cir., 1934).

The property received from the corporation was purchased by it for the stockholder and was not a dividend to the stockholder.

The evidence sustains that the purchase was by the corporation as agent for the stockholder who paid the corporation for the purchases; and the way the transactions were handled on the company's books must give way to the facts; hence, there was no dividend distribution. *Watson-Moore Co., et al.*, 30 B.T.A. 1197 (1934).

P Corp. transferred assets to S Corp. for shares of the latter, which retransferred said assets and a percentage of the profits earned thereon to P Corp. for

Sufficient evidence was not presented that S Corp. intended to distribute a dividend, which it did not formally declare, and S Corp.'s minutes indicated

Taxpayer's Position	*Court's Holding*

the shares it originally received, S Corp. remaining in business with other assets. The cash received was a dividend, as S Corp. continued in business.

The payment was not a dividend but a return of capital as stockholders bought the shares in contemplation of the dividend being paid.

Payment was made for business purposes as it increased the value of other property owned by the corporation.

Although payments to stockholders were made just prior to payment of a liquidating dividend, they were paid from earnings and were thus ordinary dividends. (1926 Act, Section 216, provided that dividends were credited for the purpose of normal tax and, therefore, measured only the surtax; amounts distributed in liquidation were subject to both the normal and surtax.)

The payment was not a dividend but a return of capital

---

that it considered the transaction a purchase of its stock with assets; hence, the distribution was in a partial liquidation and was not a dividend. *Palmetto Quarries Co.,* 30 B.T.A. 544 (1934).

Although the shares were bought shortly before the dividend was declared and it did influence the price paid for the stock, the payment received by the purchasers with respect to the shares so purchased was a dividend and not a return of capital. *Marcus Friedler,* 27 B.T.A. 1239 (1933).

Not substantiated; not shown to be real purpose of the transfer. *Security First National Bank of Los Angeles, Executor, et al.,* 28 B.T.A. 289 (1933).

What the directors may call a distribution does not alter its character; at the time of the distribution the corporation was not a going concern and dissolution was already under way; the distribution was very unusual and entirely outside the due course of the business of the corporation; it was, therefore, a liquidating dividend. *Gossett v. Commissioner,* 59 F.2d 365 (4th Cir., 1932).

Although the shares were bought shortly before the divi-

Taxpayer's Position   *Court's Holding*

C, 8. OTHER PAYMENTS TO OR WITHDRAWALS BY STOCKHOLDERS—
Continued

as stockholders bought the shares in contemplation of the dividend being paid.

dend was declared, it did influence the price paid for the stock; the payment received by the purchasers with respect to the shares so purchased was a dividend and not a return of capital. *Edward H. Moore,* 22 B.T.A. 366 (1931).

Distribution was a stock dividend and was so understood by all parties, not a purchase of stock with the proceeds of cash dividend.

Even though ultimate result was same as stock dividend, cash dividend was authorized by resolution, checks were issued, and on all evidence dividend was in cash and taxable as such. *Margaret B. Payne,* 19 B.T.A. 1305 (1930).

Withdrawals by stockholders were made after reduction in authorized capital stock.

On the facts, withdrawals were dividends. *Elizabeth Berthold, et al.,* 12 B.T.A. 1306 (1928).

The payment was not a dividend but a return of capital as stockholders bought the shares in contemplation of the dividend being paid.

Although the shares were bought shortly before the dividend was declared and it did influence the price paid for the stock, the payment received by the purchasers with respect to the shares so purchased was a dividend and not a return of capital. *Julius S. Rippel,* 12 B.T.A. 438 (1928).

Additional stock was issued to stockholders when stockholders assumed obligations of the corporation. Even though obligations were paid by corpora-

The consideration for the additional stock was assumption of the corporate liabilities. When the corporation paid the liabilities and charged the divi-

Taxpayer's Position	*Court's Holding*
tion, the transaction did not result in income to stockholders.	dend account on its books, the stockholders were in receipt of a taxable dividend. *E. B. Miller,* 7 B.T.A. 921 (1927).
Excess of receipts over cash accounted for on books charged to stockholder's personal account were bookkeeping errors.	No convincing evidence adduced that amounts were not withdrawals; hence, held to be dividends. *Max M. Barken Drug Co.,* 3 B.T.A. 277 (1925).
The corporation distributed shares of a newly formed subsidiary to which it had transferred its assets, and the receipt of those shares was not a dividend.	The stockholders of the parent corporation received assets of value severed from their capital interest in the old corporation; hence, the distribution constituted a dividend. *United States v. Phellis,* 257 U.S. 156 (1921).

D. DISTRIBUTIONS IN ALLEGED REORGANIZATIONS ("BOOT," ETC.)

The cash received was a portion of the proceeds of sale of stock in an arm's length transaction to a third-party corporate purchaser.	The transaction was an arm's length sale, and the subsequent merger of corporations sold into the purchasing corporation did not result in a statutory reorganization under which the cash received would have represented a taxable distribution of earnings and profits of the companies whose stock was sold. *Commissioner v. Johnson,* 267 F.2d 382 (1st Cir., 1959).
The issuance of the shares and debentures for the surrender of shares plus cash was in a reorganization, and was not a distribution essentially equivalent to a dividend.	The transaction did not constitute a reorganization; hence, the excess of the value of the debentures over the cash paid was a distribution essentially equivalent to a dividend. *Ort-*

Taxpayer's Position　　　　　*Court's Holding*

D. DISTRIBUTIONS IN ALLEGED REORGANIZATIONS ("BOOT," ETC.)— *Continued*

mayer v. Commissioner, 265 F.2d 848 (7th Cir., 1959).

Distribution was not made to taxpayer, nor was it constructively received by taxpayer, but was made in redemption of one half of the company's stock held by a stockholder other than taxpayer.

Unless a distribution sought to be taxed as a dividend is made to a stockholder or for his benefit, it may not be regarded as a dividend or the legal equivalent of a dividend; hence, distribution was not a dividend. *Joseph R. Holsey*, 28 T.C. 962 (1958), *rev'd*, 258 F.2d 865 (3d Cir., 1958).

The cash received by the stockholders was in connection with tax-free exchange and was not a dividend.

Taxpayer, upon the assumption that the book value of his stock was of a stated sum, exchanged his stock for stock and debentures in a new corporation. As per agreement, the stock was later re-evaluated and taxpayer was paid additional cash. This cash payment was taxable as a capital gain and not as a dividend. *Davis v. United States*, 255 F.2d 48 (6th Cir., 1958).

When M Corp. caused P Corp. to be formed and exchanged all of the shares of R Corp. for all the shares of P Corp., which it then distributed to its sole stockholder, the stockholder's receipt of the P Corp. shares was in a tax-free reorganization.

There was no business purpose for the alleged reorganization, and the transfer of R Corp. shares for the P Corp. shares had no relation to the business of any of the corporations, but was merely a device for the distribution of earnings and profits to the stockholder, who received a dividend distri-

Taxpayer's Position	*Court's Holding*
	bution, taxable as such. *Perry E. Bondy,* 30 T.C. 1037 (1958), *app. (T) pending,* 4th Cir.
Proceeds represented payment for the sale of stock by the controlling stockholders of one corporation to another corporation virtually controlled by the same group of stockholders rather than as part of a reorganization.	The substance of Section 115(g) was not extended to include cases of "brother sister" corporations until the 1954 Code; taxpayers did not receive stock in the acquiring corporation as a result of the transaction in question, and therefore there could be no reorganization; hence, proceeds did not constitute dividends. *Trianon Hotel Co.,* 30 T.C. 156 (1958).
Taxpayers sold their shares of P Corp. for short-term notes and 20-year bonds of H Corp.; and P Corp. was merged with H Corp., but the merger was not a "statutory merger"; therefore, the receipt of the notes was not essentially a dividend.	Although there was a merger of the two corporations, there was no "statutory merger" within the meaning of the Code, and taxpayers were creditors and not proprietary owners of the merged corporation; hence, the sale of the P Corp. shares was a taxable event, and the receipt of the notes was not essentially equivalent to a dividend. *W. H. Truschel,* 29 T.C. 433 (1957).
Distributions were part of a tax-free reorganization.	Distribution was not used principally as a device to distribute earnings but was in effect a tax-free "spin-off"; hence, distribution was not a dividend. *Murdock v. United States,* — F. Supp. — (D.C. Tenn., 1957).
Cancellation of stockholders' indebtedness was part of a	Cancellation of indebtedness had the earmarks of a pro rata

Taxpayer's Position   *Court's Holding*

D. DISTRIBUTIONS IN ALLEGED REORGANIZATIONS ("BOOT," ETC.)—
Continued

consolidation and had the effect of reducing stockholders' interest in the consolidation.

distribution; the notes cancelled merely evidenced nonproductive prior advances by a closely held family corporation to its shareholders for personal use, and the so-called "reduction of interest" was in reality a realignment of ownership in the new corporation to reflect its productive assets; hence, the cancellation of indebtedness was essentially a dividend. *Hawkinson v. Commissioner*, 235 F.2d 747 (2d Cir., 1956).

Payments made to stockholders of a corporation were not part of a plan reorganization, but were payments in liquidation of that corporation.

The several steps taken constituted but one reorganization transaction whereunder assets of the old corporation were transferred to a new corporation, and what the stockholders of the old corporation withdrew from it did not exceed its accumulated earnings and profits; hence, the distribution by the old corporation to its stockholders had the effect of a dividend distribution. *Liddon v. Commissioner*, 230 F.2d 304 (6th Cir., 1956).

There was a complete liquidation of the old corporation, giving rise to capital gain, as a former 20% stockholder retained no interest in the new corporation.

It is not unusual in a reorganization for minority shareholders to liquidate their interests and withdraw; hence, there was a reorganization and the old corporation's distribution of its earnings and profits had the

Taxpayer's Position

Court's Holding

effect of a dividend distribution to the remaining 80% stockholders. *Liddon v. Commissioner, supra.*

Distribution was in complete liquidation of the corporation, and the subsequent transfer by the sole stockholder of some of the assets received in the liquidation to two new corporations was a separate transaction.

The various transactions must be viewed as a whole and constituted a reorganization; hence, the distribution, to the extent of the cash and notes was pursuant to a reorganization and had the effect of a distribution of a taxable dividend. *Ethel K. Lesser, et al.,* 26 T.C. 306 (1956).

Cash distribution on liquidation of corporation, followed by incorporation of new business, was in complete liquidation of old business; business of new corporation was manufacture of different product from predecessor corporation.

Cash "boot" received in reorganization was taxable as a dividend; the fact that new business was different in nature from discontinued business does not prevent series of steps from being a reorganization. *Becher v. Commissioner,* 221 F.2d 252 (2d Cir., 1955).

Cash received constituted part of the proceeds from the sale of stock rather than "boot" in a reorganization wherein stockholder transferred all of his stock in a corporation for cash and preferred stock in the acquiring corporation which subsequently merged the acquired corporation into itself.

The principal objective of the parties was a purchase and sale of stock; taxpayer did not contemplate maintenance of a proprietary interest in the acquiring corporation. There was no reorganization and, hence, there was no boot and no dividend. *Ralph M. Heintz,* 25 T.C. 132 (1955).

The exchange by the sole stockholder of M Corp. of some of her shares for all of the shares of R Corp. (which M Corp. had formed) was made in

The transaction was a reorganization effected to accomplish a business purpose, and the exchange was part of the reorganization; hence, the receipt

Taxpayer's Position *Court's Holding*

D. DISTRIBUTIONS IN ALLEGED REORGANIZATIONS ("BOOT," ETC.)—
Continued

a tax-free reorganization in order to enable M Corp. to retain its franchise; hence, the receipt of R Corp. shares was not essentially equivalent to a dividend.

of the R Corp. shares was not essentially equivalent to a dividend. *Rena B. Farr,* 24 T.C. 350 (1955).

The receipt of debentures in exchange for preferred stock was in a tax-free recapitalization, and did not constitute dividend income.

The transaction involved was a recapitalization accomplished for good business purposes (to permit the senior security to be callable without premium and to eliminate certain voting rights); hence, under the then Code provision, receipt of the debentures was not essentially equivalent to a dividend. *Davis v. Penfield,* 205 F.2d 798 (5th Cir., 1953).

The dissolution of Corp. A and the subsequent organization of Corp. B were two separate transactions, so that earned surplus of Corp. A became paid-in or donated surplus of Corp. B, with the result that Corp. B did not have sufficient earnings to make the amount paid by it a dividend distribution.

The dissolution and subsequent incorporation were two separate transactions and not steps in only one transaction, and Corp. B's surplus was not earned but paid-in or donated; hence, the receipt was not a distribution of earnings constituting a dividend. *Charles R. Mathis, Jr.,* 19 T.C. 1123 (1953).

Assets transferred to a newly formed corporation in exchange for all of its stock, which was distributed to the shareholders of the old corporation in redemption of one half

Distribution was in pursuance of a plan of reorganization and was not essentially equivalent to a dividend. *Chester E. Spangler,* 18 T.C. 976 (1952).

Taxpayer's Position

of their stock, was all part of a tax-free reorganization.

In exchange for his stock, taxpayer received stock of another corporation and new stock of the distributing corporation; the sum of taxpayer's proprietary interest in the two corporations after the distribution was exactly the same as his proprietary interest in the old corporation; the distribution was pursuant to a plan of reorganization and hence was not equivalent to the receipt of a taxable dividend.

The receipt of debentures was part of a tax-free reorganization, and hence was not taxable as a dividend.

Distribution of liquid assets on liquidation of old corporation following transfer of operating assets to new corporation was not in a reorganization, because stockholders intended to sell business and liquidation was for shareholder rather than corporate purposes (protection of liquid assets pending such sale).

Court's Holding

The exchange was pursuant to a plan of reorganization and did not constitute the receipt of a taxable dividend. *Riddlesbarger v. Commissioner,* 200 F.2d 165 (7th Cir., 1952).

This was a reorganization and the exchange was within the scope of the Internal Revenue Code of 1939, Section 112(b)(3); hence, receipt of the debentures was not essentially equivalent to a dividend. *Wolf Envelope Co.,* 17 T.C. 471 (1951).

Although intent was to dispose of business, it was in fact continued, which is the *sine qua non* of a reorganization; distinctions between corporate and shareholder purposes is unrealistic and impractical, particularly with respect to closely-held corporations; hence, distribution had the effect of a dividend. *Lewis, et al. v. Commissioner,* 176 F.2d 646 (1st Cir., 1949).

Taxpayer's Position   *Court's Holding*

D. DISTRIBUTIONS IN ALLEGED REORGANIZATIONS ("BOOT," ETC.)—
Continued

Distribution was in complete liquidation, and the prior transfer of some assets by the old corporation to a new corporation in exchange for its stock was a separate transaction.

What took place was within a literal interpretation of the statutory definition of a reorganization, which may encompass, as one of its incidents, the liquidation of one of the corporations that was a party to the reorganization; hence, the property received from the old corporation was "boot," taxable as a dividend. *Lewis, et al. v. Commissioner, supra.*

Distribution was in complete liquidation and the prior transfer of some assets by the old corporation to a new corporation in exchange for its stock was a separate transaction.

Distribution was a step in connection with a "tax-free" reorganization, and the property received, other than stock in the new corporation, had the effect of a distribution of a dividend. *Estate of Elise W. Hill, et al.,* 10 T.C. 1090 (1948).

Distribution was made in order to complete the equalization between an indebtedness assumed by a corporation in a merger and preferred stock issued in the merger.

Distribution was part of a reorganization and not essentially equivalent to a dividend. *Georgia P. Johnson, et al.,* T.C. Memo., Docket ##7589, *et al.,* June 5, 1947.

Distribution of debentures was part of a tax-free reorganization, wherein stockholders exchanged their par value stock for no par stock and debentures.

There was no valid reorganization; nothing was accomplished that would not have been accomplished by an outright debenture dividend; hence, the distribution of the debentures was a dividend. *Adams v. Commissioner, Bazley v. Commissioner,* 331 U.S. 737 (1947).

Taxpayer's Position

Debentures were issued and distributed as part of a recapitalization which had a corporate business purpose, the hiring of competent management.

Debentures were issued and distributed as part of a recapitalization which had as its primary objective the business interests of the shareholders, and, since no tax avoidance motive is present, no separate corporate business purpose need be shown.

Distribution was in effect a purchase of the minority interest of stock, by the corporation which had been purchased by the taxpayer, so as to obtain the requisite number of shareholders to approve a merger which subsequently was consummated.

Distribution was part of a reduction of capital in a tax-free recapitalization.

Distribution was in partial liquidation, wherein stock was exchanged for cash and new

Court's Holding

Purpose of the exchange was to segregate earnings and profits and preserve them for stockholders; no corporate business purpose is shown and distribution is taxable as a dividend. *Heady v. Commissioner,* 162 F.2d 699 (7th Cir., 1947).

This contention wrongly emphasizes the motive for the transaction rather than its ultimate effect, which was to siphon off earnings and profits, thereby effecting the distribution of a dividend. *Heady v. Commissioner, supra.*

The minority stock was retained by taxpayers; the distribution of cash in the merger was pro rata and not solely to stockholders who purchased the minority interest; distribution was made to equalize the assets of the merging companies; hence, the distribution of cash and other property was essentially equivalent to a dividend. *Isabella M. Sheldon,* 6 T.C. 510 (1946).

Recapitalization does not alter the fact that the cash distribution was a dividend. *Dunton v. Clauson,* 67 F. Supp. 839 (D.C.Me., 1946).

The transaction amounted to a recapitalization, which is one form of a reorganization,

Taxpayer's Position   *Court's Holding*

D. DISTRIBUTIONS IN ALLEGED REORGANIZATIONS ("BOOT," ETC.)—
Continued

stock having less par value, for the purpose of wiping out a book deficit.

and the cash distribution pursuant to the reorganization had the effect of the distribution of a dividend. *Bedford's Estate v. Commissioner*, 325 U.S. 283 (1945).

Cash distribution in a recapitalization is "partial liquidation."

Such distribution *held* taxable as a dividend. *Bedford's Estate v. Commissioner, supra.*

Scrip issued in the amount of unpaid accumulated dividends was part of a reorganization. (Commissioner's position.)

The issuance of scrip was part of the plan of reorganization and not a separate transaction; scrip evidenced a continuing interest in the corporation so as to constitute them securities within the definition of a reorganization; hence, issuance of scrip was not a dividend. *Globe-News Publishing Co.*, 3 T.C. 1199 (1944).

The exchange by the two holders of the corporation's common stock of some of their common for preferred shares did not result in a receipt essentially equivalent to a dividend.

The transaction was an exchange; there was no distribution of earnings and profits, and both the surplus and the capital stock accounts remained unchanged in amount; hence, the issuance of preferred shares was not essentially equivalent to a dividend. *Louis Wellhouse, Jr., et ano.*, 3 T.C. 363 (1944).

Distribution was received in a tax-free reorganization.

The distribution was part of a tax-free reorganization and not essentially equivalent to the distribution of a dividend.

Taxpayer's Position	*Court's Holding*

<table>
<tr><td></td><td>Arthur J. Hooks, T.C. Memo.,
Docket #109416, Aug. 22, 1944.</td></tr>
<tr><td>The receipt of 6% debentures in exchange for 6½% preferred stock was in a tax-free recapitalization, and was not essentially equivalent to a dividend.</td><td>The transaction involved was a recapitalization accomplished to reduce the amount of interest payable and was tax-free; hence, under the Code provision then in effect, the receipt of the debentures was not essentially equivalent to a dividend. Annis Furs, Inc., 2 T.C. 1096 (1943).</td></tr>
<tr><td>The receipt by nonresident aliens of a corporation's debenture in exchange for preferred shares was pursuant to a tax-free recapitalization having a valid business purpose, the reduction of interest charges.</td><td>Distribution was made pursuant to a tax-free recapitalization which was accomplished for a good business reason; hence, distribution was not a dividend. Annis Furs, Inc., supra.</td></tr>
<tr><td>Debentures were issued as part of a recapitalization exchange.</td><td>Recapitalization plan involved the issuance of debentures and there was no ground for treating their issue as a separate and unrelated transaction; hence, not a dividend. Edgar M. Docherty, et al., 47 B.T.A. 462 (1942).</td></tr>
<tr><td>Receipt of preferred and common stock in exchange for common stock was in a recapitalization, and the receipt of preferred stock was not essentially equivalent to a dividend.</td><td>There was a recapitalization accomplished to distribute the corporation's shares more widely and promote the extension of the corporation's business; hence, receipt of the preferred stock in the recapitalization was not essentially equivalent to a dividend. Jacob Fischer, 46 B.T.A. 999 (1942).</td></tr>
</table>

Taxpayer's Position   *Court's Holding*

D. DISTRIBUTIONS IN ALLEGED REORGANIZATIONS ("BOOT," ETC.)—
Continued

Taxpayer's Position	Court's Holding
Distribution was in complete liquidation of the corporation and was a separate and distinct transaction from the reorganization wherein the corporation transferred its operating assets to two new corporations just prior to its liquidation.	The liquidation and the reorganization were all steps in a single transaction constituting a reorganization wherein boot was received and had the effect of a distribution of a dividend. *Heatley Green, et al.*, T.C. Memo., Docket ##109529–30, Dec. 23, 1942.
Distribution was part of a tax-free reorganization (Commissioner's position.)	The transaction was not essentially equivalent to a dividend. *Skenandoa Rayon Corp. v. Commissioner*, 122 F.2d 268 (2d Cir., 1941).
Exchange of old preferred for new preferred and cash was not a recapitalization, as stockholders had option to receive all cash; hence, securities received were stock dividends and dividends paid credit is allowable in full.	Clearly, corporation did not declare a stock dividend. To the extent of the exchange of securities there was a nontaxable reorganization. To the extent of the cash received the distribution had the effect of a dividend and a credit is allowable with respect thereto. *J. Weingarten, Inc.*, 44 B.T.A. 798 (1941).
Distribution was in partial liquidation, and the transfer by the old corporation of all its assets to a new corporation in exchange for the latter's stock was a separate transaction.	The transaction constituted a reorganization which required the liquidation of one of the corporations. The two steps were inseparably connected and the cash distribution was one of a series of interdependent steps and, to the extent it represented gain not in excess of the earnings and profits, it had

Taxpayer's Position	*Court's Holding*
	the effect of a distribution taxable as a dividend. *Love v. Commissioner*, 113 F.2d 236 (3d Cir., 1940).
Distribution of preferred stock was part of a tax-free reorganization.	Receipt of new preferred stock was part of a tax-free reorganization and not essentially equivalent to a dividend. *South Atlantic Steamship Line*, 42 B.T.A. 705 (1940).
Securities which were received in a tax-free reorganization were sold and later reacquired upon exercise of option to repurchase from the vendee; distribution of the reacquired securities was part of the reorganization and not a dividend.	The agreement to repurchase and the subsequent distribution of the reacquired shares were not integral parts of the reorganization transaction; hence, distribution of the reacquired shares was a taxable dividend. *Rich v. Rose*, — F. Supp. — (D.C.Ga., 1940).
The payment was received in a liquidation; there was no plan of reorganization; hence, the payment was not a step in a reorganization.	The determining element is the intention to liquidate the business, coupled with the actual distribution of cash to the stockholders; these elements being present, the payment was received in liquidation. *Kennemer v. Commissioner*, 96 F.2d 177 (5th Cir., 1938).
Taxpayer received in a statutory reorganization shares of stock that were sold at a profit, and not an interest in patents that constituted a dividend distribution from the corporate owner which was party to the reorganization.	A statutory reorganization was effected in which the taxpayer received the stock which was sold, and the reorganization transaction should not be disregarded; hence, the taxpayer was not in receipt of an interest in patents and did not receive a distribution taxable as an ordinary dividend from

Taxpayer's Position	*Court's Holding*

D. DISTRIBUTIONS IN ALLEGED REORGANIZATIONS ("BOOT," ETC.)—
Continued

	the corporate owner of the patents. *Lea v. Commissioner*, 96 F.2d 55 (2d Cir., 1938).
Payments were proceeds from the sale of stock and were not received in a tax-free reorganization, which was a transaction separate from the sale.	Two separate transactions occurred; namely, a reorganization and a sale of stock; hence, payments were not dividends. *Harris v. Commissioner*, 92 F.2d 374 (3d Cir., 1937).
Distribution was part of a reorganization, but it was essentially a dividend. (Commissioner alleged that, as to this corporate distributee, distribution was taxable as a capital gain.)	The distribution was a dividend taxable as such; the fact that in the hands of the recipient stockholder corporation such distribution was not taxable does not alter its character as a dividend. *Forhan Realty Corp. v. Commissioner*, 75 F.2d 268 (2d Cir., 1935).
Cash was received by stockholder in a corporate reorganization and is taxable as a gain.	Cash received by stockholder in a reorganization is a taxable gain, except that the portion which might have been distributed out of surplus before reorganization is taxable as a dividend. *Commissioner v. Owens*, 69 F.2d 597 (5th Cir., 1934).
Distribution was part of a tax-free reorganization.	Distribution in question was not part of the reorganization. If it had been, it would have been taxable as "boot." *H. Y. McCord, et al.*, 31 B.T.A. 342 (1934).

Taxpayer's Position	*Court's Holding*
The amount received was not a dividend, as there was no reorganization.	The several steps taken were but part of one transaction which was a reorganization, and the distribution had the effect of a dividend and is to be treated as such. *John S. Woodard,* 30 B.T.A. 1216 (1934).
Distribution was in complete liquidation of the corporation, and subsequent transfer of business to a new corporation was a separate transaction.	Liquidation of old corporation was not part of reorganization because not within literal requirement of reorganization provisions; hence, no dividend. *Rudolph Boehringer,* 29 B.T.A. 8 (1933).
The amount received was not a dividend, as there was no reorganization.	The several steps taken were but part of one transaction which was a reorganization; and the distribution had the effect of a dividend and is to be treated as such. *T. W. Henritze,* 28 B.T.A. 1173 (1933).
Distribution was part of a reorganization wherein taxpayer exchanged stock in one corporation for cash and stock in another corporation, and any recognizable gain was taxable as a capital gain.	The distribution of cash amounted to a major portion of the corporation's surplus and had the effect of a distribution of a taxable dividend. *George Woodward,* 23 B.T.A. 1259 (1931).
Distribution was part of a tax-free reorganization.	Distribution was in effect a separate transaction from the reorganization; hence, distribution was a dividend. *Fulton's Executors v. Commissioner,* 47 F.2d 436 (D.C. Cir., 1931).
The transfer to the shareholders by the corporation of	The distribution of the shares constituted a dividend.

Taxpayer's Position   *Court's Holding*

D. DISTRIBUTIONS IN ALLEGED REORGANIZATIONS ("BOOT," ETC.)— *Continued*

stock in a second corporation was part of a consolidation or merger.

Charles Owen, 3 B.T.A. 905 (1925).

E. CANCELLATION OF STOCKHOLDER'S INDEBTEDNESS TO CORPORATION

There was no indebtedness of the stockholder to the corporation which was forgiven.

On the facts, the stockholder was indebted to the corporation, as shares purchased were not purchased by him as agent for the corporation, but for his own account with money borrowed from the company; an earlier advance to the company was not a capital contribution but a loan to it; the taxpayer was both a creditor and a debtor of the corporation, and his loans to exceeded his borrowings from the corporation; hence the cancellation of all the debts did not give rise to a distribution essentially equivalent to a dividend. *Ortmayer v. Commissioner,* 265 F.2d 848 (7th Cir., 1959).

Cancellation of a debt constituted a distribution from the company's depletion reserve.

At the time of the cancellation the company had current earnings and profits; hence, the cancellation was a taxable dividend to the stockholder. *Wilson v. Commissioner,* 255 F.2d 702 (5th Cir., 1958).

Cancellation of stockholders' indebtedness was part of a

Cancellation of indebtedness had the earmarks of a pro rata

Taxpayer's Position	*Court's Holding*
consolidation and had the effect of reducing stockholders' interest in the consolidation.	distribution; the notes cancelled merely evidenced nonproductive prior advances by a closely held family corporation to its shareholders for personal use, and the so-called "reduction of interest" was in reality a realignment of ownership in the new corporation to reflect its productive assets; hence, the cancellation of indebtedness was essentially a dividend. *Hawkinson v. Commissioner*, 235 F.2d 747 (2d Cir., 1956).
Notes were cancelled to improve credit position, a business purpose.	Insufficient evidence that credit needed improvement to overcome presumptive correctness attaching to Commissioner's statutory notice of deficiency. *Thomas J. French, et al.*, 26 T.C. 263 (1956).
Cancellation of notes, given to secure loans from corporation for purchase of its stock, on surrender of stock of equivalent book value, did not constitute a dividend, as taxpayer considered notes as just "paperwork."	An obligation was incurred, and finding is dispositive of this issue. *Thomas J. French, et al., supra.*
Surrender of shares for cancellation of stockholder's indebtedness was a sale.	Stock was originally purchased by borrowing corporate funds therefor and giving notes as security; cancellation of this stock and notes left stockholders in same relative position to corporation; hence, distribution was essentially equivalent to a

Taxpayer's Position	*Court's Holding*

E. CANCELLATION OF STOCKHOLDER'S INDEBTEDNESS TO CORPORA-TION—*Continued*

	dividend. *Woodworth, et al. v. Commissioner,* **218** F.2d **719** (6th Cir., **1955**).
Debt cancelled by the corporation was not an obligation of the taxpayer.	The debt was not an obligation of taxpayer; therefore, its cancellation did not constitute a dividend. *Freeland Ham,* T.C. Memo., Docket #46310, June 21, 1955.
The dividend was not payable during the year involved and was not reportable by the stockholder for that year.	Where the dividend is applied against a stockholder's indebtedness during a particular year, it is taxable to him for that year, even though it may not be payable until the next year or is payable but recalled in the next year. *United States v. Lesoine,* **203** F.2d **123** (9th Cir., **1953**).
There was no corporate intention to pay a dividend or to cancel the stockholder's indebtedness to the corporation.	The stockholder transferred to the company securities having a value of less than his indebtedness, and the indebtedness was cancelled; hence, the stockholder was enriched and, to the extent thereof, received a dividend. *Jacob M. Kaplan, et al.,* 21 T.C. 134 (1953).
The withdrawals by the stockholder were dividends in the year withdrawn and not in the subsequent year, when there was a cancellation.	The withdrawals were loans during the years when the withdrawals were made and, during the year when the resulting indebtedness was cancelled, the stockholder derived distribution taxable as a dividend.

Taxpayer's Position	*Court's Holding*
	Wilputte Coke Oven Corp., 10 T.C. 435 (1948).
Indebtedness on account of withdrawals, written down on corporation's books pursuant to a corporate resolution, was not, in reality, released and, therefore, was not a dividend.	In the circumstances, the writedown was not a release of the indebtedness; hence, no dividend distribution. *Sala v. Commissioner*, 146 F.2d 228 (2d Cir., 1944).
Partial redemption of principal stockholder's shares was sales in reduction of his debt, thereby enabling corporation to obtain bank credit.	Net effect of the transaction was a distribution essentially equivalent to a dividend. *William W. Wood, 3rd*, T.C. Memo., Docket #109007, Nov. 23, 1943.
Stock was sold to the corporation to satisfy an existing indebtedness of the stockholder to the corporation, the consideration for the sale being applied against the indebtedness.	In the circumstances the sale was not essentially equivalent to the distribution of a dividend. *R. W. Creech*, 46 B.T.A. 93 (1942).
Transfer of shares to issuing corporation was in repayment of stockholder's debt to corporation.	Transfer was a bona fide sale of shares to the issuing corporation in discharge of stockholder's debt to corporation; hence, not a dividend. *Estate of G. A. Spang*, B.T.A. Memo., Docket #101405, Jan. 16, 1942.
Withdrawals from corporation by officer-stockholders were, in part, compensation for services and, in part, for investments in ventures made for the account of the corporation.	On the basis of the facts, the payments gave rise to debts, and were taxable as dividend income in the year written off by the corporation. *Allen & Reed Inc. v. Commissioner*, 117 F.2d 364 (1st Cir., 1941).
Distribution was made to taxpayer's testator; therefore,	Taxpayer was liable under local law upon receipt of dis-

Taxpayer's Position   *Court's Holding*

E. Cancellation of Stockholder's Indebtedness to Corporation—*Continued*

a release of the debt is not a dividend to the taxpayer.

tribution from estate; therefore, release was of taxpayer's debt and a dividend to him. *Hudson v. Commissioner,* 99 F.2d 630 (6th Cir., 1938).

The withdrawals by the stockholder were dividends in the year withdrawn and not in the subsequent year when there was a cancellation.

The withdrawals were loans during the years when the withdrawals were made, and during the year when the resulting indebtedness was cancelled, the stockholder derived distribution taxable as a dividend. *Wiese v. Commissioner,* 93 F.2d 921 (8th Cir., 1938).

Redemption of stock was made to cancel an indebtedness of the stockholder, who gained no benefit.

Stockholder received nothing of value from the corporation nor did the release and discharge of the indebtedness result in any change in its earned surplus; hence, the cancellation of the indebtedness did not amount to the distribution of a dividend. *R. J. Spencer, Jr.,* B.T.A. Memo., Docket #81472, July 11, 1938.

The dividend was not payable during the year involved and was not reportable by the stockholder for that year.

Where the dividend is applied against a stockholder's indebtedness during a particular year, it is taxable to him for that year, even though it may not be payable until the next year or is payable but recalled in the next year. *Herbert v. Commissioner,* 81 F.2d 912 (3d Cir., 1936).

Taxpayer's Position

Collection of the stockholder's debt which was cancelled was outlawed by the statute of limitations.

Court's Holding

The "statute" did not extinguish the debt; it only suspended the remedy; hence, cancellation was a dividend. *Cohen v. Commissioner,* 77 F.2d 184 (6th Cir., 1935).

Cancellation of stockholders' indebtedness not equivalent to a dividend, as the purported loans were essentially equivalent to dividends in earlier years.

No evidence that petitioners regarded loans as dividends in earlier years; hence, taxable as dividends when first action was taken by corporation to cancel the debts. *Cohen v. Commissioner, supra.*

Redemption of stock received as a stock dividend was made for the sole purpose of cancelling stockholder's indebtedness to corporation.

Not substantiated; hence, cancellation of the indebtedness was essentially a dividend to the extent of the corporation's earnings and profits. *William C. Huntoon,* 14 B.T.A. 459 (1928).

F. PAYMENTS BY CORPORATION FOR BENEFIT OF STOCKHOLDERS
1. LIFE INSURANCE PREMIUMS

Payments were premiums on life insurance policies to insure the lives of its stockholders pursuant to a stock purchase agreement.

The agreement was not one where corporate funds were used by taxpayers to increase the value of their estates; during the lifetime of the policies, the benefits accruing thereunder belonged to the corporation; any present benefits to the stockholders were not taxable incidents; hence, premiums were not dividends. *Sanders v. Fox,* 253 F.2d 855 (10th Cir., 1958).

The corporation was the owner and beneficiary of the

Although each stockholder named the other as the bene-

Taxpayer's Position   *Court's Holding*

F, 1. LIFE INSURANCE PREMIUMS—*Continued*

insurance policies on the lives of the two stockholders and payment of the premiums did not constitute income to them.

ficiary of the insurance policies, the true beneficial owner under the Massachusetts law was the corporation; hence, payment of the premiums was not a dividend to the stockholders. *Prunier v. Commissioner*, 248 F.2d 818 (1st Cir., 1957).

Premiums paid on combined life and annuity insurance policy on life of principal stockholder were not dividends to him because the benefits under the policy did not directly inure to his benefit.

The corporation possessed the right to assign the policy, change the beneficiary, receive dividends on it, and borrow on it; its creditors had a prior right to it; hence, the premium payments were not dividends to the stockholder. (Note: Corporation was entitled to death benefits although, on maturity of policy, taxpayer was to receive monthly income payments. *Casale v. Commissioner*, 247 F.2d 440 (2d Cir., 1957).

Payments of insurance premiums on stockholder's life were not income to the stockholder but were deductible business expenses of the corporation.

Stockholders were beneficiaries of the insurance; hence, premium payments constituted dividend distributions. *Paramount-Richards Theatres, Inc., et al. v. Commissioner*, 153 F.2d 602 (5th Cir., 1946).

Payments were for premiums on a life insurance policy on the life of the taxpayer-president, no part of which, including loans made thereon, and no values accounted for on

The value of the policy was treated as an asset on all corporate records and statements; after issuance of the policy the corporation received the dividends and accumulated interest

Taxpayer's Position

surrender thereof inured to the benefit of taxpayer-president.

Premium payments made by corporation on insurance policies on lives of its two stockholders were loans to the stockholders.

Where a corporation pays premiums on a policy insuring the life of an officer-stockholder, the payments do not constitute income to him if the corporation was the applicant for the policy.

A corporation's payment of insurance premiums on a policy insuring the life of an officer who owned all of the shares of the corporation does not constitute income to the officer.

Court's Holding

and all other benefits; taxpayer received nothing; hence, payments were not dividends despite the fact that taxpayer had the power to nominate a beneficiary. *Lewis v. O'Malley,* 140 F.2d 735 (8th Cir., 1944).

Not substantiated; there was no pledge of collateral or evidence of indebtedness given to corporation, and at the time of payment the corporation charged the items to expense; hence, a dividend. *Earl E. Jameson, et al.,* B.T.A. Memo., Docket ##106788–9, Jan. 22, 1942.

The presumption that insurance premiums paid by the corporation were intended as additional compensation to an officer should be indulged even though the officer-stockholder was not an applicant for the policy. *Commissioner v. Bonwit,* 87 F.2d 764 (2d Cir., 1937).

Premiums paid by a corporation on an individual insurance policy of the officer-stockholder is income to him if he is permitted to name the beneficiary and the corporation is not benefited thereby. *Yuengling v. Commissioner,* 69 F.2d 971 (3d Cir., 1934).

Taxpayer's Position   *Court's Holding*

F. PAYMENTS BY CORPORATION FOR BENEFIT OF STOCKHOLDERS—
Continued
  2. OTHER PAYMENTS FOR STOCKHOLDER'S BENEFIT

The corporation's construction of an addition to premises owned by taxpayer-stockholders did not constitute dividends to them.

Corporate expenditures for benefit of stockholders were corporate distributions taxable as dividends. *Western Supply & Furnace Co., et al.*, T.C. Memo., Docket ##57117, 57142–4, Mar. 30, 1959.

Stock of a corporation was purchased by a group with funds which they had borrowed; this loan was later repaid by the corporation when part of the stock was cancelled by it. Payment of the loan was in redemption of the stock, and is not taxable as a dividend.

On appeal, the Circuit Court held that the Tax Court's holding that the indebtedness was incurred for the benefit of the taxpayers and payment by the corporation constituted a dividend was based upon an improper consideration of evidence. The case is now pending on remand to the Tax Court. *Niederkrome v. Commissioner,* — F.2d — (9th Cir., 1958).

Amounts spent in constructing, maintaining, and operating racing boats were made in the belief that profit would accrue to the corporation; hence, these amounts were ordinary and necessary business of the corporation, and not a dividend distribution.

Such activities did not constitute a trade or business of the corporation; the money was expended for the hobby of the corporation's sole stockholder and was taxable as a dividend to him. *American Properties, Inc., et al. v. Commissioner,* 262 F.2d 150 (9th Cir., 1958).

Payments were made to a former stockholder and represented consideration for the sale of stock to the corporation.

Payments represented the price paid for stock purchased by the corporation and existing stockholders, and the arrangement had the effect as though

Taxpayer's Position	*Court's Holding*
	the sole stockholders had withdrawn funds for their own use and benefit; therefore, such payments were constructive dividends to the existing stockholders. *Zipp v. Commissioner,* 259 F.2d 119 (6th Cir., 1958).
Payments were for expenses incurred by stockholder on behalf of corporation.	Payments were for the personal expense of the stockholder; hence, they were dividends. *Lash v. Commissioner,* 245 F.2d 20 (1st Cir., 1957).
Payments represented the proceeds of a sale of stock to the corporation.	There was no business purpose of the corporation served by its acquisition of the stock, but rather an obligation of taxpayer was discharged by the payment; hence, payment was a dividend. *Ferro v. Commissioner,* 242 F.2d 838 (3d Cir., 1957).
Acquisition of farm in petitioner's name was necessary because of state law, but was corporate investment.	On the record the cost of acquisition was a diversion of corporate funds to the stockholder and a constructive dividend to him. *Archie M. Koyl,* T.C. Memo., Docket ##48336–8, July 17, 1957.
Determination of amount of constructive dividends was arbitrary, excessive, and invalid.	The corporation's funds were made available for personal use of the stockholders and under circumstances constituted constructive dividends; Commissioner's method of determining the amount thereof was reasonable. *Archie M. Koyl, supra.*
The amount paid was rental	The land was actually owned

Taxpayer's Position   *Court's Holding*

F, 2. OTHER PAYMENTS FOR STOCKHOLDER'S BENEFIT—*Continued*

to the stockholder's sons who owned the land.	by the stockholder, and to the extent that the amount paid exceeded the rental value, the stockholder was in receipt of an informal dividend. *Jolly's Motor Livery Co., et al.,* T.C. Memo., Docket ##36607, 36745, 41269–70, Dec. 16, 1957.
The amounts received were received not by the stockholder but by relatives for services rendered to the Company.	As no substantial services were rendered, the amounts involved were not salary payments to the relatives, but were informal dividends to the stockholder. *Jolly's Motor Livery Co., et al., supra.*
Corporation's payments for assets used by stockholder were business promotion expenses.	Payments were not dividends, even though property was for personal use of stockholder, because title to property remained in corporation. *Greenspon v. Commissioner,* 229 F.2d 947 (8th Cir., 1956).
The vehicles purchased by corporation for stockholder's personal use were owned by the corporation.	Amount paid by corporation to purchase this property, to which it retained title, was not a dividend to the stockholder. *Marvin T. Blackwell, et al.,* T.C. Memo., Docket #52701, Aug. 9, 1956.
Automobile expenses were properly chargeable to corporation.	Expenses were for stockholder's personal benefit and therefore, equivalent to a dividend. *Marvin T. Blackwell, et al., supra.*

Taxpayer's Position	*Court's Holding*
Expenses paid by corporation were allowable deductions of corporation.	The payments were of stockholder's personal expenses and hence, dividends. *Thomas W. Briggs, et al.*, T.C. Memo., Docket #36512, April 16, 1956.
Amounts expended by the corporation in enhancing the value of real property, which was subsequently reconveyed to stockholder, was accomplished for sound business reasons and not for the stockholder's benefit.	On the facts, the enhancement in the value of the property reconveyed to stockholder was not a dividend. *H. L. McBride, et al.*, 23 T.C. 901 (1955).
Distributions were made to controlling stockholder's relative, not to stockholder.	Distributions to controlling stockholder's relatives with his approval and consent were dividends constructively received by him. *Union Packing Co., et al.*, T.C. Memo., Docket ##29579, *et al.*, Nov. 22, 1955.
Payments to stockholder's mother were for use of her secret process.	The facts show that the payments were for use of a secret process; not dividends. *Nelson v. Commissioner*, 203 F.2d 1 (6th Cir., 1953).
Distribution was not made to controlling stockholder, but to her daughter, who was not a stockholder.	Such distribution made with stockholder's knowledge, was a dividend constructively received by stockholder. *Minnie F. Lasker*, T.C. Memo., Docket #24229, Jan. 23, 1952.
Distributions were not made to or for the account of the stockholder.	Distributions were in discharge of stockholder's obligations to third parties and were made at his direction; hence, taxable as dividends to him. *Municipal Securities Co., et al.*,

Taxpayer's Position   *Court's Holding*

F, 2. OTHER PAYMENTS FOR STOCKHOLDER'S BENEFIT—*Continued*

T.C. Memo., Docket #112287, Jan. 27, 1945.

The payment was a dividend to the old stockholder, not to the new stockholders.

Payment by the corporation did not discharge any obligation of the new stockholders to the old stockholder; hence, the new stockholders did not constructively receive any dividend. *Commissioner v. Diehl*, 142 F.2d 449 (6th Cir., 1944).

The issuance of the notes of a corporation to the sellers of its stock was not made in payment of the purchasers' obligations and therefore was not a taxable distribution to the purchasers.

The stock was purchased after the issuance of the corporate notes to the seller-stockholders; and, therefore, the sellers of the stock, and not the purchasers, received a taxable distribution. *Estate of Edward L. Koepenick*, T.C. Memo., Docket ##107653, 109915, May 24, 1943.

Payment by corporation in settlement of contested claim against itself and stockholders was not a dividend to stockholders.

Escape from personal liability in a contested matter is not income; hence, not a dividend. *Ruben v. Commissioner*, 97 F.2d 926 (8th Cir., 1938).

Payments were in settlement of protracted litigation.

Taxpayer was not enriched by having any income accrue to him or by receiving any income; merely to escape from a contested money claim by the force of circumstances or the action of others does not make a man subject to tax as though he had received income; hence, payments were not dividends.

Taxpayer's Position	*Court's Holding*
	Ruben v. Commissioner, 97 F.2d 926 (8th Cir., 1938).
Stockholder's wholly-owned corporation donated its assets to a trust for the stockholder's children.	Transfer of assets for benefit of stockholder was essentially equivalent to a dividend. Clark v. Commissioner, 84 F.2d 725 (3d Cir., 1936).
Distribution was in cancellation of stockholder's debt to a third party (Commissioner's contention).	Stockholder's debt was to a third party; hence, payment at stockholder's direction was essentially equivalent to a dividend. Duffin v. Lucas, 55 F.2d 786 (6th Cir., 1932).
Payment by the corporation was for the purchase of its shares and was not a dividend to the then sole stockholder who assigned to the corporation his contract to purchase the shares from the former stockholder.	Under applicable state law the corporation could not purchase its own shares and the assignment was null and void; and, although no dividend was formally declared, the payments fall into the same class as withdrawals made by a sole stockholder; hence, they are taxable as dividends. Ruphane B. Iverson, 29 B.T.A. 863 (1934).
Distribution of property to a trust controlled by the stockholder was a gift.	Not substantiated. Security First National Bank of Los Angeles, Executor, et al., 28 B.T.A. 289 (1933).
Payment by a corporation to its stockholders was part payment for account of a purchaser with respect to a contract of the latter to purchase from the stockholders all the stock of the corporation.	The use of the corporation as a conduit through which payment of part of the purchase price for the stock was made did not convert the payment into a dividend. William B. Aull, Jr., 26 B.T.A. 862 (1932).

Taxpayer's Position   *Court's Holding*

G. STOCKHOLDER'S BARGAIN PURCHASE

    1. OF CORPORATION'S TREASURY SHARES

Acquisitions of the corporation's treasury shares was not a "bargain purchase," but was in effect a nontaxable stock dividend.

    The acquisitions were not made in proportion to stockholdings prior to the acquisitions and were not nontaxable stock dividends but dividend distributions, to the extent that the fair market value of the shares acquired exceeded the amount paid therefor. *Joseph Scura,* T.C. Memo., Docket ##56461–2, Aug. 27, 1958.

    Gain from a purchase of property (here, treasury shares) is not realized until the property is sold.

    Such a transaction between a corporation and one of its stockholders is, in effect, a distribution of a dividend by the corporation, giving rise to income in the year it occurs. *Waldheim v. Commissioner,* 244 F.2d 1 (7th Cir., 1957).

    The purchase price by three of the corporation's five stockholders of its treasury shares was not substantially less than fair market value, and no income to stockholders resulted from such transaction.

    There was a differential between value and sales price of $35.52 per share, and the effect of the sale was to pass on to the stockholders, without cost, a part of the corporation's earnings and profits; hence, distribution of a dividend was effected. *Elizabeth Susan Strake Trust,* 1 T.C. 1131 (1943).

    A corporation issued, pro rata to holders of its common stock, rights to subscribe to newly issued preferred stock; the rights were not taxable to

    When issued, there existed a substantial spread between the market value of the right and the subscription price; when the right was exercised the cor-

Taxpayer's Position

the distributees because they did not constitute income.

Court's Holding

porate intention to distribute earnings was effected, and this distribution is taxable as a dividend. *Choate v. Commissioner*, 129 F.2d 684 (2d Cir., 1942).

G. STOCKHOLDER'S BARGAIN PURCHASE—*Continued*
  2. OF OTHER PROPERTY OF THE CORPORATION

Realty was sold by corporation at a price equal to its fair market value.

The sale price of the realty was its fair market value; hence, no part of the proceeds were essentially equivalent to the distribution of a dividend. *Southern Ford Tractor Corp.*, 29 T.C. 833 (1958).

The subsidiary's shares sold by the corporation to its stockholders were not worth more than the price at which purchased.

The government failed to produce evidence to overcome the proof that the shares sold by the corporation did not have a value in excess of the sale's price; hence, there was no distribution of a dividend. *Mauney v. United States*, — F. Supp. — (D.C.N.M., 1956).

Subsidiary sold property to stockholders of parent; profit to such stockholders upon resale was capital gain.

Price charged by subsidiary was top wholesale price permitted by OPA, and maximum profit stayed in subsidiary; hence, no anticipatory assignment of income and no dividend. *Robert Lehman*, 25 T.C. 629 (1955).

Purchase by stockholder of property leased to corporation by a third party, at what appeared to be a bargain price where corporation had first

Corporation's waiver of right to purchase the property did not bestow a property right on stockholder which can be taxed as a dividend. *Morris E.*

Taxpayer's Position ⠀⠀⠀⠀ *Court's Holding*

G, 2. PURCHASE OF OTHER PROPERTY OF THE CORPORATION— *Continued*

option to buy, did not amount to a dividend, as corporation did not provide any part of the purchase price.

Floyd, et al., T.C. Memo., Docket #49815, July 26, 1955.

The stockholders did not purchase from the corporation the shares of a second corporation; they only received the return of those shares which had been deposited as security for a loan to the stockholders, who used the money to finance the second corporation.

On the close question of fact, the stockholders made no purchase, but simply received the return of a security deposit; hence, the excess of the value of the shares over the amount of the loan repaid was not a dividend distribution to the stockholders. *Estate of Bruno P. John,* T.C. Memo., Docket ##49846–7, June 14, 1955.

Sale of assets by a trust (taxable as a corporation) to a partnership, composed only partly of all the beneficiaries of the trust, was not a distribution to the beneficiaries and therefore not taxable to them.

Sale of assets, at less than fair market value, was a sale to a partnership which included two nonbeneficiaries of the trust and did not amount to a transfer to the trust beneficiaries; hence, difference between sale price and fair market value was not a dividend. *Shunk v. Commissioner,* 173 F.2d 747 (6th Cir., 1949).

The stockholders paid the corporation the full value of the asset purchased.

Payment was made in part by delivery to the corporation of 20-year, noninterest-bearing notes, and the difference between the value of the assets acquired and the discounted value of said notes was in effect a distribution of corporate earnings, and, hence, taxable

Taxpayer's Position	*Court's Holding*
	as a dividend. *William A. Boyd*, T.C. Memo., Docket ##4988–9, Sept. 13, 1946, *aff'd no op.*, 171 F.2d 546 (6th Cir., 1948).
The sale of the corporation's assets was made, not to its corporate parent, but to the stockholders of its corporate parent.	To the extent that the corporate sale was for less than the value of the assets sold, there was a constructive dividend to the corporate parent and a dividend by the corporate parent to its stockholders who made the purchase. (Dissents by Kern, J., and Opper, J.) *V. U. Young*, 5 T.C. 1251 (1945).
The corporation's shares of a subsidiary were sold to the stockholders and not expressly declared as a dividend.	The substance of a transaction determines its character and the excess of value over purchase price is a transfer of earnings and profits; hence, such excess is taxable as a dividend. *Timberlake v. Commissioner*, 132 F.2d 259 (4th Cir., 1942).
The transfer was a "bargain purchase" by the corporate parent from its subsidiary, which gave rise to dividend income, and not a distribution in liquidation of the subsidiary.	The subsidiary's existence was continued and the excess of value of the assets transferred over the purchase price by the parent was a distribution of a dividend to the parent. *Commissioner v. American Liberty Oil Co.*, 127 F.2d 262 (5th Cir., 1942).
The shares of the subsidiary offered by the corporation to its stockholders did not have a	The shares offered did not have a value greater than that at which offered, and the sale

Taxpayer's Position   *Court's Holding*

G, 2. PURCHASE OF OTHER PROPERTY OF THE CORPORATION—
Continued

value in excess of the price at which offered.

did not result in any diminution of the corporation's net worth; hence, it was not any distribution of the corporation's profits. *Palmer v. Commissioner,* 302 U.S. 63 (1937).

There was no "bargain purchase" by the stockholders, as the shares transferred were acquired by the corporation for the shareholders.

The corporation was never the owner of the shares, but purchased them for the stockholders and turned them over to the stockholders for cost, which was less than their value; hence, there was no dividend distribution. *Commissioner v. McCloskey,* 76 F.2d 373 (5th Cir., 1935).

Payments were expended for improvements on corporate property which corporation had rented to stockholder at a fair rental.

Property was always available to corporation for the purpose for which it was acquired; corporation received a rental from stockholder for its use; hence, payments were not dividends. *O. Moorshead,* 28 B.T.A. 252 (1933).

The transaction was a purchase and, therefore, the excess of value over purchase price paid cannot be taxed as a dividend to the purchaser-stockholder who owned about 93% of the corporation's shares.

The mere fact that the purchaser is a stockholder of the vending corporation does not change the character of the transaction, there is no suggestion of fraud or any ulterior motive; hence, the bargain sale did not constitute a dividend distribution. *Commissioner v. Van Vorst,* 59 F.2d 677 (9th Cir., 1932).

Taxpayer's Position

The transaction was a sale of assets by the corporation to its stockholders and a resale by them to a second corporation.

Court's Holding

Although the sale to stockholders was at less than value, the resale was by them and not by the selling corporation which derived no gain on the resale giving rise to stockholder-transferee liability. *Fruit Bell Tel. Co.*, 22 B.T.A. 440 (1931).

The transaction was a sale by the corporation to the stockholders of shares of stock of another corporation.

A sale was made, albeit at a price less than actual value, and was not made to stockholders proportionately, and there was no testimony contradictory to the claim that the corporation needed working capital and had other business motives for making the sale; hence, there was no dividend. *Taplin v. Commissioner*, 41 F.2d 454 (6th Cir., 1930).

The property purchased from the corporation by the stockholder was worth only the purchase price.

The property purchased by the stockholder was worth more than the purchase price, and the excess constituted a dividend to the stockholder. *H. K. L. Castle*, 9 B.T.A. 931 (1927).

H. CORPORATE PROPERTY USED BY STOCKHOLDERS

The taxpayer-stockholders' occupancy of premises owned by the corporation did not result in dividends to them.

Husband and wife, sole stockholders, received benefits taxable as a dividend where premises owned by the corporation were occupied by them rent-free. *Western Supply & Furnace Co., et al.*, T.C. Memo., Docket ##57117, 57142–4, Mar. 30, 1959.

Taxpayer's Position   *Court's Holding*

H. CORPORATE PROPERTY USED BY STOCKHOLDERS—*Continued*

A sublease by the corporation to a stockholder at a rental below what the corporation would earn as lessee did not constitute a dividend to the stockholder.

The sublease involved no legitimate business purpose but only effected a shift of income; hence, a dividend. *58th Street Plaza Theatre, Inc. v. Commissioner,* 195 F.2d 724 (2d Cir., 1952).

Officer-stockholder, using corporation auto partly for noncorporate business, did not own the auto.

No part of cost of such auto is taxable as a dividend to officer-stockholder (issue of value of use not raised by Commissioner). *Joseph Morgenstern, et al.,* T.C. Memo., Docket ##39868–9, 39871–3, 39875–6, April 14, 1955) ; cf., *Henry T. Roberts,* T.C. Memo., Docket #9807, Aug. 24, 1948; *Charles A. Frueauff,* 30 B.T.A. 449 (1934), holding that value of use of property is "other income."

I. INCOME AND ASSETS OF CORPORATION DIVERTED TO STOCKHOLDERS

The amount received was from sale of taxpayers' own inventory and was not the receipt of unreported corporate earnings.

Record showed taxpayers did not own any large inventory; the sales made were of the corporation's inventory, the proceeds being appropriated by taxpayers and taxable to them as dividend distributions. *Western Supply & Furnace Co., et al.,* T.C. Memo., Docket ##57117, 57142–4, Mar. 30, 1959.

The corporation's books show all sales, and there were

Certain of the corporation's sales were not reported by it,

Taxpayer's Position	*Court's Holding*
no diversions to stockholders taxable as dividends.	having been made by the stockholder who kept the proceeds thereof, which constituted taxable income to him as dividends. *Chesterfield Textile Corp., et. al.*, 29 T.C. 651 (1958).
The corporation's books show all sales, and there were no diversions to stockholders taxable as dividends.	Certain of the corporation's sales were not reported by it, having been made by the stockholder who kept the proceeds thereof, which constituted taxable income to him as dividends. *Estate of C. J. Ginsberg*, T.C. Memo., Docket ##50034, 50657, May 26, 1958.
Income diverted to stockholders was not proportionate to stockholdings (Commissioner's position.)	Constructive dividends need not be proportionate to stockholdings; held, to be txable as dividends. *Sam Simon, et al. v. Commissioner*, 248 F.2d 869 (8th Cir., 1957).
Income diverted to stockholders was ordinary income to them (Commissioner's position.)	Distribution fits the statutory definition of dividend to the extent of available corporate earnings; hence, income diverted was a dividend. *Sam Simon, et al. v. Commissioner, supra.*
The amount of the unreported sales alleged to be informal dividends was not proved by the Commissioner.	There were unreported corporate sales, the proceeds of which went to the stockholder, the stockholder controlled the corporation, the commissioner's method of computing the amount was reasonable; hence, the amount so computed is taxable as an informal dividend to

Taxpayer's Position   *Court's Holding*

I. INCOME AND ASSETS OF CORPORATION DIVERTED TO STOCKHOLDERS
—*Continued*

the stockholder. *Gene O. Clark, et al.,* T.C. Memo., Docket ##48542–4, July 17, 1957.

Taxpayer never claimed as his own the alleged diverted checks.

The income properly belonged to the company and was diverted from it by the taxpayer-stockholder, and the taxpayer did not prove otherwise; hence, the taxpayer received a taxable dividend of the amount so diverted. *Jolly's Motor Livery Co., et al.,* T.C. Memo., Docket ##36607, 36745, 41269–70, Dec. 16, 1957.

Proceeds of a corporation's unreported sales remained the property of the corporation and were not diverted to taxpayer's personal use.

Where evidence showed that the controlling stockholder diverted corporate income to himself, such funds are taxable as constructive dividends to the extent of corporate earnings, and any excess above earnings is to be treated as a return of capital. *R. L. Bender,* T.C. Memo., Docket ##56618, 19, 22, June 28, 1957, *aff'd on another issue,* 256 F.2d 771 (7th Cir., 1958).

Funds representing income to the corporation, and subject to a 95% excess-profits tax, and which were embezzled by taxpayer-stockholders, but which were later refunded to the corporation, cannot be tax-

The stockholders diverted the corporation's funds to themselves, had complete control over such funds, there was an implied consent by the corporation; hence, to the extent of the corporation's earnings and

Taxpayer's Position

able as dividends, because the deficiencies and penalties assessed against the corporation more than exhausted earnings and profits.

Court's Holding

profits (after giving effect to the penalties and deficiencies assessed against the corporation), the stockholders were in receipt of a distribution essentially equivalent to a dividend. *Drybrough, et al. v. Commissioner*, 238 F.2d 735 (6th Cir., 1956).

Diversion of corporate funds amounted to embezzlement rather than a dividend, as all the stockholders did not participate in the receipt of funds.

The corporation and its stockholders should not be permitted to escape taxation because the distributions were technically illegal. *Drybrough, et al. v. Commissioner*, 238 F.2d 735 (6th Cir., 1956).

Proceeds of a corporation's unreported sales remained the property of the corporation and were not diverted to taxpayer's personal use.

Where evidence showed that the controlling stockholder diverted corporate income to himself, such funds are taxable as constructive dividends to the extent of corporate earnings, and any excess above earnings is to be treated as a return of capital. *Dawkins v. Commissioner*, 238 F.2d 174 (8th Cir., 1956).

There was no receipt of a dividend, as the funds were embezzled from the corporation.

Corporation could have declared a dividend and failure to do so is not sufficient to give rise to a different tax result; hence, a dividend. *Estate of Helene Simmons*, 26 T.C. 409 (1956).

Funds were embezzled from corporation.

Funds were withdrawn by principal stockholder; hence, constituted a dividend. *Mar-*

Taxpayer's Position	*Court's Holding*

I. INCOME AND ASSETS OF CORPORATION DIVERTED TO STOCKHOLDERS
—*Continued*

	vin T. Blackwell, et al., T.C. Memo., Docket #52701, Aug. 9, 1956.
The corporate taxpayer's income was correctly stated; and, therefore, the 90% stockholder did not receive unreported income from the corporation as an informal dividend.	The excess of reported sales paid directly to the stockholder in cash was a constructive dividend, since there was no evidence that the corporation retained such earnings or used them for a corporate purpose. *Cipollone's Sales & Service, Inc.,* T.C. Memo., Docket ##50082–4, Mar. 30, 1956.
Collections on behalf of corporation, retained by stockholder, were unauthorized acts constituting embezzlement, and not income.	Amounts collected were dividends as stockholder controlled all affairs of the corporation. *Paul Haimovitz,* T.C. Memo., Docket ##15929, *et al.,* Jan. 20, 1956.
Understatement of income by corporation as a result of diversions to stockholders was offset by an equal understatement of purchase costs.	The stockholders received dividend income to the extent of unreported corporate income diverted to them. *Chesbro v. Commissioner,* 225 F.2d 674 (2d Cir., 1955).
Funds represented proceeds of illegal factoring of nonexistent accounts receivable.	No evidence of which proceeds were legal and which were illegal; distribution taxable as a dividend. *William B. Benjamin,* T.C. Memo., Docket #22748, Oct. 26, 1955.
Income of partnership from sales to a related corporation was income of a bona fide part-	To the extent income was diverted from corporation, it was essentially equivalent to a

Taxpayer's Position	*Court's Holding*

nership operating independently of the corporation.

dividend. *Byers v. Commissioner*, 199 F.2d 273 (8th Cir., 1952).

Withdrawals from corporation for personal use of trustee of stockholder trust were embezzlements, not subject to income tax.

As trustee had complete control over trust and over corporation, such withdrawals are dividends. *Estate of Louis F. Buff*, T.C. Memo., Docket #4253, Dec. 20, 1945.

Taxpayer never received anything, as rebate payments were made to a corporation controlled by taxpayer.

It is not essential that taxpayer actually receive money to which he is entitled before he is required to include it in his tax return; whenever it is available to him and he is authorized to receive it or direct its payment to some other party, it is taxable to him; hence, payments were dividends. *Helvering v. Gordon*, 87 F.2d 663 (8th Cir., 1937).

Corporation owned property from which it had the right to receive oil royalties; these royalties were paid directly to stockholders and were dividends when received by the stockholders; they were not accounts receivable of the corporation at date of its liquidation.

The corporation waived its right to receive the royalty payments and authorized their payment directly to the stockholders; the royalty payments were income to the corporation when paid to the stockholders and were not an asset of the corporation at the time of the dissolution. *G. D. Rigsby*, 6 B.T.A. 194 (1927).

Collections on accounts receivable charged off as worthless by the corporation and transferred to a trustee for stockholders were part of a realignment of stock interests.

Not substantiated; the transfer of the accounts receivable to stockholders constituted dividends as collections were made. *R. G. Hubbard*, 2 B.T.A. 1287 (1925).

Taxpayer's Position   *Court's Holding*

I. INCOME AND ASSETS OF CORPORATION DIVERTED TO STOCKHOLDERS
—*Continued*

Where lessee of railroad property pays rental directly to stockholders, the corporation does not have income.

While the rent is a debt of the lessee to the lessor, as between the lessor and its stockholders, it is the lessor's income out of which dividends are paid. *Northern Ry. Co. v. Lowe*, 250 F. 856 (2d Cir., 1918); *Rensselaer & S. R. Co. v. Irwin*, 249 F. 726 (2d Cir., 1918); *West End St. Ry. Co. v. Malley*, 246 F. 625 (1st Cir., 1917).

J. DISTRIBUTION OUT OF PROCEEDS OF GOVERNMENT-INSURED LOANS

Payment was the amount by which a building loan exceeded cost of construction and was not a dividend.

To the extent that the payment was a portion of the government-insured construction loan not used in the construction, its excess of basis was not a dividend distribution but constituted capital gain. *Commissioner v. Gross*, 236 F.2d 612 (2d Cir., 1956).

The payment was a portion of proceeds of a construction loan and not of earnings and profits.

Distributions made from proceeds of the government-insured construction loan in excess of earnings and profits are not taxable as ordinary income, as either dividends or compensation. *W. H. Weaver*, 25 T.C. 1067 (1956).

The payments were made out of the proceeds of a government-insured loan and payments made to stockholders in excess of earnings of the corpo-

All other factors were present to make the redemption of stock essentially equivalent to the distribution of a taxable dividend, and to the extent that

Taxpayer's Position	*Court's Holding*
ration are not taxable as dividends.	the corporation did have earnings, the distribution is taxable as a dividend. *W. H. Weaver, supra.*
Distributions were of excess of construction loan over cost of construction, and were not dividends.	To the extent that the corporation had no earnings and profits and paid out proceeds of a government-insured construction loan, the distributions are to be applied against the stockholder's basis for the stock; any excess of such proceeds treated as capital gain; no portion is taxable as dividends. *Thomas Wilson, et al.,* 25 T.C. 1058 (1956).
Distribution to stockholders of excess of government-insured construction loan over cost of construction was not compensation for services rendered but was a partial pro rata redemption of stock paid out of capital.	To the extent that the corporation had no earnings and profits and paid out proceeds of a government-insured construction loan, the distributions are to be applied against the stockholder's basis for the stock; any excess of such proceeds treated as capital gain; no portion is taxable as dividends. *Estate of Carl C. Myers,* T.C. Memo., Docket ##51797–8, June 29, 1956.
Distribution of excess of government insured construction loan over cost of construction was not a dividend to stockholders because the property was constructed by the corporation for the account of its stockholders and for an adequate consideration.	To the extent that there were earnings and profits, the distribution was an ordinary pro rata distribution of corporate property (cash), taxable as a dividend. *Edward Pool, et al.,* T.C. Memo., Docket ##36108–14, Mar. 20, 1956, *aff'd on another issue,* 251 F.2d 233 (9th Cir., 1957).

Taxpayer's Position   *Court's Holding*

J. DISTRIBUTION OUT OF PROCEEDS OF GOVERNMENT-INSURED LOANS
—*Continued*

The payment was the excess of the amount of a building loan over cost of construction and was not a dividend.

The excess of the amount of a government-insured building loan over cost of construction was declared by the corporation as a dividend and was taxable to the stockholders as a dividend. *Wilshire-La Cienega Gardens Co., et al. v. Riddell,* 148 F. Supp. 938 (D.C.Calif., 1956).

K. DISTRIBUTION OF WARRANTS AND RIGHTS TO SUBSCRIBE

The mere issue by a corporation of rights to purchase its stock and their receipt by stockholder is not a dividend.

There was no dividend, as there was no distribution of corporate assets or diminution of its net worth in any practical sense. *Palmer v. Commissioner,* 302 U.S. 63 (1937).

Receipt of warrants to purchase stock does not constitute a dividend distribution.

Receipt of warrants to buy stock, the value of which was found to equal the offering price, does not give rise to taxable income. *Minnie T. Grippin,* 36 B.T.A. 1109 (1937).

Taxpayer-stockholders of one corporation "A" subscribed for stock of a newly-organized corporation "B"; in receiving stock warrants of "B" through their corporation "A," they received from "A" nothing which did not belong to them; hence, they did not receive a dividend from "A."

There was no distribution by "A" out of its earnings and profits, as the warrants were acquired by "A" on behalf of the stockholders of "A" and "A" parted with nothing belonging to it in delivering these warrants to the said stockholders. *Helvering v. Bartlett,* 71 F.2d 598 (4th Cir., 1934).

Taxpayer's Position	*Court's Holding*
The market value of rights issued to stockholders, to subscribe for bonds of the issuing corporations, does not constitute a taxable dividend.	The exercise of the rights was optional with the stockholders and, although the rights at all times had a market value, that does not result in their receipt constituting a taxable dividend to the stockholders. *Robert C. Cooley,* 27 B.T.A. 986 (1933), *aff'd on another issue,* 75 F.2d 188 (1st Cir., 1935).
The market value of rights issued to stockholders, to subscribe for bonds of the issuing corporations, does not constitute a taxable dividend.	The exercise of the rights was optional with the stockholders and, although the rights at all times had a market value, that does not result in their receipt constituting a taxable dividend to the stockholders. *T. I. Hare Powel,* 27 B.T.A. 55 (1932).
Receipt of subscription rights to new stock of the corporation were wholly capital.	Receipt of rights to subscribe for new stock at less than its actual value constituted no more than receipt of a stock dividend, not of income. *Mills v. Safe Deposit & Trust Co. of Baltimore,* 259 U.S. 247 (1922).

L. OTHER TRANSACTIONS

Funds received by taxpayer after sale of corporate assets and stock were received as part of the purchase price.	Taxpayer transferred beneficial ownership but retained title to stock pending ascertainment of the purchase price. Any amount received by the taxpayer was applied against the purchase price of the stock and should not be treated as a taxable dividend to him.

Taxpayer's Position   *Court's Holding*

L. OTHER TRANSACTIONS—*Continued*

Mayer v. Donnelly, 247 F.2d 322 (5th Cir., 1957).

The corporation did not make a sale of its own shares to the stockholder, but rather turned over shares which it had acquired for the stockholder and held for him until he could pay the purchase price.

Not supported by the evidence; hence, the excess of the value of the shares over the stockholder's purchase price thereof was a dividend to the stockholder. *Waldheim v. Commissioner,* 244 F.2d 1 (7th Cir., 1957).

The amounts withdrawn were not dividends, but the stockholder's profits on securities which the corporation bought and sold for the stockholder as the stockholder's agent.

The family-owned corporation bought the securities for the stockholder, the securities were held by the company, in street name, as collateral for the amounts due from the stockholder; profits, losses, and dividends were reported by stockholder in the year derived; the purchase price of the securities, gains, losses, and dividends were credited or charged currently to the stockholder; although the company did not charge for services and had title to the securities, that is not decisive; the transactions were those of the stockholder and, hence, the withdrawals were not dividends. *Jack M. Bass & Co., et al.,* T.C. Memo., Docket ##54648–51, Oct. 31, 1957.

Distribution of cash by the corporation was part of the proceeds to be received upon

Distribution was out of earnings and profits and were dividends, since there was no

Taxpayer's Position	*Court's Holding*

the sale of stock to a third party and was not an ordinary dividend.

indication of a liquidation. *Merrill C. Gilmore,* 25 T.C. 1321 (1956).

Amounts received were proceeds from the sale by taxpayer to a third party of preferred stock received as a tax-free dividend.

Taxpayer did not receive the proceeds from the corporation; the transactions involved were not fictitious or lacking in substance so as to be anything different from what they purported to be; hence, proceeds were not dividends. *Chamberlin v. Commissioner,* 207 F.2d 462 (6th Cir., 1953).

Issuance of Class A stock certificates coupled with a repurchase agreement created a profit-sharing agreement and, in effect, amounted to additional compensation, as did the dividends paid on the certificates to the officers of the corporation.

Certificate holders could not vote; had no right to share in assets upon liquidation; were not entitled to a share of earnings upon repurchase by the corporation; and were bound to accept the repurchase price set by the corporation; hence, distributions were not dividends. *A. & M. Karagheusian Inc.,* T.C. Memo., Docket #109875, Dec. 24, 1943.

Proceeds from sales of stock held by the corporation were not needed for the business of the corporation, directors therefore declared a liquidating dividend; hence, the distribution is not taxable as an ordinary dividend.

Whether a dividend is a distribution in liquidation is a question of fact and the intent of the directors of the corporation is relevant, but what the distribution may be designated is not controlling; there is no evidence to support taxpayer's contention. *Tate v. Commissioner,* 97 F.2d 658 (8th Cir., 1938).

Distribution was not in redemption but was proceeds of

Stock dividend coupled with an offer by the corporation to

Taxpayer's Position   *Court's Holding*

L. OTHER TRANSACTIONS—*Continued*

Taxpayer's Position	Court's Holding
sale to corporation of stock received as a stock dividend.	buy back part of the stock were parts of the same transaction; hence, distribution was essentially equivalent to a dividend. *Robinson v. Commissioner,* 69 F.2d 972 (5th Cir., 1934).
Payments made by stockholders of one bank to stockholders of another bank, for stock received as stock dividends, pursuant to plan of merger of the two banks, did not constitute a redemption by the corporation which issued the stock dividends.	Held, not essentially equivalent to payment of a dividend. *Silas H. Burnham,* 29 B.T.A. 605 (1933).
Distributions were proceeds of a life insurance policy on the life of a deceased corporate officer under which the stockholders were the actual beneficiaries, and the corporation, in receiving and disbursing the proceeds, was merely acting as trustee.	Not substantiated; the corporation paid the premiums and was the named beneficiary; the insurer never approved or was given notice of any change of beneficiary; hence, the distribution was a dividend. *Isaac May, et al.,* 20 B.T.A. 282 (1930).
The amounts were not dividends but, in one instance, a corporate bookkeeping entry to balance books and, in another, an incorrect charge to undivided profits.	The evidence was in support of the taxpayer's positions; hence, there was no dividend to the stockholder. *J. W. Thompson,* 10 B.T.A. 390 (1928).
There was no dividend during the taxable year, when there was a transfer from one corporate account to another.	The evidence shows a mere bookkeeping entry during the year involved; the amounts involved were subject to withdrawal in a prior year and were not paid until a subsequent

Taxpayer's Position	*Court's Holding*
	year; hence, there was no dividend during the year in question. *Charles Finsilver*, 8 B.T.A. 391 (1927).

M. Taxability of Distribution Alleged To Be Limited by Amount of Available Earnings and Profits

Cancellation of a debt constituted a distribution from the company's depletion reserve.	At the time of the cancellation the company had current earnings and profits; hence, the cancellation was a taxable dividend to the stockholder. *Wilson v. Commissioner*, 255 F.2d 702 (5th Cir., 1958).
The corporation had no surplus, but rather a deficit; therefore, a bargain purchase of its shares from it could not give rise to dividend.	The bargain sale by the corporation constituted a distribution of a dividend to the extent of its current earnings for the year in which the sale was made. *Waldheim v. Commissioner*, 244 F.2d 1 (7th Cir., 1957).
Although stockholder received diverted corporate funds, corporate earnings and profits should be reduced for each year's accrued interest on the corporation's tax deficiency liability, finally determined subsequent to the year in question here.	For purposes of determining earnings and profits, the interest is deductible yearly as it accrues. *Sidney Stark*, 29 T.C. 122 (1957).
Funds representing income to the corporation, and subject to a 95% excess-profits tax, and which were embezzled by taxpayer-stockholders, but which were later refunded to	The stockholders diverted the corporation's funds to themselves, had complete control over such funds, consent was implied by the corporation; hence, to the extent of the cor-

Taxpayer's Position   *Court's Holding*

M. TAXABILITY OF DISTRIBUTION ALLEGED TO BE LIMITED BY
AMOUNT OF AVAILABLE EARNINGS AND PROFITS—*Continued*

the corporation, cannot be taxable as dividends because the deficiencies and penalties assessed against the corporation more than exhausted earnings and profits.

poration's earnings and profits (after giving effect to the penalties and deficiencies assessed against the corporation), the stockholders were in receipt of a distribution essentially equivalent to a dividend. *Drybrough, et al. v. Commissioner,* 238 F.2d 735 (6th Cir., 1956).

As the result of unallowable losses on complete liquidation of subsidiaries, accumulated earnings were insufficient to cover dividends.

Accumulated earnings are not reduced by unallowable loss on complete liquidation of subsidiaries. *Avco Manufacturing Corp.,* 25 T.C. 975 (1956), *remanded only to recompute overpayment,* — F.2d — (2d Cir., 1957).

The dissolution of Corp. A and the subsequent organization of Corp. B were two separate transactions, so that earned surplus of Corp. A became paid-in or donated surplus of Corp. B, with the result that Corp. B did not have sufficient earnings to make the amount paid by it a dividend distribution.

The dissolution and subsequent incorporation were two separate transactions and not steps in only one transaction, and Corp. B's surplus was not earned but paid-in or donated; hence, the receipt was not a distribution of earnings constituting a dividend. *Charles R. Mathis, Jr.,* 19 T.C. 1123 (1953).

The payments received were not dividends but a return of capital, as the corporation had deficits and could not, under applicable state law, pay any dividends.

To the extent that there were earnings and profits, the payments made to stockholders proportionately were taxable dividends to them, since the Internal Revenue Code and not state law is determinative as to

Taxpayer's Position	*Court's Holding*
	what is a taxable dividend. *D. H. Wiley Lumber Co., et al. v. Commissioner,* 177 F.2d 200 (6th Cir., 1949).
The payment was out of what had been capital and was not a dividend.	Surplus had been transferred to capital and later retransferred to surplus, and the distribution thereof was equivalent to a dividend, the stockholder's proportionate interest in the corporation remaining unchanged. *Sheehan v. Dana,* 163 F.2d 316 (8th Cir., 1947).
Amounts were distributed in partial liquidation of the corporation and were not taxable as dividends because they were not paid from earnings and surplus.	The stockholder failed to show that the capital of the corporation was in any way contracted or impaired by the distributions made to him pursuant to a plan of liquidation which was never completed; therefore, taxpayer did not overcome the presumption that the distributions were made from earnings rather than from capital. *Jones v. Dawson,* 148 F.2d 87 (10th Cir., 1945).
Under state law the corporation did not have sufficient earnings to pay a legal dividend.	Amount of available earnings and profits is to be determined under provisions of Internal Revenue Code. *Commissioner v. Bedford's Estate* 325 U.S. 283 (1945).
Payment was out of corporation's capital and was not a dividend.	The corporation had large capital deficits and no accumulated earnings and profits, and wrote down capital stock to produce the surplus which was distributed; hence, there was

Taxpayer's Position   *Court's Holding*

M. Taxability of Distribution Alleged To Be Limited by
Amount of Available Earnings and Profits—*Continued*

no dividend distribution. *Page, et al. v. Haverty,* 129 F.2d 512 (5th Cir., 1942).

There were no earnings available for the distribution of a dividend, as distributions made in prior years were in excess of earnings, all of which had been reported as income.

The excess distributions in prior years was an invasion of capital and did not constitute taxable income to the recipients. No benefit can be derived for erroneous inclusion as taxable income of prior years, amounts which were, in fact, not taxable income. *Emil Stein, et al.,* 46 B.T.A. 135 (1942).

There were no profits out of which a distribution of a dividend could be made.

Not substantiated. *Hirsch v. Commissioner,* 124 F.2d 24 (9th Cir., 1941).

Distributions were not dividends, as there were no earnings and profits out of which a distribution of a dividend could be made.

Facts substantiated; hence, not a dividend. *Henderson v. United States,* 105 F.2d 461 (3d Cir., 1939).

Distribution in redemption of stock previously issued as stock dividends was not a dividend, as entire earnings were impounded and capitalized when declared, leaving none available on redemption.

Such a dividend takes the earnings out of the control of the corporation and impounds them until dissolution or cancellation of the shares; such treatment cannot be disregarded and since no other earnings are available there is no dividend. *Patty v. Helvering,* 98 F.2d 717 (2d Cir., 1938).

The distribution is not taxable as an ordinary dividend

Whether a dividend is a distribution in liquidation is a

Taxpayer's Position

as it was made from surplus accumulated prior to March 1, 1913.

Court's Holding

question of fact and neither the intent of the directors of the corporation nor what the corporation may call a "distribution" is controlling; there is no evidence to support taxpayer's contention. *Tate v. Commissioner,* 97 F.2d 658 (8th Cir., 1938).

The payment was, as the corporation had advised the stockholder, partly from earnings and surplus accumulated prior to March 1, 1913.

The earnings and profits after March 1, 1913, exceeded the amount paid, and the corporation could not make a tax-free distribution until after it had distributed its available taxable earnings and profits. *Baker v. Commissioner,* 80 F.2d 813 (2d Cir., 1936); *Leland v. Commissioner,* 50 F.2d 523 (1st Cir., 1931).

Part II. DEDUCTIBILITY BY CORPORATION

A. PAYMENTS CLAIMED AS INTEREST
  1. INTEREST ON PROMISSORY NOTES

The amount paid was interest on a note and a deductible item.

The notes issued were in direct proportion to stockholdings and were equity investment rather than indebtedness; hence, the amount paid was not deductible interest. *Gunn v. Commissioner,* 244 F.2d 408 (10th Cir., 1957).

Payments represented interest on a valid indebtedness evidenced by notes.

There was no intention to create a loan; the notes were not paid on the due date; only one note had actually been retired; the stockholders treated

Taxpayer's Position   *Court's Holding*

A, 1. INTEREST ON PROMISSORY NOTES—*Continued*

their shares of stock and the notes as a single package; hence, payment was not interest. *The Colony, Inc. v. Commissioner,* 244 F.2d 75 (6th Cir., 1956), *rev'd on other grounds,* 357 U.S. 28 (1958).

Distribution was a payment on principal of outstanding notes which represented a bona fide indebtedness with fixed maturity dates and interest payments.

Notes were subordinated to the claims of creditors; the only purpose for issuing the notes was one of tax avoidance; hence, payments were dividends. *Gooding Amusement Co. v. Commissioner,* 236 F.2d 159 (6th Cir., 1956).

Payments were interest on outstanding notes.

Note did not have a fixed maturity date; payments of interest or principal were restricted to net earnings; were subordinate to general creditors; hence, payments were dividends. *Pocatello Coca-Cola Bottling Co. v. United States,* 139 F. Supp. 912 (D.C. Ida., 1956).

Payments were interest on outstanding demand notes.

Repayment of amounts advanced for which notes were issued was never intended; admittedly the corporation could not operate to the extent it did without the advances; hence, payments were dividend distributions. *Ryan Contracting Corp.,* T.C. Memo., Docket #54335, Aug. 17, 1956.

Payments were interest on

Corporation began business

Taxpayer's Position	*Court's Holding*
outstanding demand promissory notes.	with no stated capital; present debt to capital ratio was 2,500 to 1; hence, payments were not interest. *Robert L. Osborne*, T.C. Memo., Docket #40735, April 30, 1954.
Payments were interest on outstanding notes.	Notes represented a bona fide indebtedness; bore a fixed maturity date and a fixed rate of interest; did not result in a high ratio of indebtedness to equity capital; hence, payments were interest. *Gazette Telegraph Co.*, 19 T.C. 692 (1953), *aff'd on other grounds*, 209 F.2d 926 (10th Cir., 1954).
Payments were interest on notes that were issued in exchange for preferred stock.	Notes had a fixed maturity date; payment of principal and interest was not dependent upon a particular source; noteholders had no right to participate in management; interest was paid when due; exchange of preferred stock for notes eliminated voting rights of preferred stockholders; hence, payments were interest. *H. E. Fletcher Co.*, T.C. Memo., Docket #28105, Oct. 26, 1951.
Payments were interest on outstanding notes of the corporation.	Notes had a definite maturity date; were unsecured and ranked with general creditors; were transferable and the transaction was not lacking in substance; hence, payments were interest. *Chas. Schaefer & Son, Inc.*, T.C. Memo., Docket #24160, Nov. 21, 1950.

Taxpayer's Position	*Court's Holding*

A, 1. INTEREST ON PROMISSORY NOTES—*Continued*

Payments were interest on outstanding notes issued in satisfaction of an extra dividend declaration.	Notes had a fixed maturity date; interest was payable in all events; parties intended to create an indebtedness; hence, payments were interest. *Echota Cotton Mills v. Allen,* 97 F. Supp. 800 (D.C.Ga., 1951).
Payments were interest on outstanding promissory notes.	Notes represented a bona fide indebtedness as evidenced by the intent of the parties; hence, payments were interest. *Wilshire & Western Sandwiches, Inc. v. Commissioner,* 175 F.2d 718 (9th Cir., 1949).
Payments were interest on outstanding registered notes issued in a recapitalization in exchange for 80% of the outstanding stock.	Notes provided for a variable interest rate dependent upon earnings; were issued only to stockholders in exchange for stock alone; issuance did not affect control of the corporation and was motivated by tax avoidance; hence, payments were dividends. *Talbot Mills v. Commissioner,* 326 U.S. 521 (1946).
Payments were interest on outstanding notes issued in partial payment for the acquisition of certain assets.	Principal and interest were payable on demand and not restricted to earnings; notes represented a valid indebtedness even though subordinate to certain other debt; hence, payments were interest. *Page Oil Co. v. Commissioner,* 129 F.2d 748 (2d Cir., 1942).

Taxpayer's Position	*Court's Holding*
Payments were interest on outstanding promissory notes.	Notes provided for a definite principal and a specified rate of interest; provided limitations on additional liabilities by the company; had a fixed maturity date; had no voting rights; hence, payments were interest. *The Tennessee Co. v. Commissioner,* 111 F.2d 678 (3d Cir., 1940).
Payments were interest on notes distributed to stockholders in lieu of a cash distribution of profits.	Distribution of profits in the form of notes created a legal indebtedness; hence, payments on such notes were interest. *Miller Mill Co. v. Commissioner,* 102 F.2d 599 (5th Cir., 1939).
Payments were interest on outstanding past-due notes rather than dividends on preferred stock which was issued to noteholders to meet their demands for an increased rate of interest.	Notes were never discharged or issued in exchange for stock and continued to carry a fixed rate of interest; hence, payments were interest. *Paramount Knitting Mills,* 17 B.T.A. 91 (1929).
Payments were interest on notes that were subsequently converted into preferred stock.	Notes carried a fixed interest and were payable on demand; hence, payments were interest until the notes were converted into preferred stock; thereafter, they constituted dividends. *L. Z. Dickey Grocery Co.,* 1 B.T.A. 108 (1924).

A. PAYMENTS CLAIMED AS INTEREST—*Continued*
   2. INTEREST ON DEBENTURES

| Disbursements were deductible interest on debentures. | The so-called "debentures" were not intended to be nor were they in fact a genuine in- |

Taxpayer's Position   *Court's Holding*

A, 2. INTEREST ON DEBENTURES—*Continued*

debtedness; the formal attributes of an instrument are not conclusive, the important point is whether the moneys are put at the risk of the business; payment of the "interest" was continually postponed upon consent; based on the facts and circumstances, the disbursement was not deductible interest. *Hoguet Real Estate Corp.*, 30 T.C. 580 (1958).

Interest on its bonds was deductible by corporation.

Based upon the facts involved, the bonds represented a bona fide indebtedness and not equity contribution; hence, the interest was deductible. *Leach Corp.*, 30 T.C. 563 (1958).

The amount paid by the corporation to its sole stockholder was interest on its unsecured 20-year, 5% debentures and was deductible.

Although in form the debentures were evidences of indebtedness, on consideration of the entire record, including the extent to which the debentures were subordinated to general creditors, the failure to pay the entire "interest" due, the failure to show that the stock-debenture ratio was to permit employees to acquire shares, the write-up of values, there was no intention to establish a debtor-creditor relation between the corporation and the stockholder; hence, there was no indebtedness and the amount paid as "interest" is not de-

Taxpayer's Position	*Court's Holding*
	ductible. *Texoma Supply Co.,* T.C. Memo., Docket #52401, Feb. 28, 1958.
The amount paid was deductible interest on sinking-fund debentures.	The stockholders transferred assets to the corporation for stock and debentures, but the corporation was capitalized adequately, was formed for valid business reasons, and functioned effectively; hence, the debentures evidenced a bona fide indebtedness and interest paid thereon is deductible. *Dennis Corp. v. United States,* — F. Supp. — (D.C.Va., 1958); *Dominion Oil Co., Inc. v. United States,* — F. Supp. — (D.C.Va., 1958).
The disbursement was deductible interest paid on debentures.	The jury found that part of the advances represented loans, so that payments thereon were deductible as interest. *Mill Ridge Coal Co. v. Patterson,* — F. Supp. — (D.C.Ala., 1958).
Payments were for interest on outstanding preferred debentures.	Debentures had no fixed maturity date; were not issued for new capital; had a face value nearly 10 times the stockholder's equity; were subordinate to claims of general creditors; hence, payments were not interest. *Beaver Pipe Tools, Inc. v. Carey,* 240 F.2d 843 (6th Cir., 1957).
Payments were interest on outstanding debentures issued in payment of a dividend deduction.	Debentures contained all the necessary features of instruments of indebtedness and none of the features associated with

Taxpayer's Position	*Court's Holding*

A, 2. INTEREST ON DEBENTURES—*Continued*

	equity interests; the fact that debenture holder was parent corporation of taxpayer did not effect creditor relationship; the issuance of debentures did not cause a disproportionate ratio of debt to capital and the fact that debentures were neither issued for borrowed money nor against accumulated earnings did not affect the relationship; hence, payments were interest. *Kraft Foods Co. v. Commissioner*, 232 F.2d 118 (2d Cir., 1956).
Payments constituted interest on outstanding debentures.	Debentures had a fixed maturity date; they afforded no basis for participation in management; they carried a fixed rate of interest; there was no unusual imbalance in petitioner's ratio of equity capital to indebtedness; hence, payments were not dividends. *John W. Walter, Inc.*, 23 T.C. 550 (1954).
Payments were interest on outstanding debentures which were issued in exchange for preferred stock and accumulated dividends in a recapitalization.	Debentures had a fixed maturity date; a fixed rate of interest not dependent on earnings; hence, payments were interest. *Bemis Hardwood Lumber Co. v. United States*, 117 F. Supp. 851 (D.C.N.C., 1954).
Payments were interest on outstanding debentures issued	Debentures had a fixed maturity and interest dates; ratio

Taxpayer's Position	*Court's Holding*
in exchange for preferred stock.	of borrowed capital to invested capital remained low; debentures were also owned by employees and other nonstockholders; hence, payments were interest, not dividends. *Garrett Freightlines, Inc.*, T.C. Memo., Docket #33845, Mar. 31, 1953.
Payments were interest on outstanding debentures issued by the corporation upon its organization and for which it received full value in assets.	Debentures were issued with intent to create an indebtedness; corporation had paid substantial dividend on its common stock; corporation received slightly less than value of stock and bonds in assets transferred to corporation upon its organization; hence, payments were interest. *Harvey Investment Co. v. Scofield,* — F. Supp. — (D.C.Tex., 1953).
Payments were part interest and part principal on outstanding debentures.	Debentures were issued for good business reasons and represented a bona fide indebtedness; hence, payments were not dividends. *Harvey v. United States,* — F. Supp. — (D.C. Tex., 1953).
Payments were interest on outstanding debentures issued in exchange for preferred stock.	Debentures were issued in registered form; had a fixed maturity date; principal was unqualifiedly payable; payment of interest did not depend upon anyone's discretion; holders had no voice in management; were secured by a trust indenture and had sinking fund provisions; intention of the

Taxpayer's Position   *Court's Holding*

A, 2. INTEREST ON DEBENTURES—*Continued*

parties in exchanging preferred stock for debentures was that holders would become creditors; hence, payments were interest. *Roosevelt Hotel, Inc.,* T.C. Memo., Docket #25810, May 22, 1953.

Payments were interest on outstanding income debentures issued in exchange for preferred stock.

In the circumstances the payments were interest on a valid indebtedness. *United Theatres, Inc.,* T.C. Memo., Docket #21749, June 30, 1953.

Payments were interest on outstanding debentures.

Debentures had a fixed maturity date; interest was cumulative and payable regardless of earnings; debentures were not held pro rata by the stockholders; hence, payments were interest. *B. M. C. Manufacturing Corp.,* T.C. Memo., Docket #31588, April 16, 1952.

Payments were interest on debenture notes issued to stockholders to cover open accounts representing unpaid dividends, salaries, and advances.

Debentures had a fixed maturity date; no restriction as to the source of payment; payment could be enforced; debentures were not issued in proportion to stockholdings; they represented a genuine indebtedness; hence, payments were interest not dividends. *Graves Brothers Co.,* 17 T.C. 1499 (1952).

Payments constituted interest on outstanding debentures.

Debentures were issued pursuant to a reorganization and were supported by assets; they had fixed maturity and interest

Taxpayer's Position	*Court's Holding*
	dates; hence, payments were not dividends. *The Tribune Publishing Co.*, 17 T.C. 1228 (1952).
Payments were interest on outstanding debentures.	Debentures carried no right to vote; had a fixed maturity date; were freely transferable without regard to the stock; were issued for a good business purpose and represented a valid indebtedness; hence, payments were interest. *Ruspyn Corp.*, 18 T.C. 769 (1952).
Payments were for interest on outstanding debentures.	Debentures had a fixed maturity date; contained no right to participate in management; were subordinate to creditors; although interest was payable out of available earnings, this did not relieve the corporation of liability, as interest was cumulative; hence, payments were interest. *Lansing Community Hotel Corp. v. Commissioner*, 187 F.2d 487 (6th Cir., 1951).
Payments constituted interest on outstanding debentures.	Debentures carried fixed interest and maturity dates; evidence showed intent to create a debt and not to place the funds at risk of business; hence, payments were not dividends. *Sabine Royalty Corp.*, 17 T.C. 1071 (1951).
Payments were interest on outstanding income debentures.	Debentures had a fixed maturity date; were carried on the books as a liability; holders' rights were not limited; hence,

Taxpayer's Position   *Court's Holding*

A, 2. INTEREST ON DEBENTURES—*Continued*

payments were interest. *Pierce Estates, Inc.,* 16 T.C. 1020 (1951), *rev'd on other issues,* 195 F.2d 475 (3d Cir., 1952).

Payments were interest on outstanding debentures even though payable out of available net operating income.

Debentures had fixed maturity and interest dates; holders did not have any right to participate in management; payment of interest was not within the corporate discretion; hence, payments were interest. *Lansing Community Hotel Corp. v. Commissioner,* 187 F.2d 487 (6th Cir., 1951).

Payments were interest on outstanding debenture notes.

Notes were not issued for borrowed money; represented no new contribution to capital; were subordinate to claims of creditors; interest was dependent on earnings and payments were at discretion of board of directors; hence, payments were dividends. *Wetterau Grocer Co., Inc. v. Commissioner,* 179 F.2d 158 (8th Cir., 1950).

Distributions on preferred stock were in effect payments of interest on debentures.

Securities had no fixed maturity date; redemptions were required but only out of surplus; remedy for nonpayment was a prohibition on the declaration of common dividends and an increase in voting rights for the preferred; holders could not sue to recover an indebtedness; hence, distribution was a

Taxpayer's Position

Court's Holding

dividend. *The Rappold Co.*, T.C. Memo., Docket #23393, Nov. 8, 1950.

Payments were interest on outstanding debentures that were originally issued in exchange for preferred stock.

There was a good business reason for the issuance of the debentures, which had a fixed maturity date; a fixed rate of interest payable regardless of earnings; were assignable without restriction; hence, payments were interest. *Hemenway-Johnson Furniture Co. v. Commissioner*, 174 F.2d 793 (5th Cir., 1949).

Payments were interest on outstanding debentures.

Debentures had a fixed maturity date; part of the interest was fixed; were on parity with other creditors; holders had no voice in management; stockholders did own debentures in proportion to their stock; there were good reasons for the debenture issue; hence, payments were interest not dividends. *New England Lime Co.*, 13 T.C. 799 (1949).

Payments were interest on outstanding debentures.

Debentures did not provide for a fixed maturity date; were subordinate to general creditors; payments were required to be made out of profits; hence, payments were dividends. *The Jordan Co. v. Allen*, 85 F. Supp. 437 (D.C. Ga., 1949).

Payments were interest on an outstanding "debenture-preferred stock."

Securities had no fixed maturity date; were held by the stockholders in control of the

Taxpayer's Position	*Court's Holding*

A, 2. INTEREST ON DEBENTURES—*Continued*

	corporation; would not, in effect, be collected on default until liquidation; resulted in a debt to capital ratio of 29 to 1; interest was to be paid only out of earnings; hence, payments were dividends. *Mullin Building Corp. v. Commissioner*, 167 F.2d 1001 (3d Cir., 1948).
Payments were interest on outstanding debentures.	Debentures were absolute as to the payment of both principal and interest in all events and at definite times; hence, payments were not dividends. *Toledo Blade Co. v. Commissioner*, 180 F.2d 357 (6th Cir., 1950).
Payments were interest on outstanding debentures.	Debentures were owned by stockholders in proportion to their stockholdings; were unsecured; were subordinate to all creditors; there was no identification of amounts contributed for stock and debentures; hence, payments were dividends. *1432 Broadway Corp. v. Commissioner*, 160 F.2d 885 (2d Cir., 1947).
Payments were interest on outstanding income-debentures.	Debentures in effect had no maturity date; they were unsecured and subordinate to all creditors; interest payment, although cumulative, were dependent on earnings; although callable they were in reality uncollectible until dissolution;

Taxpayer's Position

Court's Holding

they effected an obviously excessive debt structure; hence, payments were essentially dividends on preferred stock. *Swoby Corp.*, 9 T.C. 887 (1947).

Payments were interest on outstanding debenture bonds issued in a reorganization.

Debentures contained a fixed maturity date; a fixed annual payment from earnings; contained no right to participate in management; were assignable without regard to any transfer of stock; hence, payments were interest. *John Kelley Co. v. Commissioner*, 326 U.S. 521 (1946).

Payments were interest on outstanding gold debentures.

Payments were made only out of net income and payable only on declaration; without such declaration there could be no default; the trust indenture was not recorded; hence, payments were dividends. *Petit Anse Co. v. Commissioner*, 155 F.2d 797 (5th Cir., 1946).

Payments were interest on outstanding Class A debentures issued in exchange for stock in a reorganization.

Debentures had a fixed maturity date; a fixed rate of interest payable regardless of earnings; had no voting rights; hence, payments were interest. *Elliot-Lewis Co. v. Commissioner*, 154 F.2d 292 (3d Cir., 1946).

Payments were interest on outstanding Class B debentures issued in exchange for stock in a reorganization.

Interest rate of 50% was excessive and was equal to the amount of dividends paid on the stock exchanged for the

Taxpayer's Position	*Court's Holding*

A, 2. INTEREST ON DEBENTURES—*Continued*

	debentures; hence, payments were dividends. *Elliot-Lewis Co. v. Commissioner, supra.*
Payments were interest on outstanding debentures issued in a reorganization.	Debentures had a fixed maturity date; were freely transferable independently of stock, interest was payable in all events; hence, payments were interest. *Cleveland Adolph Mayer Realty Corp.,* 6 T.C. 730 (1946).
Payments were interest on outstanding debentures issued in payment for assets.	Debentures were issued for value and represented a legal obligation to pay; hence, payments were interest. *Dade-Commonwealth Title Co.,* 6 T.C. 332 (1946).
Payments were interest on outstanding junior debentures issued as a dividend.	Debentures were issued as a dividend to conserve cash and were taxable when issued; they represented a legal obligation to pay, hence, payments were interest. *Dade-Commonwealth Title Co., supra.*
Payments were interest on outstanding debentures.	Debentures had a fixed maturity date; a fixed rate of interest payable at definite intervals regardless of earnings; contained proper safeguards in case of default; were superior to subsequent indebtedness and were secured; hence, payments were interest. *Andersen Corp.,* T.C. Memo., Docket #6893, May 23, 1946.

Taxpayer's Position	*Court's Holding*
Payments were interest on outstanding debentures.	Debentures had no fixed maturity date; were unsecured; were uncertain as to source and amount of payment; were subordinate to claims of general creditors; hence, payments were dividends. *The Briggs Co.*, T.C. Memo., Docket #6582, May 14, 1946.
Payments were interest on outstanding debentures which were issued in exchange for preferred stock pursuant to a reorganization.	Debentures had a fixed maturity date; a fixed rate of interest payable monthly regardless of earnings; carried the right to enforce payment of principal and interest; on dissolution holders ranked with other unsecured creditors to the exclusion of stockholders; hence, payments were interest. *250 Hudson Street Corporation*, T.C. Memo., Docket #7468, Aug. 9, 1946.
Payments were interest on outstanding debentures.	Debentures had no fixed maturity date; payments were not cumulative and were payable within discretion of the board; no provision for interest on unpaid dividends; no recourse in default of payment; subordinated to creditors; hence, payments were dividends. *Green Bay & W. R. Co. v. Commissioner*, 147 F.2d 585 (7th Cir., 1945).
Payments were interest on outstanding debenture certificates.	Debentures had a fixed maturity date; were issued for a good business reason; interest payments had fixed dates and

Taxpayer's Position   *Court's Holding*

A, 2. INTEREST ON DEBENTURES—*Continued*

were not dependent upon earnings; holders had no share in corporate assets upon liquidation; hence, payments were interest. *Clyde Bacon, Inc.,* 4 T.C. 1107 (1945).

Payments were interest on outstanding debentures.

Debentures were subordinate to claims of all creditors; were unsecured; and interest was payable only at the option of the corporation; hence, payments were dividends. *Charles L. Huisking Co.,* 4 T.C. 595 (1945).

Payments were interest on outstanding debenture stock.

Debentures had a fixed maturity date; a fixed rate of interest; were subordinate to creditors but superior to common stockholders; were retireable on any interest date by payment of principal and unpaid interest; hence, payments were interest. *Idaho Lumber & Hardware Co.,* T.C. Memo., Docket #4792, Mar. 8, 1945.

Payments were interest on outstanding debentures.

Debentures had a fixed maturity date; interest was payable quarterly out of earnings but was cumulative and payable absolutely in event of call or maturity, irrespective of earnings; holders had no voting rights; hence, payments were interest. *Hood & Sons, Inc. v. Commissioner,* 141 F.2d 467 (1st Cir., 1944).

Taxpayer's Position	*Court's Holding*
Payments were interest on outstanding debentures even though payable only if there were sufficient earnings.	Debenture had a fixed maturity date; a fixed interest rate; was preferred over stockholders in liquidation; had no right to participate in management; could not share in profits with stockholders; hence, payments were interest. *S. Glaser & Sons, Inc.,* T.C. Memo., Docket #2897, May 22, 1944.
Payments were interest on outstanding debentures.	Debentures did not have a fixed maturity date nor a fixed principal amount; carried a participation in profits; hence, payments were dividends. *Bonds, Inc.,* T.C. Memo., Docket #5074, Nov. 11, 1944.
Payments were interest on outstanding debenture preferred stock.	Debentures had a fixed maturity date; a fixed rate of interest not restricted to earnings; were preferred in liquidation and had no voting rights; hence, payments were interest. *Idaho Department Stores, Inc.,* T.C. Memo., Docket #923, Feb. 24, 1944.
Payments were interest on outstanding debenture preferred stock.	Debentures did not have a fixed maturity date; were issued in exchange for old preferred stock so that no new capital was paid into or lent to the corporation; were treated as part of the capital structure in tax returns; hence, payments were dividends. *Golden Belt Lumber Co.,* 1 T.C. 741 (1943).
Payments were interest on outstanding debenture pre-	Debentures were issued in a reorganization and did not rep-

Taxpayer's Position   *Court's Holding*

A, 2. INTEREST ON DEBENTURES—*Continued*

ferred stock which had a fixed maturity date.

resent new capital; were included as part of corporation's authorized capital; were listed in tax return as capital stock; hence, payments were dividends. *Rolfe Building Materials Co.*, T.C. Memo., Docket #110268, Aug. 30, 1943.

Payments were interest on outstanding debentures.

Payments were payable only out of net income; owners could and did share in the profits in excess of interest and had a veto power over election of directors; creditors had preference; hence, payments were dividends. *Hale-Justis Drug Co.*, T.C. Memo., Docket #110117, May 10, 1943.

Payments were interest on outstanding debentures which were issued in exchange for preferred stock pursuant to a recapitalization.

Debentures had a fixed maturity date; a fixed rate of interest payable without regard to earnings; were superior to the stockholders in dissolution; payment could be enforced; hence, payments were interest. *Annis Furs, Inc.*, T.C. Memo., Docket #110894, Jan. 28, 1943.

Payments were interest on outstanding income bonds.

Income bonds had no definite maturity date; interest was payable out of earnings and only when directors declared it to be payable; hence, payments were dividends. *Ticker Publishing Co.*, 46 B.T.A. 399 (1942).

Taxpayer's Position	*Court's Holding*
Payments were interest on outstanding debentures.	Debentures had a fixed maturity date; bore a fixed rate of interest; carried no voting rights; payments were not limited to earnings and payment of interest and principal could be enforced by general action; hence, payments were interest. *Chas. Olson & Sons, Inc.*, B.T.A. Memo., Docket #109980, Nov. 10, 1942.
Payments were interest on preferred debentures.	Preferred debentures had a fixed maturity date; no voting rights; interest was not restricted to corporate earnings; holders had the right to compel payment of principal and interest in event of default by suit; holders were entitled to principal and cumulative unpaid interest in event of dissolution; hence, payments were interest. *Western Dredging Company*, B.T.A. Memo., Docket #105842, Nov. 19, 1942.
Payments were interest on outstanding debenture preference stock.	Debentures had a fixed maturity date; carried no right to vote; on dissolution debenture holders could only receive par and could sue for principal and interest if default occurred for two years; hence, payments were interest. *Fidelity Finance Service, Inc.*, B.T.A. Memo., Docket #107146, Aug. 19, 1942.
Payments were interest on outstanding debentures issued under a refinancing plan to	Debentures had no fixed maturity date; were subordinate to general creditors; interest

Taxpayer's Position	*Court's Holding*

A, 2. INTEREST ON DEBENTURES—*Continued*

former holders of cumulative preferred stock.	was payable only out of profits; hence, payments were dividends. *Commissioner v. Schmoll Fils Associated, Inc.,* 110 F.2d 611 (2d Cir., 1940).
Payments were interest on outstanding debentures.	Debentures had a fixed maturity date; were a definite ascertainable obligation and holders had no right to participate in management; hence, payments were interest. *O. P. P. Holding Corp. v. Commissioner,* 76 F.2d 11 (2d Cir., 1935).
The payment by the company was interest on bonds issued by it.	The payment by the company was a dividend to its shareholder, and not a deductible interest payment. *George D. Mann, et al.,* 33 B.T.A. 281 (1935).
Payments were interest on outstanding debenture stock which contained a fixed maturity date.	Payments were cumulative and were to be made only out of earnings; debentures were treated as part of capital stock structure; hence, payments were dividends. *Kentucky River Coal Corp. v. Lucas,* 63 F.2d 1007 (6th Cir., 1932).

A. PAYMENTS CLAIMED AS INTEREST—*Continued*
    3. INTEREST ON PREFERRED STOCK

Payments were for interest on a debt and preferred stock issued to debtors was issued merely as security for the payment of the debt.	Securities were referred to as preferred stock; were carried on corporate books as capital stock rather than as an indebtedness; were subordinate to creditors; dividends were pay-

Taxpayer's Position

Court's Holding

able from earnings; hence, payments were dividends. *Crown Iron Works Co. v. Commissioner*, 245 F.2d 357 (8th Cir., 1957).

Payments were for interest on outstanding preferred stock that was merely evidence of an indebtedness.

Certificates did not have a fixed maturity date; were subordinate to general creditors; interest was payable from earnings and only when declared; hence, payments were dividends. *Kingsmill Corp.*, **28** T.C. 330 (1957).

Payments were for interest on outstanding preferred stock.

Certificates were called "preferred stock" and treated as such on the corporate books; were subordinate to general creditors; payments were to be made only out of net profits; hence, payments were dividends. *Lee Telephone Co. v. Commissioner*, 260 F.2d 114 (4th Cir., 1958).

Payments were for interest on outstanding preferred stock which in effect represented an indebtedness that had to be retired at fixed dates.

Preferred stock was unsecured and subordinated to claim of all creditors; liability for payment of interest was not absolute; was treated on books as preferred stock; hence, payments were dividends. *Confidential Loan Corp.*, T.C. Memo., Docket #59890, Jan. 31, 1957.

Payments were interest on outstanding preferred stock that in fact represented an indebtedness maturing on a definite date.

Certificates were treated as preferred stock in all corporate records and tax returns; were subordinate to general creditors; payments were limited to

Taxpayer's Position	*Court's Holding*

A, 3. INTEREST ON PREFERRED STOCK—*Continued*

	earnings; hence, payments were dividends. *Crawford Drug Stores, Inc. v. United States,* 220 F.2d 292 (10th Cir., 1955).
The amount paid was deductible interest on debenture preferred stock.	The company needed to borrow money, the certificate constituted a definite obligation to pay a certain sum and accrued cumulative interest at a definite date. The holders had no privilege or control in the corporation except upon default; hence, there was a corporate indebtedness, and payment of interest thereon is deductible. *Motor & Industrial Finance Corp. v. Scofield, et al.,* — F. Supp. — (D.C.Tex., 1955).
Payments were interest on outstanding preferred stock that in effect was merely evidence of an indebtedness.	The so-called "preferred stock" was not issued for sale to the public but to an insurance company, under terms and restrictions prescribed by the insurance company to insure repayment of a definite amount within a definite period; stock had no voice in the operation of the business; hence, payments were deductible interest. *Choctaw, Inc.,* T.C. Memo., Docket #36173, Dec. 8, 1953.
Payments were interest on outstanding preferred stock that was exchanged, pursuant to contract, for an outstanding mortgage to change the form of	Dividend payments were guaranteed, as was payment of the obligation, in fixed amounts on fixed dates; parties intended only to change form of indebt-

Taxpayer's Position	*Court's Holding*
indebtedness for credit purposes.	edness; hence, payments were interest. *Bowersock Mills & Power Co. v. Commissioner,* 172 F.2d 904 (10th Cir., 1949).
Payments were interest on outstanding preferred stock which was exchanged for common stock and which was redeemable with accumulated unpaid dividends at a fixed date.	Preferred stock represented original capital investment, contributed, not as a loan but at risk of the business; payments were always treated as dividends; change in stock structure was made only to facilitate a sale of the business which was never consummated; hence, payments were dividends. *Messenger Publishing Co. v. Commissioner,* 168 F.2d 903 (3d Cir., 1948).
Payments were interest on an outstanding debenture preferred stock.	Securities had no fixed maturity date; were held by the stockholders in control of the corporation; would not, in effect, be collected on default until liquidation; resulted in a debt to capital ratio of 29 to 1; interest was to be paid only out of earnings; hence, payments were dividends. *Mullin Building Corp. v. Commissioner,* 167 F.2d 1001 (3d Cir., 1948).
Payments were interest on outstanding debenture preference stock issued after incorporation for the purpose of paying off a prior indebtedness which accrued to the corporation.	Stock had no fixed maturity date; participated in profits after common stock requirements were met; was subordinate to general creditors; hence, payments were dividends. *Pottstown Finance Co., Inc. v. United States,* 73 F. Supp. 1011 (D.C.Pa., 1947).

Taxpayer's Position	*Court's Holding*

A, 3. INTEREST ON PREFERRED STOCK—*Continued*

Payments were interest on outstanding preferred stock which was in fact an indebtedness.	Certificates had no maturity date; had no prior right to payment except as to holders of common stock; were inferior to general creditors; there was no unconditional liability to pay any sum; payments were dividends. *Hercules Gasoline Co., Inc.,* T.C. Memo., Docket #111038, July 31, 1944.
Payments were interest on outstanding preferred stock that in reality represented an indebtedness, and preferred stock terms were amended so as to provide for a maturity date.	Payments were due only out of profits; certificates were treated as capital stock; evidence indicated that the intent of the parties was to issue preferred stock; hence, payments were dividends; amendment not controlling. *Verifine Dairy Products Corporation of Sheboygan, Inc.,* 3 T.C. 269 (1944).
Payments were interest on outstanding guaranteed prior preference stock which was in effect an indebtedness, as payments were due regardless of earnings.	Certificates had no fixed maturity date; carried voting privileges; did not provide for right to sue in event of default; hence, payments were dividends. *Texas Drivurself System, Inc.,* T.C. Memo., Docket #112159, Mar. 31, 1944.
Payments were interest on outstanding preferred stock which was issued in cancellation of a corporate indebtedness.	Preferred stock did not contain a fixed maturity date; was subordinate to general creditors; hence, payments were dividends. *John Wanamaker, Philadelphia v. Commissioner,* 139 F.2d 644 (3d Cir., 1943).

Taxpayer's Position	*Court's Holding*

Payments were interest on outstanding preferred stock which in effect was an indebtedness.

Preferred stock was carried on books as part of capital structure; there was no fixed maturity date; dividends were payable only when declared; holders had no priority in dissolution; hence, payments were dividends. *First Mortgage Corporation of Philadelphia v. Commissioner*, 135 F.2d 121 (3d Cir., 1943).

Payments were interest on outstanding preferred stock which in fact represented an indebtedness as agreed upon between the corporation and certificate holders.

Stock had a fixed redemption date; interest was cumulative; was not treated as invested capital; was not sold with other stock; had no voting rights; was not obtained in combination with voting stock; parties agreed that it was to represent an indebtedness; hence, payments were interest. *United States v. Title Guarantee & Trust Co.*, 133 F.2d 990 (6th Cir., 1943).

Payments were interest on preferred stock which was in reality evidence of an indebtedness, since it provided for a fixed maturity date and a guaranty by the common stockholders of payment of a fixed amount of dividends and redemption price.

Payments could be made only out of net earnings; redemption could be made only without impairing capital; hence, payments were dividends. *Northern Refrigerator Line, Inc.*, 1 T.C. 824 (1943).

Payments were interest on outstanding debenture preference shares issued in a reorganization in exchange for notes.

In the circumstances the payments were dividends. *The Buckeye Cereal Co.*, T.C. Memo., Docket #112589, July 5, 1943.

Taxpayer's Position   *Court's Holding*

A, 3. INTEREST ON PREFERRED STOCK—*Continued*

Taxpayer's Position	Court's Holding
Payments were interest on outstanding preferred stock which was in effect an indebtedness, as the company was required to redeem a certain amount of shares per year.	Certificates had no par value; provided for dividend payments; carried voting rights; were treated in tax returns and books of account as part of the capital structure; hence, payments were dividends. *Parisian, Inc. v. Commissioner,* 131 F.2d 394 (5th Cir., 1942).
Payments were interest on preferred stock which was converted to a debt by corporate resolution.	Articles of incorporation and stock certificates indicated that the preferred stock was not a debt; there was no fixed maturity date; hence, payments were dividends. *Gallatin Farmers Co. v. Commissioner,* 132 F.2d 706 (9th Cir., 1942).
Payments were interest on preferred stock that in fact represented an indebtedness having a definite maturity date.	Payments were restricted to earnings; certificate holders were subordinate to general creditors and had no remedy for failure to receive payments; hence, payments were dividends. *Meridian & Thirteenth Realty Co. v. Commissioner,* 132 F.2d 182 (7th Cir., 1942).
Payments were interest on outstanding preferred stock that was in reality an indebtedness.	Payments were to be made out of profits; both parties intended the relation to be proprietary rather than that of creditor and debtor; hence, payments were dividends. *Pacific Southwest Realty Co. v. Commissioner,* 128 F.2d 815 (9th Cir., 1942).

Taxpayer's Position

Payments were interest on outstanding debenture preferred stock issued in a recapitalization.

Court's Holding

Debentures had a fixed maturity date; fixed rate of interest with priority over dividends on preferred and common stock, and provided for suit to enforce payment of principal and interest; hence, payments were interest. *Commissioner v. J. N. Bray Co.*, 126 F.2d 612 (5th Cir., 1942).

Payments represented interest on preferred stock and was deductible.

The payment was not deductible as interest as the preferred stock did not represent an indebtedness; there was no fixed maturity date for payment of principal, no right on dissolution to share in the assets with creditors, the security was called "preferred stock" and payments thereon "dividends," which were payable only out of earnings and the holders of preferred could elect one director. *The Ernst Kern Co.*, 1 T.C. 249 (1942).

Payments were interest on preferred stock which were in effect demand notes.

Certificates were designated as preferred stock and called for payment of cumulative dividends; were treated as preferred stock in all corporate articles, certificates and resolutions provided for payment of dividends; hence, payments were dividends. *Spahn & Rose Lumber Co.*, T.C. Memo., Docket #106747, Dec. 8, 1942.

Payments were interest on outstanding debenture pre-

The certificates had no fixed maturity date; had no prefer-

Taxpayer's Position   *Court's Holding*

A, 3. INTEREST ON PREFERRED STOCK—*Continued*

ferred stock issued in a reorganization of the company.

ence over creditors; were
treated as part of the capital
structure and not as a debt;
were not issued for money
loaned but in lieu of common
stock and were merely new evidence of funds placed at risk of
the business; hence, payments
were dividends. *Brown-Rogers-
Dixson Co. v. Commissioner,*
122 F.2d 347 (4th Cir., 1941).

Payments were interest on
outstanding preferred stock
which constituted an indebtedness of the corporation.

Securities were called and
treated as preferred stock in the
articles of incorporation, the
tax returns, and the capital
stock tax returns; hence, payments were dividends and not
interest. *Leslie-James, Inc.,*
B.T.A. Memo., Docket #100756,
April 16, 1941.

Payments were interest on
outstanding preferred stock
that in reality was an indebtedness.

Payments, and amounts set
aside in retirement sinking fund
were to be made only out of
earnings; there was no fixed
maturity date and there was no
right to force payment as a
debt in event of default; hence,
payments were dividends.
*Haffenreffer Brewing Co. v.
Commissioner,* 116 F.2d 465
(1st Cir., 1940).

Payments were interest on
outstanding preferred stock
which in effect represented an
indebtedness.

Preferred stock had a fixed
maturity date; payments of a
fixed amount were not dependent on earnings; hence, payments were interest. *Diamond*

Taxpayer's Position	*Court's Holding*
	Calk Horse Shoe Co. v. United States, 116 F.2d 284 (8th Cir., 1940).
Payments of guaranteed dividends secured by a mortgage on outstanding preferred stock were in effect interest payments.	Stock was subordinate to general creditors; guaranteed dividends were not to be paid in any event but only out of profits; hence, payments were dividends. *Dayton & Michigan R. Co. v. Commissioner,* 112 F.2d 627 (4th Cir., 1940).
Payments were interest on outstanding preferred stock which in effect was an indebtedness.	Preferred stock was received as consideration for a sale and was accepted as security and not an investment; it was to be liquidated in 20 instalments and payments of 6% on deferred instalments; hence, payments were interest. *Palmer, Stacy-Merrill, Inc. v. Commissioner,* 111 F.2d 809 (9th Cir., 1940).
Payments were interest on outstanding preferred stock issued to retire a bonded indebtedness.	Preferred stock had no fixed maturity date and facts showed that the corporation intended in the refinancing to substitute stock liability for debt liability; hence, payments were dividends. *United States v. South Georgia Ry. Co.,* 107 F.2d 3 (5th Cir., 1939).
Payments were interest on outstanding debenture preference stock.	In the circumstances, the debenture preference stock represented an indebtedness; hence, payments were interest. *The Proctor Shop, Inc. v. Commissioner,* 82 F.2d 792 (9th Cir., 1936).

Taxpayer's Position   *Court's Holding*

A, 3. INTEREST ON PREFERRED STOCK—*Continued*

The amount paid was deductible interest on the corporation's obligation, and not a dividend on preferred stock.

The corporation purchased assets upon agreement to pay a sum of money with interest at 7%, the preferred stock in a like amount was given as security and the company's agreement to repurchase it was in payment of the debt; hence, the 7% paid was not a dividend on preferred stock, but deductible interest on a debt. *National Cottonseed Products Corp. v. Commissioner,* 76 F.2d 839 (6th Cir., 1935).

Payments were interest on preferred stock which was essentially equivalent to a bond because of the many restrictions in its terms.

There was no obligation to repay principal or interest; no fixed maturity date; hence, payments were dividends. *Greensboro News Co.,* 31 B.T.A. 812 (1934).

Payments were interest on outstanding preferred stock which in fact represented an indebtedness.

Preferred stock was not entitled to a fixed rate of return; was subordinate to creditors; payments were to be made from earnings; hence, payments were dividends. *Finance & Investment Corp. v. Burnet,* 57 F.2d 444 (D.C. Cir., 1932).

Payments were interest on outstanding preferred stock which was in reality a debt.

There was no definite obligation to repay a specified sum of money; no provision for retirement at a definite date; payments were to be made only out of profits; hence, payments were dividends. *Elko Lamoille Power Co. v. Commissioner,* 50 F.2d 595 (9th Cir., 1931).

Taxpayer's Position	*Court's Holding*
Payments were interest on preferred stock which in reality represented borrowed funds.	The stock had no fixed maturity date; no fixed rate of interest; payments could be made only out of earnings; general creditors were senior to preferred stockholders; hence, payments were dividends. *Badger Lumber Co.*, 23 B.T.A. 362 (1931).
Payments were interest on preferred stock, as they were paid irrespective of earnings; and the corporation had agreed to limit its indebtedness.	In the circumstances the preferred stock did not represent an indebtedness; hence, payments were dividends. *McCoy-Garten Realty Co.*, 14 B.T.A. 853 (1928).
Payments on Class A preferred stock were interest, as the stock was merely evidence of an indebtedness.	The preferred stock had no fixed maturity date; they were not secured; hence, payments were dividends. *Northern Fire Apparatus Co.*, 11 B.T.A. 355 (1928).
Payment was in fact deductible interest, the preferred shares simply being used to cover a usurious loan.	On the facts the first preferred shares actually were a loan, and the payments in question were interest and not dividends. As between the government and the taxpayer, the true relationship of debtor and creditor controls, rather than what the transaction is called. *Arthur R. Jones Syndicate v. Commissioner*, 23 F.2d 833 (7th Cir., 1927).
Payments made on preferred stock were deductible as interest, as the holders of preferred stock were in effect creditors not stockholders.	Payments were to be made only out of surplus and net profits; upon dissolution, the preferred stock was preferred only as to common stock; hence,

Taxpayer's Position   *Court's Holding*

A, 3. INTEREST ON PREFERRED STOCK—*Continued*

payments were dividends. *William Cluff Co.*, 7 B.T.A. 662 (1927).

Payments were interest on outstanding preferred stock which was in effect a loan to the corporation.

The certificate represented a part of the corporation's authorized capital stock; was issued in form of a preferred stock certificate; provided for a quarterly dividend; was not secured by a mortgage or otherwise; hence, payments were dividends. *Leasenhold Realty Co.*, 3 B.T.A. 1129 (1926).

A. PAYMENTS CLAIMED AS INTEREST—*Continued*
   4. INTEREST ON OTHER FORMS OF INDEBTEDNESS

The amount paid was deductible interest on an instalment sales contract.

Debt-stock ratio standing alone is not sufficient to justify treating an instalment sales contract as equity investment; although ratio was 50 to 1, the company was adequately capitalized; hence, payment was of deductible interest. *J. I. Morgan, Inc., et al.*, 30 T.C. 881 (1958).

Payments were interest on income notes.

The amount purporting to be a debt was in effect placed at the risk of the business and therefore did not represent a valid debt; hence, the payments were dividends. Notes did not provide for a fixed rate of interest; interest was dependent on earnings and noncumulative; hence, payments were

Taxpayer's Position	*Court's Holding*
	dividends. *Gregg Company of Delaware v. Commissioner*, 239 F.2d 498 (2d Cir., 1956).
Payments were interest on advances made to the corporation.	Advances were evidenced by promissory notes which provided for a fixed maturity date, provided for semiannual payment of interest and were not subordinate to general creditors; hence, payments were for interest. *Associated Investors, Inc. v. United States*, — F. Supp. — (D.C.Kan., 1956).
Payments were interest on investment certificates.	Certificates were cast in the form of interest-bearing obligations; there was a need for more capital, and former preferred stockholders were reluctant to invest further unless an absolute obligation was offered; hence, payments were interest. *G. W. Onthank Co.*, T.C. Memo., Docket #42593, Mar. 31, 1954.
Payments under agreement were deductible interest on debt.	On the facts, the corporation did not desire nor obtain a loan; hence, the payment was not deductible interest. *Heymann Mercantile Company, Inc.*, T.C. Memo., Docket #14883, Nov. 18, 1948.
Payments were interest on certificates of beneficial ownership.	Certificates contained no fixed maturity date; were not in the form of an indebtedness; contained no right to force payment of principal as a debt in event of default; hence, payments were dividends. *Indus-*

Taxpayer's Position   *Court's Holding*

A, 4. INTEREST ON OTHER FORMS OF INDEBTEDNESS—*Continued*

	trial Addition Association v. Commissioner, 149 F.2d 294 (6th Cir., 1945).
Payments were interest on liquidation certificate.	Certificates had a fixed amount of principal; a fixed rate of interest payable in all events and payment was capable of being enforced; hence, payments were interest. *Staked Plains Trust, Ltd. v. Commissioner,* 143 F.2d 421 (5th Cir., 1944).
Payments were interest on liquidation rights certificates.	Rights did not represent an obligation in a specific sum; interest payments were not due or payable; hence, payments were dividends. *Staked Plains Trust, Ltd. v. Commissioner, supra.*
Payments were interest on a contract of purchase of assets necessary to operate the business.	The obligation to make payments had no fixed payment date and called for payment of all earnings; hence, payments were dividends. *Fontana Power Co. v. Commissioner,* 127 F.2d 193 (9th Cir., 1942).
Payment was deductible interest on certificates of deposit, upon which there was an unconditional obligation to pay interest.	The holders of the certificates had put their money at the risk of the business, and what the instrument was called is immaterial; there was no obligation to make payments indefinitely into the future; hence, the payments were dividends and not deductible interest. *Bakers' Mutual Coopera-*

Taxpayer's Position	*Court's Holding*
	tive Ass'n. of Newark, N. J. v. Commissioner, 117 F.2d 27 (3d Cir., 1941).
Payments were interest provided for in a collateral agreement executed as security to a former stockholder who had been induced to exchange his notes for preferred stock.	In the circumstances the payments were interest. *The Brush-Moore Newspapers, Inc.,* 37 B.T.A. 787 (1938).
Payments on certificates of 2½% of insurance renewal payments were interest.	Payments were to continue whether or not indebtedness was retired; hence, payments were dividends, as there could be no interest after payment of principal debt. *Manhattan Mutual Life Insurance Co.,* 37 B.T.A. 1041 (1938).
Payments on certificates of 6% of par value were interest on a surplus guaranty fund.	Interest was guaranteed in a fixed amount payable annually; the guaranty fund was an outstanding indebtedness; hence, payments were interest. *Manhattan Mutual Life Insurance Co., supra.*
Payments were interest on outstanding guaranteed stock which was in effect an outstanding indebtedness, even though there was no fixed maturity date.	Interest and principal were payable in any event, became first liens on assets, and had priority over secured and general creditors; stock was treated by taxpayer and Internal Revenue Service as outstanding debt for Excess Profits Tax purpose; hence, payments were interest. *Richmond, Fredericksburg & Potomac Railroad Co. v. Commissioner,* 90 F.2d 971 (4th Cir., 1937).

Taxpayer's Position   *Court's Holding*

A, 4. INTEREST ON OTHER FORMS OF INDEBTEDNESS—*Continued*

Taxpayer's Position	Court's Holding
Payments were interest on shares of special common stock, which were in effect certificates of indebtedness.	Payments were to be made only out of profits; certificates provided that it was part of a capital stock issue; hence, payments were dividends. *Perrine & Buckelew, Inc.*, 32 B.T.A. 168 (1935).
Payment on redemption of stock issued as security for a loan was, to the extent that it exceeded the loan, interest on an outstanding indebtedness.	In the circumstances the amount paid in was for capital stock rather than a loan, and the redemption was equivalent to a dividend. *Colorado Life Co.*, 29 B.T.A. 950 (1934).
Payments were interest on outstanding property interest certificates.	Interest was payable out of profits; corporation had no outstanding issue of capital stock but only the property interest certificates which represented an investment and not an interest-bearing obligation; hence, payments were in effect dividends. *Artesia Alfalfa Growers Assn.*, B.T.A. Memo., Docket #68867, Aug. 24, 1934.
Payments were interest on advances made to the corporation, and, although stock was issued to cover the advances, it was never intended to convert the loans to any other form, as the stock was issued only as a convenience.	Loans were treated as invested capital; same rate of "interest" was paid to all stockholders; securities were always treated as stock; hence, payments were dividends. *Angelus Building and Investment Co. v. Commissioner*, 57 F.2d 130 (9th Cir., 1932).
Payments were interest on outstanding withdrawable stock.	Payments were to be made out of earnings; hence, payments were dividends. *Guar-*

Taxpayer's Position	*Court's Holding*

anty State Savings & Loan Co.,
14 B.T.A. 72 (1928).

A. PAYMENTS CLAIMED AS INTEREST—*Continued*
 5. INTEREST ON INDEBTEDNESS NOT EVIDENCED BY INSTRUMENT

The amount paid by the corporation is interest on an indebtedness due to stockholders and a deductible item.	The amount advanced to the corporation constituted not a loan but an equity investment, and "interest" paid thereon is not deductible. To be considered in determining whether an advance is a capital contribution instead of a loan are the debt-equity ratio, the fact that money was needed to commence business and for working capital; advances were proportionate to stockholdings; a disinterested person would not make a loan; the stockholders could not have expected repayment; demanding payment would ruin the company to the loss of the same individuals. *Lockwood Realty Co. v. Commissioner,* 264 F.2d 241 (6th Cir., 1959); *Harkins Bowling, Inc. v. Knox,* 164 F. Supp. 801 (D.C.Minn., 1958), *app. (T) pending,* 8th Cir.; *Canton Tool Mfg. Co.,* T.C. Memo., Docket #55518, Aug. 19, 1957.
Payments were interest on loans payable.	Loans were not evidenced by instrument of indebtedness; no security was given; there was no formal corporate action taken authorizing the creation of the debt nor the payment of

Taxpayer's Position   *Court's Holding*

**A, 5. INTEREST ON INDEBTEDNESS NOT EVIDENCED BY INSTRUMENT
—Continued**

interest; capital structure was wholly unrealistic as ratio of debt to equity capital ranged from 64 to 1 to 71 to 1; hence, payments were dividends. *U. S. Asiatic Co.*, 30 T.C. 1373 (1958).

Payments were interest on advances made to the corporation.

Advances had no maturity date; were not evidenced by any writing; represented part of purchase price of some of corporate properties; were exactly proportionate to stock-holdings; resulted in a debt to capital ratio of 600 to 1; repayment was dependent upon future earnings; hence, payments were essentially dividends. *241 Corp. v. Commissioner*, 242 F.2d 759 (2d Cir., 1957).

The payment made was deductible interest on an instalment purchase.

The newly formed corporation was not a "thin corporation," and its acquisition of property from the incorporators was an instalment purchase; hence, interest on the instalment purchase arrangement is deductible. *Perrault v. Commissioner*, 244 F.2d 408 (10th Cir., 1957).

Payments were interest on a corporate loan.

Loan was not evidenced by any note; it had no maturity date or method of repayment; interest payments and amounts varied; it was subordinate to all other creditors; there was

Taxpayer's Position	*Court's Holding*
	no corporate action confirming the understanding of indebtedness; hence, payments were dividends. *Artistic Venetian Blind Corp.*, T.C. Memo., Docket #50420, Feb. 24, 1956.
Payments were interest on amounts loaned to the corporation.	Corporate records evidenced an intent to make a loan; corporation was not undercapitalized; hence, payment was interest. *Bakhaus and Burke Inc.*, T.C. Memo., Docket #49166, Aug. 12, 1955.
Payments were interest on advances made by a stockholder to the corporation.	Advances were acknowledged as loans by the corporation; they were carried on the books as loans payable; conduct of the parties had been consistent with the characterization of the advances as loans; hence, payments were interest. *Pier Management Corp.*, T.C. Memo., Docket ##50756, 50820, June 20, 1955.
Payments were interest on advances made by the stockholders to the corporation.	Ratio of debt to capital was excessive; advances were in proportion to stockholdings; loans had no maturity date, were unsecured, and payment of interest was dependent on earnings; hence, payments were dividends. *Two-L Realty Co., Inc.*, T.C. Memo., Docket #50962, Oct. 31, 1955.
Loan, upon which payments of interest was made, was created pursuant to an agreement among stockholders.	Not pertinent. *Robert L. Osborne*, T.C. Memo., Docket #40735, April 30, 1954.

Taxpayer's Position   *Court's Holding*

A, 5. INTEREST ON INDEBTEDNESS NOT EVIDENCED BY INSTRUMENT
—*Continued*

Payments were interest on advances made to the corporation.

Advances were in proportion to the stock interests; resulted in a debt to capital ratio of 1000 to 1; hence, payments were dividends. *Kipsborough Realty Co.*, T.C. Memo., Docket #27676, Sept. 28, 1951.

Payments to partnership consisting of corporation's stockholders was ordinary and necessary payment for providing needed capital.

Funds advanced were a contribution to capital and the payments were dividends on preferred stock. *Heymann Mercantile Company, Inc.*, T.C. Memo., Docket #14883, Nov. 18, 1948.

Payments were interest on advances made to the corporation.

Advances were not evidenced by notes; had no fixed maturity date; were carried as stock assessments on tax returns; hence, payments were dividends. *Minden Compress Co., Inc.*, T.C. Memo., Docket #109431, Aug. 4, 1944.

The disbursement was deductible interest on a loan received from a stockholder.

The loan made by the stockholder provided for no interest and, therefore, the corporation was under no obligation to pay it; hence, the deduction is not allowed (see dissenting opinion). *Transportation Service Associates, Inc.*, T.C. Memo., Docket #110653, Feb. 11, 1944, *aff'd on other issues*, 149 F.2d 354 (3d Cir., 1945); *Miller Safe Co., Inc.*, 12 B.T.A. 1388 (1928).

Taxpayer's Position

Payments were interest on advance to corporation by stockholders made after preferred stock was retired.

Payments were interest on cash advance to corporation.

Payments were interest on advances made to the corporation by the stockholders.

Payments were interest on outstanding loans made to the corporation's predecessor by the stockholders.

Payments were interest on advances made by the stockholders to the corporation.

Court's Holding

Transaction was a sham and no indebtedness existed; hence, payments were dividends. *The Humko Co.*, T.C. Memo., Docket ##112235, 79, Dec. 11, 1943.

Under the circumstances, a debtor-creditor relationship was created when advances were made; hence, payments were interest. *The Humko Co., supra.*

Advances were subject to withdrawal on demand; were not in proportion to stockholdings; interest was paid regularly; hence, payments were interest. *J. W. Fales Co.*, B.T.A. Memo., Docket #88242, Sept. 22, 1937.

Loans were made to the corporation's predecessor and assumed by the corporation; payments of interest were made regularly; hence, loan was a valid indebtedness and payments were deductible interest. *Wax Paper Products Co.*, B.T.A. Memo., Docket #71977, Sept. 23, 1935.

Advances were recorded on the corporate books as loans; were not in proportion to stockholdings; interest was paid regularly; hence, payments were interest. *Bogota Land Co.*, B.T.A. Memo., Docket #54161, Aug. 2, 1934.

Taxpayer's Position | *Court's Holding*

A, 5. INTEREST ON INDEBTEDNESS NOT EVIDENCED BY INSTRUMENT —*Continued*

Taxpayer's Position	*Court's Holding*
Amounts paid were deductible interest.	The obligation was that of the company's shareholders, and the payments were dividends to them and not interest. *Morris Plan Bank of Binghamton,* 26 B.T.A. 772 (1932).
Payments were interest on deferred dividends on preferred stock.	No indebtedness existed until payment of dividend was authorized; the payments were measured by the dividends; hence, so-called interest for period prior to declaration of dividend is not deductible. *Drayton Mills,* 19 B.T.A. 76 (1930).
Payments were interest on loans made to the corporation by its stockholders.	Payments were based on stockholdings; hence, payments were dividends. *Cloquet Co-operative Society,* 21 B.T.A. 744 (1930).
Payments were interest on an outstanding loan and were not payments on preferred stock which was held as security for the loan.	In the circumstances, the payments constituted interest. *Overland Knight Co., Inc.,* 15 B.T.A. 870 (1929).
Payments were interest on undivided profits.	There was no obligation to pay interest on undivided profits as the profits do not belong to stockholders until distributed; hence, payments were dividends. *West Music Co.,* 14 B.T.A. 158 (1928).

Taxpayer's Position   *Court's Holding*

B. PAYMENTS CLAIMED AS OTHER EXPENSES
   1. COMPENSATION FOR SERVICES

Payments were for services performed by the stockholder-doctors.

Payments to the extent of the stockholders' billings were reasonable compensation, but payments in excess of the billings constituted distribution of dividends. *Klamath Medical Service Bureau,* 29 T.C. 339 (1957).

The amount paid was deductible compensation for services rendered by relatives of the stockholder.

No substantial services were performed and the "salaries" were unreasonably high; hence, deduction for the payment thereof is not allowable. *Jolly's Motor Livery Co., et al.,* T.C. Memo., Docket ##36607, 36745, 41269–70, Dec. 16, 1957.

Authorization of the payment of reasonable salaries to officers-stockholders gave rise to a valid corporate deduction; and nonwithdrawal of the salaries and the subsequent issuance of stock in lieu of payment thereof does not alter the nature of the payments.

Payments to officers-stockholders were distributions of corporate profits and not deductible salaries, as the distributions were based on the ratio of stock ownership. *Jacksonville Paper Co.,* T.C. Memo., Docket ##14884, *et al.,* July 30, 1954.

Taxpayer received nothing from the corporation.

Salary paid to stockholder's son who rendered practically no services to the company was essentially equivalent to the distribution of a dividend to the stockholder. *Goodman v. Commissioner,* 176 F.2d 389 (2d Cir., 1949).

Payment was deductible

The payment was recorded

Taxpayer's Position   *Court's Holding*

B, 1. COMPENSATION FOR SERVICES—*Continued*

salary to the 75% stockholder-officer and not a dividend.

by the company and reported by the individual as a dividend, and, even though dividends were not paid to the holders of other 25% of stock, it was a dividend and not a deductible salary payment. *S. Lachman Co.,* T.C. Memo., Docket ##105243–4, Feb. 24, 1943.

The amounts paid were deductible "bonuses" to the company's two officers.

Each officer owned 27 of the company's 55 shares, each received the same year-end payment although one did far more work for the company and assumed more responsibility, practically all profits were paid out; hence, the payments were distributions of profits and not deductible bonuses for services. *Rivoli Operating Corp.,* T.C. Memo., Docket #103260, Jan. 28, 1942.

Payments were commissions.

Not substantiated; under the circumstances there was a distribution of dividends. *McKeever v. Eaton,* 6 F. Supp. 697 (D.C.Conn., 1934).

Payments to stockholders were commissions and deductible as an ordinary and necessary expense.

Actual facts, and not the form of the transaction, determine whether a payment is a distribution of profits. In looking to the substance of the transaction, part of the payment was a dividend. *Alexander Sprunt & Son, Inc. v.*

Taxpayer's Position	*Court's Holding*
	Commissioner, 64 F.2d 424 (4th Cir., 1933).
The amounts paid were deductible salaries and not dividends on stock owned by the employees.	The stock was transferred to the employees by the company's president, sole stockholder, as an incentive, and the company had no obligation to make any incentive payments; hence, the amounts paid were dividends and not deductible salaries. *Kennington v. Donald,* 50 F.2d 894 (5th Cir., 1931).
Distributions were payments of commissions for work sent to corporation by stockholders.	Not substantiated, as commissions earned had already been paid. *United Tailors & Cleaners Co.,* 10 B.T.A. 172 (1928).
Distribution represented additional salary.	Not substantiated. *Joseph Goodnow & Co.,* 5 B.T.A. 1154 (1927).
Distributions were bonuses or additional compensation.	Not substantiated. *R. E. Kennington Realty Co.,* 8 B.T.A. 1030 (1927).
Distributions were commissions for negotiating a sale.	Not substantiated. *The Times-News Co.,* 3 B.T.A. 1251 (1925).
Payments to stockholders in exchange for agreement to exchange preferred stock for common were compensation for personal services.	Payments were dividends inasmuch as paid under contract to reimburse stockholders for dividends on preferred stock exchanged for common. *American Textiles, Inc.,* 2 B.T.A. 186 (1925).

Taxpayer's Position   *Court's Holding*

B. Payments Claimed as Other Expenses—*Continued*
  2. Rents

Taxpayer's Position	Court's Holding
Amounts paid represented a fair rental for the property.	On the basis of the record the amount paid represented a fair rental; hence, it was deductible as rent and no part was essentially equivalent to the distribution of a dividend. *Southern Ford Tractor Corp.,* 29 T.C. 833 (1958).
The amount paid was deductible rental for land owned by the stockholder's sons.	The amount paid as rental exceeded the rental value of the land, and to the extent of such excess was not deductible rental. *Jolly's Motor Livery Co., et al.,* T.C. Memo., Docket ##36607, 36745, 41269–70, Dec. 16, 1957.
Amounts were rent payments to stockholder.	No evidence to support rental arrangement; hence, amounts were dividends. *Marvin T. Blackwell, et al.,* T.C. Memo., Docket #52701, Aug. 9, 1956.
Rental paid under a contract not made at arm's length was nevertheless fair and reasonable and deductible as a business expense.	Not substantiated; excess over fair rental was equivalent to a dividend. *Floridan Hotel Operators, Inc.,* T.C. Memo., Docket ##24426, 27033, Feb. 16, 1953.
Rental payments to stockholders were not excessive and were deductible by the corporation as an expense rather than the distribution of a dividend.	Rental between corporation and stockholder was lacking in reality and was merely a device to reduce taxes; hence, the excessive portion was equivalent to the distribution of a dividend. *Stanwick's, Inc. v. Com-*

Taxpayer's Position	Court's Holding
	missioner, 190 F.2d 84 (4th Cir., 1951).
Payments were for rent of property under a valid sale and leaseback of machinery to provide lessee with additional working capital.	Based on facts, there was no valid sale and leaseback arrangement. (Rents for three months exceeded the sales price of the property.) *Armston Co., Inc. v. Commissioner*, 188 F.2d 531 (5th Cir., 1951).
The payments made by the corporation were deductible rents.	The corporation was under no obligation to pay the "rental"; the payments were proportional to stockholdings, although the agreement was with only one of them; hence, the payments were not deductible rents. *D. H. Wiley Lumber Co., et al. v. Commissioner*, 177 F.2d 200 (6th Cir., 1949).
Payments to stockholders constituted a fair rental for property leased to corporation by stockholders.	Rents were excessive; excess over a reasonable amount of rent was distribution of a dividend. *Limericks, Inc. v. Commissioner*, 165 F.2d 483 (5th Cir., 1948).
Payments made by corporation in amount required by contract to sole stockholder for use of his property are deductible business expenses.	Such payments, although paid under binding contract, are deductible only to extent they are reasonable. *Greenspun, et al. v. Commissioner*, 156 F.2d 917 (5th Cir., 1946), *on remand*, T.C. Memo., Docket ##108233, *et al.*, July 22, 1948.
Entire amount of payments made by corporation to sole stockholder for use of his property is deductible business ex-	Payments by corporation to stockholder in excess of minimum rental required by contract are not deductible, since

Taxpayer's Position   *Court's Holding*

B, 2. RENTS—*Continued*

pense, as contract permitted corporation to increase rental.

Payments by corporation to sole stockholder for use of property transferred to stockholder, which was originally acquired by corporation from stockholder, were not dividends but were rent and deductible as business expenses.

Payments were rents.

Additional payments by corporation to manufacturing stockholders were deductible as rent and were not distribution of net profits.

not paid pursuant to an obligation. *Greenspun, et al. v. Commissioner, supra.*

No tax-avoidance motive since corporation had rented all such property since before 1913; also property transferred was only a small part of similar property so used; therefore, transfer had substance and must be recognized. *Greenspun, et al. v. Commissioner, supra.*

Payments were in excess of a fair rental value; hence, the excess over the fair rental value was a dividend. *Iron City Industrial Cleaning Corp., et al.,* T.C. Memo., Docket ##10417, *et al.,* Nov. 12, 1947.

Payments were deductible rents, even though paid to stockholders on percentage of net profits, since the base rent was below normal and the payments were based on amount of film actually furnished and not on proportion of stock owned. *In re General Film Corp., United States v. Kellogg,* 274 F. 903 (2d Cir., 1921).

B. PAYMENTS CLAIMED AS OTHER EXPENSES—*Continued*
   3. ROYALTIES

The grants by a stockholder to a controlled corporation of

The portion of the payments in excess of a reasonable rate

Taxpayer's Position	Court's Holding
exclusive patent rights in exchange for a percentage of sales under the patent were bona fide and arm's length agreements.	constituted dividends. *Roy J. Champayne*, 26 T.C. 634 (1956).
Payments to stockholders were royalties pursuant to contract.	Royalty payments were not necessary as the corporation had the right to mine coal under a previous lease and the payments were not necessary for the continuation or the development of the business; corporation was reorganized solely for the purpose of exacting a royalty; hence, payments were dividends. *Ingle Coal Corp. v. Commissioner*, 174 F.2d 569 (7th Cir., 1949); see also *Ingle Coal Corp. v. United States*, 127 F. Supp. 573 (Ct. Cl., 1955).
Payments were deductible as royalties paid to the corporation's stockholders who owned the patents.	The patents were distributed to the stockholders as dividends in kind and the payments made under license granted by the stockholders-distributees were necessary expenses allowable as deductions. *Stearns Magnetic Mfg. Co. v. Commissioner*, 208 F.2d 849 (7th Cir., 1954).
Payments were royalties, not dividends.	Corporation rather than taxpayer owned the mine; hence, payments could not be royalties but were dividends. *Tressler v. Commissioner*, 206 F.2d 538 (4th Cir., 1953).
Royalty payments were an ordinary and necessary expense of the corporation.	The payments were made to the stockholders in almost the same percentage as their stock-

Taxpayer's Position　　　　　*Court's Holding*

B, 3. ROYALTIES—*Continued*

holdings. In the circumstances, the payments were not royalties but dividends. *Granberg Equipment, Inc.*, 11 T.C. 704 (1948).

The disbursement to the stockholder was a deductible royalty.

The stockholder had transferred the coal mine to the corporation for its stock and its agreement to pay 10¢ per ton mined; the 10¢ per ton was payable regardless of profits and was a fixed obligation of the corporation; hence, the disbursement is deductible either as royalty or as expense necessary to conduct business. *Buffalo Eagle Mines, Inc.*, 37 B.T.A. 843 (1938).

Payments were royalties from subsidiary for use of assets.

Assets had previously been sold outright to the subsidiary. *Washburn Wire Co.*, 26 B.T.A. 464 (1932), *rev'd and remanded on another issue*, 67 F.2d 658 (1st Cir., 1933).

Royalty payments were for right of subsidiary to obtain working capital from parent.

Insufficient to support royalty payment. *Washburn Wire Co., supra.*

Royalty payments were made under contract between parent and subsidiary.

Parent fixed royalty payments in a non-arm's length transaction. *Washburn Wire Co., supra.*

Intention of parties was that payments were royalties.

Uncontradicted testimony that intention was to obtain earnings without declaration of dividends is evidence of divi-

Taxpayer's Position	*Court's Holding*
	dend. *Washburn Wire Co.,* *supra.*
The disbursement to the stockholder was deductible royalty.	The stockholder had no such property interest as would support a claim of royalty; hence, the item is not deductible. *L. Schepp & Co.,* 25 B.T.A. 419 (1932).
The disbursements were deductible royalties.	The taxpayer failed to prove that the disbursements to its stockholders were royalties rather than dividends; hence, the deduction is disallowed. *W. N. Thornburgh Mfg. Co.,* 17 B.T.A. 29 (1929).
Payments were for royalties for the use of a secret process.	Taxpayer did not possess any particular method which could be the subject of a secret process; hence, payments were dividends. *Peterson & Pegau Baking Co.,* 2 B.T.A. 637 (1925).

B. PAYMENTS CLAIMED AS OTHER EXPENSES—*Continued*
   4. OTHER EXPENSES

Amounts spent in constructing, maintaining, and operating racing boats were made in the belief that profit would accrue to the corporation; and, hence, these amounts were ordinary and necessary business expenses of the corporation.	Such activities did not constitute a trade or business of the corporation; the money was expended for the hobby of the corporation's sole stockholder and was not a deductible corporate expense. *American Properties, Inc. v. Commissioner,* 262 F.2d 150 (9th Cir., 1958).
Deduction was for amortization of financing fees.	Since existence of a bona fide indebtedness was shown, the deductions are allowable as

Taxpayer's Position   *Court's Holding*

B, 4. OTHER EXPENSES—*Continued*

	ordinary and necessary expenses. *Leach Corp.,* 30 T.C. 563 (1958).
Corporation's payment of expenses of stockholder were business promotion expenses.	Payments represented dividends inasmuch as items were stockholder's personal expenses and there was no intention to repay. *Greenspon v. Commissioner,* 229 F.2d 947 (8th Cir., 1956).
Payments were for traveling expenses advanced and were not dividends.	Not fully substantiated; a portion allocated to expense. *B. F. Crabbe, et al.,* T.C. Memo., Docket ##44359–60, Mar. 5, 1956.
Payment was of legal expenses on behalf of corporate officer indicted for acts on behalf of corporation.	Payments were such; hence, they were not dividends. *B. F. Crabbe, et al., supra.*
The disbursement to the stockholder was for deductible business expenses.	The stockholder prevented the corporation from keeping adequate books and records of the alleged expenditures, which could not be proved and, therefore, were not permitted to be deducted. *Joseph Zukin, et al. v. Riddell,* — F. Supp. — (D.C. Calif., 1955).
Payment was for legal expenses incurred in suit against dissident stockholder.	Amounts expended on legal fees for stockholder were distributions essentially equivalent to a dividend. Amounts expended on behalf of corporation were not. *Holloway v.*

Taxpayer's Position	Court's Holding
	Commissioner, 203 F.2d 566 (6th Cir., 1953).
Expenditures made by principal stockholder and reimbursed by corporation were corporate selling expenses.	Payments to stockholder on account of the nonbusiness portion of expenses were essentially equivalent to dividends. *Chester Distributing Co., Inc. v. Commissioner*, 184 F.2d 514 (3d Cir., 1950).
The payment was a deductible expense for looking after property.	The property belonged to a stockholder and, hence, the payments were not deductible as ordinary and necessary expenses. *D. H. Wiley Lumber Co., et al. v. Commissioner*, 177 F.2d 200 (6th Cir., 1949).
Payments of insurance premiums on stockholder's life were deductible business expenses of the corporation.	Stockholders were beneficiaries of the insurance; hence, premium payments constituted dividend distributions, and are not deductible. *Paramount-Richards Theatres, Inc., et al. v. Commissioner*, 153 F.2d 602 (5th Cir., 1946).
Payment was of a business expense, and not of stockholder's personal obligation.	Not substantiated; payment was a dividend. *Mark Kleeden*, T.C. Memo., Docket #1715, Oct. 25, 1944.
The payments made were of state taxes and are deductible.	The taxes paid were those of the shareholders for which the corporation was not liable; hence, the payment is not deductible. *Eastern Gas & Fuel Associates v. Commissioner*, 128 F.2d 369 (1st Cir., 1942).
Amounts paid by corporation were business expenses re-	The stockholders agreed to make the payments in order to

Taxpayer's Position   *Court's Holding*

B, 4. OTHER EXPENSES—*Continued*

imbursed to the shareholders who had made payment to the company's creditors.

preserve their own company, and the obligation was theirs; hence, payment to them in reimbursement of the amount they paid was payment of a dividend and not of an expense. *Peoples Bank,* 43 B.T.A. 589 (1941).

The payment by the company were deductible expenses for legal fees.

The legal fees were for services rendered to the company's stockholder and were not deductible corporate expenses. *George D. Mann, et al.,* 33 B.T.A. 281 (1935).

Payments were a bonus for making loans and were represented by notes.

There was no consideration for the alleged bonus; stockholders were entitled to profits in either event and motive for bonus was tax avoidance; hence, payments were in effect dividends. *West v. Commissioner,* 68 F.2d 246 (3d Cir., 1933).

Distribution was pursuant to an agreement of stockholders to pledge property to improve corporation's credit in consideration of one half of corporation's earnings and such distribution was, therefore, deductible as an ordinary expense.

Distribution was pro rata and would have the same effect if the company had paid out the money by regular dividends; hence, distribution was essentially a dividend. *R. L. Heflin, Inc. v. United States,* 58 F.2d 482 (Ct. Cl., 1932).

Payment out of profits to stockholders in proportion to their stockholdings in return for their pledging of private securities for the corporation's

Not substantiated; it was not shown that the credit was used or needed. *R. L. Heflin, Inc.,* 7 B.T.A .1002 (1927).

Taxpayer's Position	*Court's Holding*
credit was an ordinary and necessary expense and not the distribution of a dividend.	
Payments were made to its shareholders for guaranteeing the corporation's loans and credits and were deductible as ordinary and necessary business expense.	The amounts were paid in proportion to stockholdings; since most of the guarantors-stockholders had no assets, they risked nothing; the stockholders were also indebted to the corporation for more than the credit guaranteed; hence, the payment was a distribution of profits and not a deductible expense. *Universal Milking Machine Co.*, 4 B.T.A. 506 (1926).
The legal fee was a deductible necessary expense of the corporation.	The payment of the legal fee was not a corporate expense, although the corporation did benefit from the services, but the satisfaction of a personal expense of the stockholder-officer. *Forty-Four Cigar Co.*, 2 B.T.A. 1156 (1925).

B. Payments Claimed as Other Expenses—*Continued*
  5. Refunds and Rebates

Corporation was obligated by amendments of bylaws and certificate to pay "patronage dividends," which were deductible as proper business expenses.	In the absence of an obligation to make such payments, existing at the time when the income was received, refunds of profits, by whatever name called, are not deductible. *Associated Grocers of Ala., Inc. v. Willingham*, 77 F. Supp. 990 (D.C.Ala., 1948); *United Butchers Abattoir, Inc.*, T.C. Memo., Docket #6746, Jan. 21, 1946.

Taxpayer's Position	*Court's Holding*

B, 5. REFUNDS AND REBATES—*Continued*

Bylaws and written agreement in effect prior to earning of income required corporation to make refunds to stockholders, which are deductible.	On these facts, payments were refunds rather than dividends and are deductible. *Peoples Gin Co.*, T.C. Memo., Docket ##111436 and 111452, June 21, 1943.
Corporation was obligated by amendments of bylaws and certificate to pay "patronage dividends," which were deductible as proper business expenses.	In the absence of an obligation to make such payments, existing at the time when the income was received, refunds of profits, by whatever name called, are not deductible. *Peoples Gin Co., Inc. v. Commissioner*, 118 F.2d 72 (5th Cir., 1941).
Distribution was pursuant to contract requirement that "entire net profit . . . as and when declared by the Directors" be distributed among those executing similar contracts in proportion to goods sold to corporation, and was deductible.	Provision had the effect of authorizing a dividend, and distribution was pursuant to resolution of directors. Even if distribution were made pursuant to contract it would still be a dividend, as contracts were between shareholders and an entity of their own creation and, therefore, subject to change; only shareholders had such contracts, and distribution was in fact made to them as shareholders. *Juneau Dairies, Inc.*, 44 B.T.A. 759 (1941).
Payments were deductible rebates made as an inducement to obtain advertisers.	The amounts paid were not taxed as income when received by the corporation, and although paid pursuant to an agreement and not in propor-

Taxpayer's Position	*Court's Holding*
	tion to stockholdings, to which the stockholders agreed, they were in the nature of dividends and were not deductible. *Cleveland Shopping News Co. v. Routzahn,* 89 F.2d 902 (6th Cir., 1937).
The payments were deductible refunds and not dividends.	The corporation was formed by several insurance companies to print insurance forms and agreed (with the stockholders-insurance companies for whom the corporation did printing) to refund to each that portion of its net profit as business provided by each bore to total net profits; the refund was made under the agreement and was deductible and not a dividend distribution. *Uniform Printing & S. Co. v. Commissioner,* 88 F.2d 75 (7th Cir., 1937).

Chapter 4

STEPS TO BE TAKEN

The extraordinarily large number of court cases (digested in Chapter 3) involving disputes between taxpayers and the Internal Revenue Service as to when a transaction constitutes a "distribution" from a corporation which is to be treated as "essentially equivalent to a dividend" is an indication of the complexity and difficulty of finding satisfactory answers to the two questions: What is a corporate "distribution"? When is it treated as a dividend?

This chapter on "Steps to Be Taken" could commence with examples of how a stockholder can get cash into his hands, representing corporate profits, without being taxed at once on the amount received, or, if taxable, pay only at the long-term capital gain rate. Such examples can be helpful, and some will be given later in this chapter, but experience has shown that a thorough analysis of the relevant principles of law and of court decisions illustrating their application in specific circumstances, forms a valuable background for sound and effective tax planning and minimizing. This chapter, then, will commence with a statement of basic principles; follow with a discussion of their application to various elements of problems that may be encountered in planning to avoid distributions being taxed as dividends; and conclude with suggestions of steps to take to avoid pitfalls and obtain advantages under the provisions of the present Code.

248

Restatement of Basic Principles

Whenever a payment or a transfer of property, not in the form of or intended to be a dividend, is made by a corporation to or for the benefit of a stockholder, including a forgiveness of a debt owed by a stockholder, the possibility should be kept in mind that the Internal Revenue Service may allege that there is a "distribution" which is "essentially or substantially equivalent to or has the effect of" a dividend, taxable as such to the stockholder. Hence, every such transaction should be considered from the viewpoint of being prepared to show that, depending upon the nature of the transaction:

1. No income results to the stockholder, or
2. If there is any income to the stockholder, it is exempt (paid out of earnings and profits accumulated prior to March 1, 1913), or
3. If the stockholder has realized income, it is in the nature of a gain which is "not recognized," "tax-free," or
4. If there is a gain which is to be "recognized" and the stockholder is an individual, the gain is taxable to the stockholder as a capital gain, or
5. If there is a gain which is to be "recognized" and the stockholder is a corporation, the gain is taxable to the stockholder as a dividend or as a capital gain, whichever is, under the particular circumstances, the more desirable; and/or
6. The amount of the payment or transfer of property to the stockholder is allowable as a deduction in computing the taxable income of the distributing corporation.

In such consideration of any proposed payment or transfer of property to a stockholder, it will be found helpful to start with an analysis of the transaction from the viewpoint of substance *and* form:

As to the Stockholder

1. Has the stockholder given or will he give the distributing corporation any consideration for what he is to receive,

and, if so, what is the fair market value of such consideration?

2. If any consideration has been or is to be given by the stockholder to the corporation, does or did such consideration have any statutory "adjusted basis" in his hands?

3. Will the stockholder give up, as consideration for what he receives, all or any portion of his stock interest in the corporation?

4. Can the transaction qualify as wholly or partially "tax-free" under any of the "Reorganization" provisions in Subchapter C of the Code?

5. If the stockholder is an individual and the transaction cannot qualify as "tax-free," can it be handled so as to qualify, under Section 302 or Section 346 or any other provision of Subchapter C, as an "exchange," so that any resulting gain would be taxable as a capital gain?

6. If the stockholder is a corporation, and the transaction cannot qualify as "tax-free," can it be handled so as to constitute the receipt of a dividend, if the resulting tax would be less than if the transaction gave rise to a capital gain?

7. If the transaction results in a "distribution," will all or any portion thereof be out of earnings and profits accumulated prior to March 1, 1913, and, hence, not taxable?

As to the Corporation

1. Will any consideration or benefit be received by the corporation for the payment or transfer made by it, and, if so, what is the fair market value or reasonable value of such consideration or benefit?

2. If an interest deduction is to be claimed, is there, in fact, an indebtedness of the corporation with respect to which such interest is payable?

3. If the deduction is to be claimed as compensation, are services being rendered to the corporation by the stockholder, and, if so, what is the value of such services?

As to Both Stockholder and Corporation. Can the transaction be shown to be, in fact, something other than a distribution of corporate profits?

The "form vs. substance" principle is usually applied to pierce form and ascertain substance, and then to determine tax liability based upon the substance of the transaction involved. But when the issue involved is whether the transfer is "essentially equivalent to a dividend," the planner cannot stop with his conclusion that in substance there is no dividend. Even if in substance the transaction is not a dividend and does not come squarely within any specific provision of the Code making it taxable as such, extreme care must be taken to make sure that the *form* which the transaction takes will not result in the application of the "essentially equivalent" doctrine. In *Wall v. United States*, 164 F.2d 462 (4th Cir., 1947), Wall and another person were each 50 per cent stockholders of Rosedale and, after the other person's death, his estate sold his shares to Coleman, who was the principal owner of the stock of Rosedale's competitor. Wall wanted to get Coleman out of Rosedale. A purchase of all of Coleman's stock in Rosedale was negotiated for a cash payment plus a balance payable over ten years, but Wall, instead of Rosedale, was the purchaser. About a year and a half later, Wall transferred the purchased shares to Rosedale which agreed to and did make the payments due to Coleman. The court held that the Rosedale payments to Coleman were constructive dividends to Wall. The importance of form in the transaction is made apparent by the following language used in that case by the Fourth Circuit Court of Appeals: "The final contention of the taxpayer is that the two transactions, that is, the transfer from Coleman to Wall in 1937 and the transfer from Wall to Rosedale in 1939, should be treated as parts of a single transaction whereby Coleman sold his stock to Rosedale without the intervention of Wall. This, it is said, is the true meaning of what the parties did, and, hence, Wall incurred no tax liability; and we are asked to reach this conclusion since taxation is a practical matter which requires that regard be had to the substance rather than to the form of the taxpayer's acts. This argument must also be rejected. In the first place, the effect of the two transactions is not identical to the situation that would have arisen had the stock been purchased directly by Rosedale, for in that event no personal obligation would have been incurred by Wall. As it actually was, he did incur such an obligation to Coleman, and it is precisely the payment of that obligation by Rosedale which constitutes income to him. Wall deliberately elected to attain his objective by two distinct transactions and there is no evidence that he was merely acting as an agent for Rosedale when he made the purchase. As was stated in Woodruff v. Commissioner, 5 Cir., 131 F.2d 429, 430, where a similar contention was advanced and rejected, 'if a taxpayer has two legal methods by which he may attain a desired result, the method pursued is determinative for tax purposes without regard to the fact that different tax results would have attached if the alternative procedure had been followed.' " *Wall v. United States,* 164 F.2d 462, 465 (4th Cir., 1947). Had the *form* been different in the *Wall* case, the result would have been different.

Thus, where the "essentially equivalent" issue is present, the tax planner must be concerned, not merely with "form *versus* substance," but with form *and* substance.

A review of the digests of cases in Chapter 3, which are classified in such a way as to facilitate such review, will be found helpful in determining what steps should be taken in connection with a prospective transaction to establish that it is what it is desired to be; what is to be avoided in order that it may *not* be held to be something other than was intended; and, what should be done to minimize the probability of attack by the Internal Revenue Service.

Such a review, and a reading of relevant cases located in Chapter 3, will reveal circumstances the courts have considered to be favorable to the taxpayer's position, and those which have been considered harmful.

In addition, it is of course essential to determine what statutory provisions may be applicable in determining whether the transaction might constitute a distribution taxable as a dividend or as ordinary income or, on the other hand, qualify, under some specific provision of the Code, for more favorable treatment. The following brief description of relevant Code provisions will be found helpful for this purpose:

1954 Code Section	Subchapter C	1939 Code Section
301	General rules prescribing treatment of distributions of cash or other property by a corporation to a shareholder with respect to his stock, including a radically new rule as to the receipt by a corporation of a property or "in kind" dividend.	22(e) 115(j)
302	General rules prescribing treatment of distributions by a corporation in redemption of its stock, under which a redemption may be treated as a distribution in part or full payment in exchange for the stock redeemed.	115(c) 115(g)(1)
303	Redemption of stock to pay death taxes and funeral and administration expenses without dividend consequences.	115(g)(3)
304	Redemptions of stock through the use of related corporations.	115(g)(2)
305	Treatment of distributions by a corporation of stock and stock rights.	115(f)(1), (2)
306	Redemptions or sales of certain preferred stock or stock received in a "tax-free" exchange, which may give rise, not to capital gains or dividend income, but to ordinary income.	New
312(j)	Distribution of proceeds of loan insured by the United States.	New
316	Definition of "dividend."	115(a),(b)
317	Definition of the terms "property" and "redemption of stock."	New
318	The general rules as to constructive ownership of stock.	New

1954 Code Section	Subchapter C	1939 Code Section
331	Recognition of gain or loss to shareholders in complete or partial liquidation of a corporation.	115(c)
332	Recognition of gain or loss upon complete liquidation of a subsidiary.	112(b)(6)
333	Election of shareholders as to recognition of gain in certain one-month corporate liquidations, under which part of the gain may be taxable as a capital gain and part as a dividend.	112(b)(7)
337	Effect of certain 12-month corporate liquidations.	New
341	Treatment of sale of stock or liquidation of a collapsible corporation which may give rise, not to capital gains or dividend income, but to ordinary income.	117(m)
342	Liquidation of certain foreign personal holding companies which may give rise, not to dividend income, but to short-term capital gain.	115(c)
346	Definition of a partial liquidation and distinction between stock redemptions which qualify as partial liquidations, subject to capital gain treatment, and stock redemptions which may have dividend consequences.	New
354	Treatment of exchanges by stockholders and security holders in reorganizations.	112(b)(3)
355	Treatment of distributions of stock and securities of a controlled corporation.	112(b)(3), (11)
356	Treatment of the receipt of additional consideration in certain reorganizations and distributions which may have dividend consequences.	112(c)

1954 Code Section	*Subchapter C*	*1939 Code Section*
357	Treatment of the assumption of liabilities in certain corporate organizations and reorganizations.	112(k)
361	Treatment of the exchange of property by a corporation pursuant to a reorganization.	112(b)(4) 112(d) 112(e)
371	Treatment of gain or loss in certain receiverships and bankruptcy proceedings.	112(l) 112(b)(10)
374	Treatment of gain or loss in certain railroad reorganizations.	New

Other Relevant Sections

547	Treatment of deficiency dividend for personal holding company purposes.	506
551	Treatment of undistributed foreign personal holding company income.	337

Having analyzed the substance and form of a proposed transaction, consider what steps must be taken and what must be avoided to obtain the desired result. For this purpose, the following suggestions are offered:

Redemptions and Distributions in Partial or Complete Liquidation. In dealing with redemptions of stock, which include any purchases by a corporation of shares of its own stock, subsequent to 1953, Section 317(b), it is necessary to start with the many new rules incorporated by Congress in the 1954 Code in pursuance of its expressed intention to do away with the uncertainties as to when a redemption will be treated as a sale rather than as a distribution taxable as a dividend.[1]

---

[1] "Under present law it is not clear when a stock redemption results in capital gain or ordinary income. . . . Your Committee's bill sets forth definite conditions under which stock may be redeemed at capital gains rate . . ." House Report No. 1337 on H.R. 8300, at p. 35.

The general scheme laid down in the Code, Sections 301(a), 302(d), is to treat *all* distributions in redemption of stock as dividends unless they meet certain tests, some of which are specified in the Code (see the list of Code sections above).

REDEMPTIONS OF STOCK IN PARTIAL LIQUIDATION. Unfortunately, though unavoidably, the first test laid down as to whether a redemption of a portion of a corporation's stock is to be treated as a "distribution in partial liquidation of a corporation," Section 346(a)(2), and, hence, as a sale, Section 331(a)(2), requires the taxpayer to establish that the redemption is *not* "essentially equivalent to dividend," and, hence, brings us right back to the problem under prior law. Nevertheless, qualification of a redemption of stock as a "distribution in partial liquidation" affords a degree of certainty difficult to attain under most of the other Subchapter C provisions.

A redemption of a portion of the stock of a corporation is afforded the benefit of treatment as a "distribution in partial liquidation" under Section 346 if:

A

1. The distribution is not essentially equivalent to a dividend,
2. Is pursuant to a plan, and
3. Occurs within the taxable year or within the succeeding taxable year, or

B

1. The distribution
   a. is attributable to ceasing to conduct, or
   b. consists of the assets of, a trade or business, and
2. Such trade or business
   a. has been actively conducted throughout the five-year period immediately before the distribution, and
   b. was not acquired by the distributing corporation within such period in a transaction in which gain or loss was recognized in whole or in part, and
3. Immediately after the distribution the distributing cor-

poration is actively engaged in the conduct of a trade or
business which was:

    a. actively conducted throughout the five-year period
       ending on the date of the distribution, and

    b. not acquired by the distributing corporation within
       such period in a transaction in which gain or loss was
       recognized in whole or in part, and

4. Such distribution need not be pro rata with respect to
   all of the shareholders of the distributing corporation.

It is to be noted that where the assets so distributed were
acquired by the distributing corporation in a reorganization in
which "boot" was also received and, at the time of such acquisition, it distributed to its shareholders the "boot" so received,
its receipt of the "boot" would not, under Section 361, give rise
to recognizable gain to it. Hence, a distribution of such assets
would meet the test of Section 346 as a partial liquidation of
assets not acquired in a transaction in which gain or loss was
recognized, in whole or in part, to the distributing corporation.

It will be seen that the tests set forth above under *A* and *B*
are not the same.

To qualify under *A* it is necessary to establish that the distribution is *not* "essentially equivalent to a dividend." The
Code provides no definition of this phrase or explanation of its
meaning. Hence, all the decisions under prior law (condensed
in Chapter 3, under "Distributions in Partial or Complete Liquidation"), bearing on the question of when a distribution is
"essentially equivalent to a dividend," are pertinent and must
be considered in determining whether a distribution (not
within the rules set forth above under *B*) intended to be in partial liquidation of a corporation, qualifies, under Section 346(a)
(2), for treatment as such. If it does *not* so qualify, distribution will, generally, be taxable as a dividend. (*Caveat:* A distribution coming within the scope of the "collapsible corporation" provisions of the Code, Section 341, may be taxable as
"ordinary" income, rather than as a dividend.)

If the redemption of shares of stock of a corporation can be
established as being "not essentially equivalent to a dividend,"

the two other tests (set out under *A*) are simple and easily met, and the transaction will then be treated as a sale of the shares redeemed.

The tests set out under *B* likewise appear to be simple, but meeting them depends, in the first place, upon facts which have existed during the five-year period preceding the redemption, as to which there is no means of turning back the hands of the clock. Unless, at the date of the distribution, the distributing corporation, or another corporation from which it acquired the assets in a "tax-free" exchange, has for the preceding five years been actively conducting at least *two* separate and distinct trades or businesses meeting the requirements of the Code, Sections 346(b)(1),(2), a distribution in redemption of its shares cannot qualify, under the tests set forth above under *B*, Section 346(b), as a distribution in partial liquidation entitled to treatment, under Section 331(a)(2), as in part or full payment in exchange for the shares redeemed. This, then, raises the question: What is a separate trade or business, as distinguished from a *part* of a single trade or business?

The Code throws no light on this problem; it is, therefore, necessary to have recourse to the reports of the Congressional tax committees, the Regulations, and Internal Revenue Service rulings, as there are as yet no decisions dealing with this precise issue. Further discussion of this point is beyond the scope of this work. It must be pointed out, however, that this is "a question of fact," as to which no ruling can be obtained from the Internal Revenue Service in the case of a prospective transaction.

If the past history of the corporation making the distribution is such as to meet the *B* tests, then, in order that a redemption of a portion of its shares may be treated as a sale by the stockholder, it is necessary for the distributing corporation to retain and to continue to operate (for an adequate but undefined period of time) at least *one* such trade or business, and, with respect to *another* such trade or business, distribute to all or some of its stockholders:

    1. The assets other than inventory used in such other trade or business and, within prescribed limitations, Regula-

tions §1.346-1(b), the inventory of such other trade or business, or

2. The proceeds from the sale of such assets other than inventory and, within prescribed limitations, of such inventory.

Where assets are distributed, the other trade or business must be actively conducted until immediately before the distribution, and, where proceeds of sale are distributed, distribution must be made as soon after the sale as is reasonably possible, Regulations §1.346-1(c).

Here again, as to the amount attributable to such a discontinuance of operations, guidance can be found in decisions under prior law, condensed in Chapter 3 under the heading, "Alleged Distribution in Partial or Complete Liquidation," and subheading, "Alleged Contraction of Business."

Where all the stock of a corporation is owned by individuals and not by another corporation, if a payment or transfer of property is made to all the stockholders, without a complete liquidation of the corporation, see to it, if possible, that the redemption is in a partial liquidation of the corporation under and in compliance with the requirements of Section 346, so as to assure capital gain treatment.

REDEMPTIONS OF STOCK NOT IN A "PARTIAL LIQUIDATION." If a redemption, including any purchase, by a corporation of a portion of its shares of stock, whether or not the shares are retired, Section 317(b), does not qualify as a "distribution in partial liquidation," such redemption may nevertheless be treated as a sale of the shares not giving rise to dividend income, if the redemption meets the tests prescribed in Section 302(b)(2), (3), and (4) *or* if it is "not essentially equivalent to a dividend," Section 302(b)(1).

As to the latter test, here again we must look for guidance to decisions under prior law, condensed in Chapter 3.

It is to be noted that the degree of certainty present in a Section 346(b) partial liquidation is also present where there is a substantially disproportionate redemption of stock within the meaning of Section 302(b)(2), or a termination of the shareholder's interest in the corporation within the meaning of Section 302(b)(3) or where the redemption is with respect to stock issued by a railroad corporation in certain reorganizations under Section 302(b)(4).

If a partial liquidation under Section 346 is not possible, then see to it, if possible, that there is a substantially disproportionate redemption of the corporation's outstanding shares under Section 302(b)(2), so as to assure capital gain treatment, if that result is desirable. (Note: Where the stockholder-taxpayer is a corporation, treatment as a dividend may be more desirable.)

If a payment or transfer of property to an individual stockholder takes the form of a redemption in which there is a termination of the individual stockholder's interest in the corporation, the Code, Section 302(b)(3), assures that the transfer to the stockholder will not be taxable as essentially equivalent to a dividend.

Subsection (d) of Section 302 warns that a redemption of stock which does not meet the above-mentioned tests will be taxable as a dividend, unless such redemption comes within some other provisions of Subchapter C providing for different treatment.

In considering whether a redemption, including any purchase, of its shares by a corporation meets the other tests set forth in Section 302(b)(2), (3), and (4), special attention must be given to the rules of attribution of ownership of the stock of the corporation making the redemption, Sections 302 (c) and 318. For example, it will not be sufficient merely to determine whether there is a disproportionate redemption with respect to one of the shareholders of the corporation, Section 302(b)(3); it will be necessary to determine whether the shareholder's interest in the corporation is terminated, which necessitates a compliance with the requirements embodied in Section 302(c) and Section 318 and the Regulations thereunder.

Where the redemption is of all the shareholder's stock of the corporation, however, the attribution rules in Section 318(a) (1) do not apply if the requirements set forth in Section 302 (c)(2) are met. Hence, where husband and wife each owns shares of a corporation, it may be possible to redeem all the stock of the husband at capital gain rates, and leave the wife with her shares, through which the husband could still retain effective control.

Care must be taken to avoid the additional tax assessment for the year of redemption of all of a stockholder's interest in a corporation, which could occur in the event such stockholder reacquires an interest, other than by bequest or inheritance, during the ensuing *10 years,* Section 302(c)(2)(A). It is to be noted, in this connection, that, under the Regulations, §1.302-4(c), it likewise is essential for the retiring shareholder not to acquire an interest in a parent, subsidiary or successor of the corporation which redeems its shares.

For example, a stockholder, all of whose stock has been redeemed in such a way as not to realize dividend income, who remains a creditor of the redeeming corporation, should not, upon the corporation's default, reacquire shares of the redeeming corporation in connection with the enforcement of his rights as a creditor, Section 302(c)(2). Nor should he retain, as a creditor, a right to name anyone to the corporation's board of directors, Rev. Rul. 59–119, 1959–1 C.B. 68. Otherwise, the amount of the distribution, received by such stockholder in redemption of the shares, might become subject to tax as a dividend, assessable at any time within ten years after the distribution, Section 302(c)(2)(A).

It is to be remembered that not all distributions in partial liquidation, or redemptions of stock otherwise meeting the tests in Section 302(b), are treated as sales of a capital asset eligible for long-term capital gain treatment. For example, gain on redemptions of stock coming under Section 306 will be treated as "ordinary" income, and, in the case of a loss, no deduction will be allowed.

It is to be noted, however, that the provisions of Section 306 do *not* apply to a redemption of Section 306 stock in a distribution in partial or complete liquidation under Subchapter C, Part II, Sections 331 through 346.

It also is noteworthy, that, although due to the collapsible corporation provisions in Section 341, a gain usually treated as a long-term capital gain may end up treated as ordinary income, a short-term capital gain does not lose its character by reason of that section and will remain available as an offset against a capital loss.

Before deciding upon any redemption or liquidation, Subchapter C, see list of sections given above, should, in view of these complexities, be carefully reviewed to determine whether any provisions thereof, applicable to the proposed transaction, would deprive it of the benefit of any provisions of Sections 302 or 346 otherwise applicable thereto.

As pointed out earlier, every distribution which meets the tests of a "distribution in liquidation," partial or complete, of a corporation necessarily involves a redemption of its stock. However, not every redemption of stock does necessarily involve a liquidation. This distinction is important because, under the Code, there is a substantial difference between the treatment of a redemption in liquidation, as defined therein, and of a redemption not involving a "liquidation."

REDEMPTION OF STOCK TO PAY DEATH TAXES. A redemption of stock in circumstances which might otherwise result in its being taxable as a dividend may be treated as a sale if it meets the tests prescribed in Section 303 with respect to redemptions to pay death taxes and funeral and administration expenses. Such treatment may result in little or no tax, where the stock is sold shortly after the date of the estate tax valuation, which determines the statutory "basis" of the shares sold, Section 1014.

In planning that the estate and beneficiaries of a taxpayer may be entitled to the benefits of Section 303, care should be taken to insure that the percentage of the taxpayer's ownership of stock of any closely held corporation(s) will equal or exceed the required amount(s), Section 303(b)(2).

SALE OF STOCK TO A RELATED CORPORATION. Where one or more individuals control Corporations A and B, a sale of some of his or their shares of stock of Corporation A to Corporation B may be governed by the provisions of Section 304. Under that section such a transaction is deemed to be, not a purchase by Corporation B of the Corporation A shares, but a redemption by Corporation B of its own shares, which might constitute a distribution by Corporation B taxable as a dividend under Section 302. In such case, "... the determination of the amount which is a dividend shall be made solely by reference to the earnings and profits of the acquiring corporation," Section 304(b)(2)(A).

In a transaction such as described above, occurring after 1953, care must be taken not to rely on cases decided under the 1939 Code, but rather to seek guidance in the relevant provisions of the 1954 Code and the Regulations issued pursuant thereto.

SECTION 305 DISTRIBUTIONS OF STOCK. The tax-free nature of stock dividends (that is, their nonincludibility in gross income) is provided in Section 305. This section is broader than the comparable provisions in 1939 Code, Section 115(f). Under the 1954 Code, no distributions by a corporation of its stock or of rights to subscribe to its stock are includible in gross income, with only the two exceptions mentioned in Section 306(b).

SECTION 306 REDEMPTIONS. Sections 302, 303, and 346 prescribe tests which, if met, result in the redemption of a portion of the shares of a corporation being treated as a sale of the stock redeemed, and thus not taxable as a dividend. Section 306, however, is designed to deny capital gain treatment to the proceeds from certain sales or redemptions of what the Code itself designates as "Section 306 stock," and to tax such proceeds as ordinary income or as a dividend. All that can be done here is to study carefully the provisions of that section, and avoid making any redemption coming within their scope. These provisions do not apply any of the principles applicable in determining when a distribution is "essentially equivalent to a dividend," and hence require no further discussion here.

It is to be noted, however, that the provisions of Section 306 do *not* apply to a redemption of Section 306 stock in a distribution in partial or complete liquidation under Subchapter C, Part II, Sections 331 to 346. Nor do the provisions of Section 306 apply where the disposition of the "Section 306 stock" results in a termination of the shareholder's interest in the corporation, Section 306(b)(1).

Moreover, the tax planner should bear in mind that a charitable contribution of "Section 306 stock" and its subsequent sale does not result in taxable income to the donor, who may, subject to the percentage-of-income limitations, deduct the fair market value of the stock at the time of contribution as a charitable deduction, Rev. Rul. 57-328, 1957-2 C.B. 229.

And, in certain circumstances, the sale of "Section 306 stock" is not within the purview of Section 306(a) where the agreement of sale was entered into before the reorganization in which the "Section 306 stock" was received, Rev. Rul. 56-223, 1956-1 C.B. 162.

As the definition of "Section 306 stock" is, in the case of an individual shareholder, limited to stock distributed to the shareholder who sells or otherwise disposes of it, Section 306 (c)(1)(A), a sale thereof by such shareholder's estate would not appear to be within the purview of Section 306(a); and hence such sale will give rise only to capital gain or loss and not ordinary income, Regulations §1.306-3(e) (last sentence).

SECTION 312(j) DISTRIBUTIONS. Section 312(j) of the 1954 Code embodies a provision wholly new to the taxing statute. It is a legislative change of the interpretation of prior law applied in *Commissioner v. Gross,* 236 F.2d 612 (2d Cir., 1956), and subsequent cases, whereunder the distribution of an FHA "windfall," the amount by which the loan insured by the government exceeded the cost of construction for which the loan was made, was held to be a return of capital and not a dividend to the extent that the amount distributed exceeded the earnings and profits of the corporation.

Under Section 312(j), if the corporation distributes property with respect to its stock, and at the time of such distribution there is an outstanding loan to the corporation made, guaranteed, or insured by the United States, or an agency or instrumentality thereof, and the amount of the outstanding loan exceeds the adjusted basis of the property constituting security for such loan, the corporation's earnings and profits are deemed to be increased by the amount of such excess. The result is that the amount of any distribution attributable to such excess received by the stockholders is taxable to them as a dividend, Section 312(j)(1).

Under Section 312(j) the adjusted basis of the property is to be determined without regard to any adjustment under Section 1016(a)(2) for depreciation, etc.

It is to be noted that Section 312(j) applies only when there is an existing loan which is made, guaranteed, or insured by the government. Thus, the benefits accorded under *Commissioner v. Gross* may still be obtainable where the loan obtained by the corporation is of a kind which does not fall within the provisions of the statute.

COMPLETE ONE-MONTH LIQUIDATIONS. Whenever the benefits afforded by Section 333 in a one-month liquidation are sought, it is necessary to keep in mind that, in addition to the benefits it affords, the section also carries with it the possible detriment of leaving the qualified electing individual shareholder with dividend income. In a one-month liquidation under Section 333, so much of the individual stockholder's gain "as is not in excess of his ratable share of the earnings and profits of the corporation accumulated after February 28, 1913" is to be treated as a dividend, Section 333(e)(1).

Before deciding upon a Section 333 liquidation, a careful study must be made of the corporation's profit and loss statements to ascertain the amount of earnings and profits which may be subjected to dividend income tax liability, the portion thereof which will be taxed as dividend income, and the amount of the resulting tax. It will then be possible to weigh, against the benefits afforded by liquidation under this section, the detriment of some portion of the gain being taxed as dividend income instead of at the capital gain rate. Thereafter, and only thereafter, can a conclusion be reached as to whether or not a liquidation under Section 333 is advisable.

FOREIGN PERSONAL HOLDING COMPANY LIQUIDATIONS. Where the corporation to be liquidated is a "Foreign Personal Holding Company," Section 552(a), special attention must be given to Section 342. Under the provisions of that section gain upon the liquidation of certain foreign personal holding companies is to "be considered as a gain from the sale or exchange of a capital asset held for not more than six months." While the section does not treat the gain as dividend income, it deprives the gain of "long-term capital gain" treatment which is contemplated in the usual case where a corporation is liquidated. Accordingly, it may be desirable not to liquidate such a foreign personal holding company unless a resulting short-term capital gain can be offset by capital losses with respect to other transactions, or to defer the liquidation until a future year when such an offset will be possible.

"SPIN-OFF" DISTRIBUTIONS. Section 355 provides a general rule that where a corporation distributes to its stockholders shares of a corporation controlled by the distributing corporation, in what is generally called a "spin-off," gain shall not be recognized to the stockholder on the receipt of such shares. The general rule does not apply unless a number of prescribed conditions are met, one of which is that "the transaction was not used principally as a device for the distribution of earnings and profits" of either the distributing corporation or the controlled corporation, Section 355(a)(1)(B). While the requirements of Section 355(b) must be met in order that Section 355(a) apply, the meeting of the Section 355(b) requirements alone will not necessarily satisfy the Section 355(a) conditions.

Whenever a corporation distributes to its stockholders shares of stock in another corporation which it controls, the stockholder may find that what he has received will be taxable to him as a dividend, Section 356(a)(2). In order to avoid such a result, it is necessary that the transaction be one which is "not used principally as a device for the distribution of the earnings and profits of the distributing corporation or the controlled corporation or both," Section 355(a)(1)(B).[2]

If the transaction was not so used and if other requirements set forth in Section 355 are met, then no gain or loss on the transaction is to be recognized to the shareholder, Section

---

[2] See Chapter 1, *supra*.

355(a)(1). Careful study of that section must precede any distribution by a corporation of stock and securities of another corporation it controls.

Three varieties of qualifying distributions fall within the provisions of Section 355. They are frequently designated as "spin-offs," "split-offs," and "split-ups," and may be briefly described as follows:

1. Where a corporation owns all the shares of stock of a subsidiary which operates its own separate business, and the former distributes to its stockholders all the shares of the subsidiary without having the stockholders surrender any of their shares, the corporation has effected a "spin-off" of the shares of stock of its subsidiary. Frequently, the subsidiary is formed for the purpose of effecting the "spin-off," the parent corporation first exchanging assets for the shares of the newly organized subsidiary. However, there is no requirement that the subsidiary be newly formed.

2. Where the transaction is the same as described in (a) except that the shareholder is required to surrender *some* of his shares of the distributing corporation, a "split-off" is thereby effected.

3. A "split-up" is effected by the distributing corporation where its stockholders are required to surrender *all* of their shares and receive shares in two or more corporations. The distributing corporation may own all the shares of stock of two subsidiaries, each conducting its own business. A "split-up" may then be effected by distributing all the shares of the two subsidiaries, which may or may not be newly formed for that purpose, to shareholders of the distributing corporation in exchange for all the shares of the latter, which is then dissolved.

The question whether or not a particular distribution will qualify as a "spin-off," "split-off," or "split-up" is outside the scope of this book and, for that reason, is not dealt with herein, although it must be studied carefully by anyone confronted with the problem of determining whether the proposed distribution is a "device for the distribution" of a dividend.[3]

In order that a distribution along the lines set forth above be one as to which gain will not be recognized, and not be taxable as the receipt of a dividend, it is essential to comply with a number of requirements which are specifically set forth in Section 355. Both the distributing corporation and the subsidiary must each be engaged in the active conduct of a trade or business immediately after the distribution, Sections 355(a)(1)(C) and 355(b)(1); or, immediately before the distribution, the distributing corporation must have had no assets other than stock or securities of its subsidiaries and each subsidiary must be engaged in the active conduct of a trade or business immediately after the distribution, Sections 355(a)(1)(C) and 355(b)(2). Regulations §1.355–1 contains the requirement that each trade or business must have been separate and actively conducted throughout the five-year period ending on the date of distribution, but in *Edmund P. Coady, et ux.*, 33 T.C., No. 87 (1/29/60), the Tax Court held, with six dissents, that Regulations §1.355–1 is invalid under the statute, and that separate businesses before the distribution were not necessary and the division of a single business is valid under Section 355. The trade or business cannot have been acquired within the five-year period in a transaction in which gain or loss was recognized in whole or in part, Section 355(b)(2)(C). Control of a corporation conducting the trade or business must have been acquired in a particular way, Section 355(b)(2)(D).

Not all businesses will satisfy the "active business" requirement set forth in Regulations §1.355–1(c) and (d), which must be studied.

If the distributing corporation does not distribute all of the shares of its subsidiary, it must distribute at least 80 per cent thereof and satisfy the Secretary or his delegate that the retained shares of the subsidiary were not retained in pursuance of a plan having as one of its principal purposes the avoidance of federal income tax, Sections 355(a)(1)(A)(i)–(ii).

---

[3] For a discussion of what is a "spin-off," etc., see *inter alia*, Robert S. Holzman, *Corporate Reorganizations* (2d ed., rev. prtg.; New York: The Ronald Press Co., 1956), pp. 8·21, *et seq.*

Even where all other stated requirements are met, it will still be essential to show that the transaction was not used as a device to distribute earnings or profits, Section 355(a)(1) (B). The Code does not define what is or is not a "device," and, here again, the Regulations must be studied. Where the stockholder arranged to sell the distributed shares before their distribution, Section 355 will not apply, Regulations §1.355-2(b)(1). Nor will Section 355 apply where the distribution is carried out for purposes not germane to the business of the corporations, Regulations §1.355-2(c).

The Regulations state that, in considering whether a transaction was used principally as a device, all the facts and circumstances will be given consideration, Regulations §1.355-2(b)(3).

This brings the tax adviser back to the cases summarized in Chapter 3 for guidance as to what are facts and circumstances as to which the effect of a transaction will or will not be deemed "essentially equivalent to a dividend."

"Do's" and "Don't's"

FOR TRANSACTIONS WHICH MAY BE SPECIFICALLY COVERED BY CODE PROVISIONS RELATING TO DISTRIBUTIONS TAXABLE AS DIVIDENDS

"Do's" and "Don't's" with respect to prospective transactions not intended to be distributions "essentially equivalent to a dividend," but which, under specific provisions of Subchapter C, might nevertheless be held to be taxable as such, or as ordinary income, are set forth below in the same order as the relevant provisions of the Code.

These brief reminders of what to do and what not to do, to avoid undesired tax consequences and to secure the most advantageous tax results with respect to the receipt, by a stockholder as such, of money or other property, are intended to be no more than that—*reminders* of possible effects of relevant provisions of the Code, dealt with in greater detail elsewhere in this and other chapters, and of principles established in decisions under prior law, digested in Chapter 3, which, in certain circumstances, are still significant in determining when a transaction is "essentially equivalent to a dividend."

Do not rely initially or solely upon principles established under the law in effect prior to the 1954 Code to establish that a distribution, redemption of shares, or partial liquidation is *not* "essentially equivalent to a dividend"; first determine whether the transaction is one specifically covered by any provision of the Code and, if so, the effect of the provision.

On the other hand, where the Code specifically requires a determination as to whether a transaction is "essentially equivalent to a dividend" or "has the effect of the distribution of a dividend," or is a "device" to distribute earnings and profits, reference should be made to principles established under prior law, which not only afford a guide but should be controlling.

Redemptions and Distributions in Liquidation

REDEMPTIONS QUALIFYING UNDER SECTIONS 302(a) and 303. To qualify a redemption of a portion of the shares of stock of a corporation for capital gain treatment under Section 302:

1. Make sure that the shares to be redeemed are not "Section 306 stock," unless the redemption qualifies under Section 302(b)(3).
2. Where there is a Section 302(b)(3) redemption of all the shares of stock of a stockholder, make sure that he does not retain any interest, other than as a creditor, in the corporation.

    In a recent ruling, Rev. Rul. 59-119, 1959-1 C.B. 68, it was held that a stockholder, all of whose stock was retired but who remained a creditor of the corporation and retained the right to name a director to the company's board to look after his interest as a creditor, would be treated as having retained an interest in the corporation, thereby subjecting the payments he received from the corporation in redemption of his stock to treatment as distributions essentially equivalent to a dividend. Note, however, that the ruling states that all the remaining stockholders were related to the retiring stockholder. *The Tax Barometer,* Vol. 16 (May 2, 1959), ¶966, states that the Internal Revenue Service has indicated that if the remaining stockholders had been strangers, the redemption would not have been disqualified under Section 302(c)(2)(A)(i).

3. Make sure that the redemption does not result in ordinary income under the "Collapsible Corporation" provisions of Section 341.

4. If the redemption is of shares included in determining the value of the gross estate of a decedent, remember that Section 303 permits, in the circumstances therein prescribed, the amount received in a redemption of stock to be treated as the proceeds of a sale of such stock and, hence, eligible for capital gain treatment to the extent that the amount received is not in excess of the sum of all death taxes imposed and of all administration and funeral expenses allowable as a deduction, Regulations §1.303-2(g). Section 303 applies whether the shares redeemed are held by an executor or administrator or a beneficiary of the estate of the decedent, without need to qualify under any other provisions of the Code, *unless* the person holding the shares acquired them from the executor in satisfaction of a specific monetary bequest, Regulations §1.303-2(f), or is a surviving spouse who received the shares by reason of a marital deduction bequest, Rev. Rul. 56-270, 1956-1 C.B. 325. Before deciding upon any Section 303 distribution, it is imperative that the tax adviser make sure that the value of the shares of stock of the corporation included in the decedent's estate is more than 35 per cent of the gross estate of the decedent or more than 50 per cent of the taxable estate, Section 303(b)(2), and that the distribution is made within the prescribed period of time, Section 303 (b)(1).

It is important to note that a Section 303 redemption may be made where shares of more than one corporation are involved, if the statutory requirements are met, Section 303(b)(2)(B).

Furthermore, where a common stock is involved and a Section 303 redemption may be effected, the executors may obtain the benefit of this provision through a sale to the corporation's wholly-owned subsidiary, Rev. Rul. 55-592, 1955-2 C.B. 573.

5. To the extent that the amount received in a redemption otherwise qualifying under Section 303 exceeds the sum of the death taxes, administration and funeral expenses, such excess will be treated as a distribution taxable as a dividend, unless the transaction qualifies for capital gain treatment under some other provision of the Code.

6. In making a determination regarding a redemption under Section 302 where the percentage of ownership by the taxpayer of stock of the redeeming corporation is significant, be sure to give full effect to all relevant rules in Section 318 as to *constructive ownership of stock*.

7. Remember that a distribution is taxable as a dividend only to the extent that it does not exceed earnings and profits accumulated subsequent to February 28, 1913, or earnings and profits of the year in which the distribution is made, Section 316. Hence, the amount of such earnings and profits, not necessarily equal to the book "surplus" of the distributing corporation, should be checked wherever it is possible that such amount might be less than the distribution in question.

8. In determining the amount of a distribution, including amounts received as a "redemption" of stock, which is taxable as a dividend, consideration is to be given to the rules applicable to special situations such as personal holding company deficiency dividends, Section 547, and adjustments required to be made with respect to accumulated earnings and profits of an electing small business corporation, Section 1377, and the effect of a loan to the corporation made, guaranteed, or insured by the United States, Section 312(j).

SALE OF STOCK TO A RELATED CORPORATION. A sale of stock to a corporation other than the issuer of the stock may, under

Section 304, be deemed to be a redemption of stock by the corporation acquiring such shares.

Here it can only be said: study carefully the extremely complicated and "tricky" provisions of Section 304, and the Regulations thereunder, before reaching any conclusion as to the tax effect of any sale of shares of stock of one corporation to another corporation which might, under the provisions of that section, be deemed to be related.

Note, however, that a redemption which qualifies under Section 303 is not disqualified by reason of being in the form of a sale to a subsidiary, Rev. Rul. 55-592, 1955-2 C.B. 573.

DISPOSITIONS OF SECTION 306 STOCK. Any stock acquired in a transaction which was "tax-free" in whole or in part *may* be "Section 306 stock" and, if so, the amount realized from its sale *or other disposition* may be treated as gain from the sale of property which was *not* a capital asset or, in the case of redemptions, with one exception, as a taxable dividend.

In the case of every sale or other disposition of such stock it is, therefore, essential to determine whether such stock is, in fact, "tainted"; that is, "Section 306 stock." Such "tainted," "Section 306," stock includes: preferred stock received as a nontaxable distribution; stock of any kind received, in a taxable year ending after 1953, in a "tax-free" or partially "tax-free" transaction such as is described in Section 306(c); and stock received for "Section 306 stock" in a "tax-free" or partially "tax-free" exchange. However, if at the time of a stock's receipt in a transaction which determines its character, money had been received "in lieu of the stock," and no part of the money so received would have been a dividend, then the stock so received is not "Section 306" stock.

If the stock in question *is* "Section 306 stock," it is then necessary to determine whether, under the elaborate provisions of that section, the amount realized upon its sale or other disposition would be treated as a gain from the sale of a noncapital asset or as a taxable dividend.

A complete analysis of the provisions of Section 306 and the

Regulations thereunder is beyond the scope of this work. The following reminders are, however, presented below:

1. A loss on a disposition of "Section 306 stock" will not, in general, be recognized.
2. Subject to certain exceptions, a redemption of "Section 306 stock" is taxable as a dividend.
3. One such exception is a redemption in partial or complete liquidation under Part III of Subchapter C (Sections 331 through 346), discussed further below.
4. One means of disposing of "Section 306 stock" without adverse consequences is by means of a deductible contribution to a charitable, etc., organization, Rev. Rul. 57-328, 1957-2 C.B. 229.
5. "Section 306 stock" can be transferred in an exchange under Section 306(b)(3) without being subject to the general rules regarding the manner in which sales and exchanges of such stock are taxable, Section 306(b)(3).
6. It may be possible to transfer "Section 306 stock" to another corporation, as a contribution to the capital of the latter, without realizing taxable gain or income under Section 306.[4]
7. Apparently the tax effect of a sale of "Section 306 stock" received from a decedent by reason of death is not governed by Section 306 (see Regulations §1.306-3(e), last sentence).
8. The special rules regarding stock rights and convertible stock, Section 306(d) and (e), should be studied if such securities are involved in any transaction to which Section 306 might be applicable.
9. If stock, received in a year ending prior to 1954, which would have been Section 306 stock under that section, is "disposed of or redeemed" after June 21, 1954, the effect of such distribution is to be determined under the relative provisions of the Internal Revenue Code of 1939, *without regard* to Section 306.

[4] See Revised Report of the Advisory Group on Subchapter C, December, 1958, p. 18.

PARTIAL LIQUIDATIONS. Acquisitions by a corporation of shares of its own stock are, by Code definition, Section 317(b), "redemptions." Subchapter C, however, in prescribing conditions under which redemptions will be treated as sales of the stock redeemed, Section 302, impliedly excludes the type of redemption termed a distribution in partial liquidation, Section 302(e)(3) [referring to Section 331], as to which there are separate rules, Section 331, as to the circumstances in which the distribution is to be treated as in part or full payment for the stock, Section 331(a), and, hence, generally give rise to capital gain or loss.

Certain Other Liquidation Distributions

LIQUIDATION OF SUBSIDIARIES. No gain or loss, Sections 1001, 1222, Regulations §1.302-1(b), will be recognized where there is a complete liquidation of a domestic corporate subsidiary, if such liquidation qualifies under the rules in Section 332.[5]

ONE-MONTH LIQUIDATIONS. Another exception to the general rule as to the effect of stock redemptions is in Section 333, which provides that, where the statutory requirements are met, the amount of gain realized by an individual who is a "qualified electing" stockholder, on the complete liquidation of a domestic corporation in one calendar month, is to be taxed as follows:

1. As a dividend, to the extent of his share of earnings and profits of the corporation accumulated after February 28, 1913.
2. At capital gain rates, to the extent of:
   a. The amount received in money and in securities acquired by the corporation after December 31, 1953, less
   b. The amount taxed as a dividend.

If the "qualified electing" stockholder is a corporation, the taxable portion of its *gain* is the greater of the two following:

1. The amount received in money and in securities acquired

[5] See Section 367 regarding the case where one of the corporations is a foreign corporation.

by the liquidating corporation after December 31, 1953, or

2. Its ratable share of the earnings and profits of the liquidating corporation accumulated after February 28, 1913.

Note that no portion of the gain realized by a corporate stockholder is taxable as a dividend, but the entire amount is taxable as a short-term or long-term capital gain, as the case may be, Regulations §1.333-4(c)(1), last sentence.

Any portion of gain realized by the stockholder in excess of the foregoing (e.g., as a result of the receipt of property having a fair market value in excess of its adjusted basis in the hands of the liquidating corporation) is not taxable at the time of receipt of the distribution, but only if and when such property is subsequently sold or exchanged for an amount in excess of such basis, adjusted for any changes during the period held by the taxpayer.

A warning must be sounded: before making an election under Section 333, be certain that the amount of earnings and profits of the liquidating corporation, accumulated after February 28, 1913, has been accurately determined; then compute the tax *with* and *without* application of the election permitted by Section 333; then consider the tax effect of any contemplated disposition of any of the property, other than the money and securities, received in the one-month liquidation. The results of these computations should speak for themselves.

In order to be sure of obtaining the benefits of Section 333, it is essential to comply meticulously with all the requirements spelled out in that section and the Regulations thereunder, and to keep the required records and file the required information with the return, Regulations §1.333-5.

LIQUIDATION OF COLLAPSIBLE CORPORATIONS. The next exception to the general rule as to distributions in liquidation is that set forth in Section 341, relating to collapsible corporations, which is not discussed here, since the result of the application of that section is to tax as ordinary income what otherwise would be treated as capital gain.

"SPIN-OFF" DISTRIBUTIONS. Section 355 provides for the "tax-free" distribution of shares of one corporation to stockholders of another corporation. How this must be done, to avoid having the receipt with respect to such shares taxed as a dividend, is dealt with above in this chapter at length, and need not be repeated here. It is well, however, to keep in mind that the "tax-free" status of such a distribution cannot be relied upon, unless it can be established, aside from meeting all other requirements, that the distribution is not a "device" for the distribution of a dividend.

DEFINITION OF PARTIAL LIQUIDATION. Finally, Section 346 lays down rules for the determination of what *is* a distribution in "partial liquidation" for the purposes of that section, and, hence, treated as in part or in full payment for the stock, Section 331, rather than taxable as a dividend.

What to do and not to do, in order to qualify a distribution as one in partial liquidation under Section 346, and hence a transaction which may be eligible for capital gain treatment, has been set out at length at the beginning of this chapter, and need not be repeated here.

Receipt of "Boot" in a Reorganization. Where an exchange in a reorganization would be "tax-free" (i.e., one with respect to which no gain or loss would be recognized) if not for the receipt, in addition to stock or securities which could be received "tax-free," of money or other property, the latter is generally termed "boot." As a general rule, any gain on such an exchange is taxable, but not in excess of the amount of the "boot" received, Section 356.

Aside from mentioning that no *loss* is recognized (i.e., allowable as a deduction or as an offset to another gain) as a result of such an exchange, Section 356(c), the many problems connected with the "Reorganization" provisions of the statute, other than the treatment of "boot" as dividend income, are not touched upon here, as they are dealt with exhaustively in the book on that topic forming a part of the "Tax Practitioners' Library." [6]

[6] Robert S. Holzman, *op. cit.*

Care must be taken that the exchange in such a case *is* within the scope of the reorganization provisions of Subchapter C, and that the gain thereon, if any, *is* taxable in an amount not in excess of the "boot" received. If it is, then such amount may, under Section 356, be taxable:

1. As a dividend, or
2. As gain from the exchange of property, Section 356 (a) (2).

The portion of such gain taxable as a dividend is not in excess of the distributee-stockholder's "ratable share of the undistributed earnings and profits of the corporation accumulated after February 28, 1913," and any excess of the taxable gain over the amount taxable as a dividend is to be treated as gain from the exchange of property.

From the foregoing it can be seen that the "boot" received in a reorganization exchange may *not* be taxable *as a dividend* if, and to the extent that, it can be shown that the amount of the "boot" is:

1. In excess of the gain realized in the exchange, i.e., excess of value of all that is received, over statutory adjusted basis of all that is given;
2. Attributable to the recipient-stockholder's ratable share of the corporation's earnings and profits accumulated prior to March 1, 1913, or
3. In excess of the recipient-stockholder's ratable share of the corporation's earnings and profits accumulated after February 28, 1913.

Hence, all these factors must be considered and investigated if there is any possibility that any of them would affect the amount taxable to the stockholders as a dividend.

In the case of a corporation which receives "boot" in an otherwise "tax-free" exchange, it will not have any taxable gain as a result of such exchange, if it "distributes it in pursuance of the plan of reorganization." Section 361(b)(1)(A).

In the case of a corporation, a party to a "reorganization," it must also be kept in mind that, if a liability owing by it is assumed by another party, or property transferred by it is subject to a liability, and the Internal Revenue Service alleges that the purpose of such assumption or transfer was: (1) "to avoid Federal income tax on the exchange," or (2) "not a bona fide business purpose," the amount of the liability will be treated as the receipt of money (and hence treated as "boot"), unless the taxpayer can overcome the presumption of the correctness of the Service's finding.

Assumption of Liability of the Taxpayer in an Otherwise Wholly "Tax-Free" Reorganization. Ordinarily, the assumption of a liability of the taxpayer, in a reorganization exchange transaction otherwise qualifying as "tax-free," does not deprive the transaction of its "tax-free" status, Section 357(a). If, however, the circumstances are such that it appears that the principal purpose of the taxpayer was to avoid tax or "was not a bona fide business purpose," the amount of the liability assumed (or subject to which an asset is taken by the taxpayer) will be treated as money received by the taxpayer, Section 357(b). This may mean that such amount will be treated as a receipt of "boot" by the taxpayer. As noted above, this may in turn result in the taxpayer being deemed to have received a distribution "essentially equivalent to a dividend" and, hence, taxable as such.

The circumstances in which the Internal Revenue Service may seek to hold a taxpayer liable on this theory in such a case are many and varied. Here, again, recourse is to be had principally to decisions of the courts under the 1939 Code and earlier laws, digested in Chapter 3, in which the issue was whether the transaction was "essentially equivalent to a dividend."

A word of warning—in case of a finding by the Commissioner of Internal Revenue that an assumption of a liability, in what otherwise would be a "tax-free" reorganization exchange, was made for tax-avoidance reasons or for what was not a bona fide business purpose, such finding not only is supported by the usual presumption of correctness in the Commissioner's favor, but the specific statutory provision, Section 357(c), that the taxpayer's burden of proving such finding erroneous "shall not be considered as sustained unless the taxpayer sustains such burden by the clear preponderance of the evidence," Section 357(b)(2). This is a heavy burden, and stresses the need of careful consideration wherever liabilities are involved in what is intended to be a "tax-free" reorganization transaction.

"TAXABLE DIVIDENDS" WHERE THERE IS NO DISTRIBUTION. Unlike all other situations dealt with in this book, a stockholder owning stock of a "holding company" may be held taxable as though he had received a taxable dividend even though there has been *no* distribution, actual or constructive, of money or property.

In the case of a domestic corporation meeting the definition of a "personal holding company," Section 542, a stockholder may agree to treat as a taxable dividend all or any portion of the amount which he might have received as a dividend with respect to the shares (other than shares of certain preferred stock) of such corporation owned by him, Section 565.

This means of avoiding the extremely heavy penalty tax otherwise payable by such a corporation upon its "undistributed personal holding company income," Section 541, may be useful in certain circumstances. It is to be kept in mind, however, that the amount so taxed to the stockholder is considered as contributed by him to the capital of the corporation, Section 565(c)(2), and, therefore, cannot thereafter be withdrawn tax-free until and unless all other accumulated earnings and profits, including earnings and profits of the current year, have first been distributed by the corporation, Regulations §1.316-2(a).

In the case of a "Foreign Personal Holding Company" the stockholder (if a U.S. citizen or resident alien) is taxable each year, without any choice in the matter, upon his share of the corporation's "undistributed foreign personal holding company income" to the same extent as if it had been distributed to him as a dividend, Section 551(b).

The "do's" and "don't's" here are very simple: do become thoroughly acquainted with all the consequences of becoming taxable as the stockholder of such a corporation—and then don't fall into the trap if it is possible to avoid it.

Do's and Don't's

Regarding Transactions Not Specifically Covered by Any Code Provisions Relating to Distributions Taxable as Dividends

Even if a transaction does not come within the scope of any provision of the Code relating specifically to distributions or to dividends, such a transaction may constitute a distribution taxable as a dividend if it is, in substance, a payment or transfer of money or other property to or for the benefit of a stockholder as such, without the receipt by the corporation of full and adequate consideration in exchange for the money or other property paid or distributed by it. Here again, decisions under prior law will furnish a guide and may be controlling in determining whether the facts are such that the transaction is, in effect, a distribution taxable as a dividend.

Loans to Stockholders. The Internal Revenue Service may assert that any loan to a stockholder is "essentially equivalent to a dividend." Hence, every precaution should be taken to insure that the genuineness of the loan, as such, can be established.

The cases summarized in Chapter 3, Part I, Subpart B, give an indication of how frequently such an attack is made, and what factors are considered by the courts in reaching a decision. Favorable factors include: evidence of indebtedness in the form of a promissory note; definite maturity date or dates; interest payable by stockholder; obligation recorded as such on corporation's books; security given for loan; repayment in part or in full; finally, the "existence of the intent to repay."

Unfavorable factors, aside from absence of any of the favorable factors listed above, include: loans in proportion to stockholdings; notes given only after Revenue Agent questioned loans; conduct of the parties indicating that they did not regard the transaction as a loan.

Payments of Money or Transfers of Property to Stockholders, Not in the Form of Dividends. It would hardly seem necessary to point out that a payment of money or a transfer of property to a stockholder may be taxable as a dividend even though there was no formal declaration of a dividend, or the distribution was not made in the ordinary course of business. Yet, it can be seen, as in cases in Chapter 3, that many taxpayers have unsuccessfully asserted these as reasons why such actual distributions should not be taxed as dividends. No reliance should be placed upon such grounds to escape dividend taxation of a payment or transfer of property received by a stockholder.

Distributions Not Proportionate to Stockholdings. Similarly, the argument that distributions disproportionate to stockholdings should not be taxed to the stockholders as dividends is not, in and of itself, an adequate defense.

Payments to Stockholders Alleged To Be in Repayment of Loans by Them to the Corporation. The essence of the problem here is to establish that the amount alleged to have been advanced to the corporation was advanced to it as a loan; that the corporation was indebted to the stockholder; and that the repayment was in satisfaction of such debt.

These issues are technically "questions of fact," and involve evidentiary material. However, a study of the cases in Chapter 3, involving such transactions, will reveal that the decision as to the nature of the transaction may depend to a considerable degree upon establishing what was the underlying intent, as to which there can seldom be proof, but only an opinion reached in the light of the significant facts.

Accordingly it is essential, in order to be able to defend a taxpayer against an assertion by the Internal Revenue Service that a payment of money or a transfer of property is a distribution taxable as a dividend, to be prepared to prove all relevant facts, and in the case of a prospective transaction to use such instruments and forms as will most likely support the desired conclusion as to their intent, and therefore their effect.

Where money is loaned by a stockholder to a corporation, for example, the following steps should be taken:

1. Have it give a promissory note or some other evidence of

indebtedness to the lender, specifying a due date or dates of payment and rate of interest.

2. Record the transaction properly in the accounts of both borrower and lender, including, if practicable and appropriate in the light of the amount involved, the adoption and entry, in the minutes of a stockholder's meeting, of a resolution authorizing the borrowing;

3. Have the corporation give security for the loan;

4. Have the corporation pay interest periodically in accordance with the terms of the obligation, which payments *should not be dependent upon the amount of the corporation's annual earnings;*

5. Have the corporation make payments on the obligation in accordance with its terms, which should be such as might reasonably be agreed upon between an unrelated borrower and lender.

Yet, with all these precautions, if:

1. The amounts loaned to the corporation were in proportion to stockholdings, and

2. The total debt was too large in proportion to the capital of corporation,

the taxpayer might be unable to overcome a charge by the Internal Revenue Service that the amount paid by the corporation in liquidation of the alleged loans was, in fact, a distribution equivalent to a redemption of stock (rather than a payment of a debt) and, as such, essentially equivalent to, and taxable as, a dividend. This issue is often referred to as the problem of "thin incorporation," which is the title of another book in this series.[7] Factors favorable to the taxpayer which have been given weight by the courts in this regard include:

1. The fact that the corporation was adequately capitalized;

2. Acceptable evidence that there was no intent to place the amount of the loan at the risk of the business;

[7] Martin M. Lore, *Thin Capitalization* (New York: The Ronald Press Co., 1958).

3. The fact that the amounts advanced by the stockholders were not proportionate to their stockholdings; and

4. Existence of particular circumstances requiring the corporation to borrow the money.

Payments to Stockholders for Property Purchased by the Corporation. Here, the question is one of actual facts: Did the corporation acquire the property for which the alleged payment was made and, if so, was the amount paid by the corporation actually paid for such property (i.e., did the corporation receive value for the amount paid by it)?

The cases in Chapter 3 show that the courts have been willing to decide in favor of taxpayers in those instances where the essential facts could be proved.

In one instance the court held that payments for property were not dividends to a stockholder even though the property purchased was for the personal use of such stockholder, and grounded its decision upon the fact that title to the property remained in the corporation, *Greenspon v. Commissioner*, 229 F.2d 947 (8th Cir., 1956).

In another instance the court sustained the taxpayers, where they had sold to a corporation controlled by them stock in another corporation immediately prior to the declaration of a dividend by the latter, *Charles Dreifus Co. v. United States*, 140 F. Supp. 499 (D.C.Pa., 1956). In a case such as the latter, however, it is necessary to take into consideration relevant provisions of the present Code (e.g., Section 304) which were not in effect in the year for which such decision was made.

Other Payments or Transfers of Property to Stockholders. A taxpayer's position that money or other benefit received from a corporation was not received by reason of stock ownership, but for some adequate consideration passing to the corporation, may be rejected by the Internal Revenue Service and not sustained by the courts. For example, payments to three widows, who collectively owned 63 per cent of the shares of stock of a family-owned corporation, characterized by the corporation as a "gratuity" for past services, were, in a recent decision held to be taxable as dividends, with the explanation: "We cannot escape the conclusion that by legislative definition they were 'dividends,' " *Lengsfield v. Commissioner*, 241 F.2d 508 (5th Cir., 1957).

On the other hand, the Tax Court has held that a payment by the corporation was a gift to the widow of the corporation's deceased president, and that, because it was *intended* as a gift, it was *not* taxable income, *Estate of John A. Maycann*, 29 T.C. 81 (1957).

Sometimes it is difficult to distinguish the cases. They do stand as a warning, and as a reminder, of the unpredictable results of the law's uncertainties. Do not place reliance on the general holding of any particular case; make sure you limit the holding to the facts involved in it.

A review of the cases in Chapter 3 under the same heading as this paragraph will serve to point out transactions, not intended to be dividends, which were held to be taxable as such; affording guidance as to what should be done or avoided. Where a tax has been, or is believed likely to be, proposed as a result of such a transaction, you will find it helpful to review these digests, and make a thorough study of those cases involving facts and issues most similar to those in your own case. It will be seen, however, that most of these cases turn on questions of fact—such as the underlying intent—and where the facts were favorable to the taxpayer, and could be proved, the result was favorable.

Cases in which the facts were adverse to the taxpayer's position, or not sufficient to overcome the proposal to treat the transaction as a distribution taxable as a dividend, afford a guide to what to avoid in prospective transactions. For example, in the life insurance cases it will be seen that, if the proceeds of insurance on the life of an officer to be received by stockholders are not to be taxed to them as dividends, it is essential that the insurance policies be not owned by the corporation, *Thomas F. Doran, et al.*, T.C. Memo., Docket #51880, May 18, 1956; *Cummings, et al. v. Commissioner*, 73 F.2d 477 (1st Cir., 1934). For guidance as to what facts and what evidence in proof of such facts may be required in this regard, make sure that you study the cases in this field.

Alleged Receipt of "Boot" in Reorganization Transactions. The cases in Chapter 3 under this heading fall into two classifications:

1. Those few cases in which the taxpayer alleged that he did not, in fact, receive "boot," and
2. Those cases where the facts were not in dispute, but the question was whether there was a reorganization giving rise to "boot," taxable as a dividend.

Of the cases falling within the second classification, the more numerous are those in which the taxpayer took the position that there were two separate transactions involved: first, a complete liquidation of a corporation, giving rise to capital gain; and second, an entirely separate transaction in which some part of the property received in the liquidation was transferred to another corporation, organized either before or after the liquidation.

The Commissioner's position in these cases was that there was but one transaction, a reorganization; and that whatever the taxpayer received from the "liquidating" corporation and did not transfer to the second corporation constituted "boot," taxable as a dividend.

The issue in these cases was neither as to the facts, nor as to the interpretation of the provisions of the Code (in these cases, the 1939 Code) relating to the receipt of "boot" in a reorganization. The issue was whether the taxpayer's contention that there were two transactions, a complete liquidation and the organization of a new corporation, was correct; or whether, as alleged by the Commissioner, the liquidation and organization of a new corporation constituted two steps in but a single reorganization transaction in which "boot," taxable as a dividend, was received by the taxpayer.

It will be seen that in all the cases, except one decided in 1933, *Rudolph Boehringer,* 29 B.T.A. 8 (1933), in which the foregoing issue was involved, the taxpayer was held to have received a taxable dividend. Do not, therefore, use such a device in the hope of thereby withdrawing, at capital gain rates, some or all the earnings of a corporation, as it is unlikely to be successful. The 1954 Code contains no provision which specifically requires such steps to be treated as parts of a single transaction, but such a provision was included in Section 357 of H.R. 8300 as originally introduced. It was omitted from the Code as enacted, because of the expressed belief that such a situation "can appropriately be disposed of by judicial decision or by regulation within the framework of the other provisions of the Bill." [8]

Cancellation of Stockholder's Indebtedness to Corporation. Cases under this heading fall into two categories:

1. Where the indebtedness of the stockholder to the corporation is cancelled without receipt by the corporation of adequate consideration.
2. Where the stockholder surrenders shares of stock of the corporation in exchange for the cancellation of his debt to it.

Regardless of the category, if the stockholder was in fact indebted to the corporation, the forgiveness of the debt is given the same effect, for the purpose of determining whether such cancellation is a distribution taxable as a dividend, as the payment to the stockholder of a like amount of money.

Hence, the tax effect of such a forgiveness must be determined in the same manner as if cash was, or was to be, paid to the stockholder, *unless* the transaction which gave rise to the indebtedness was essentially equivalent to a dividend *and* had already been taxed or was taxable as such in a prior year.

Payments by Corporations for Benefit of Stockholders. One of the common situations is a corporation's payment of premiums for insurance policies on the life of an officer-stockholder where the corporation is not the beneficiary of the policy. If these are the facts, the tax consequences are the same as if the cash for the premium were paid to the stockholder instead of to the insurance company. (This situation is

---

[8] Conference Report (No. 2543, 83d Congress), to accompany H.R. 8300, p. 41.

to be distinguished from that involving the receipt of the proceeds of an insurance policy, discussed above.)

Where the corporation pays what is, in fact, an expense of a stockholder, such payment is treated, for the purpose of determining if it is taxable to him as a dividend, in the same manner as if the payment had been directly to him. Wherever such a transaction may be involved, ask yourself this question: Whose expense was it? If the expense was the stockholder's, the tax consequences to be expected are a taxable dividend to the stockholder and a disallowed deduction for the corporation. If you believe the expense to be that of the corporation, make every effort to assemble the evidence necessary to prove that fact in the event that the item is questioned by the Internal Revenue Service. This problem is dealt with further below, from the viewpoint of the corporation's deduction. Expenses of a relative of a stockholder, paid by the corporation, are taxable as if paid to the stockholder.

In what might be considered a rather liberal decision, the Tax Court held that a stockholder did *not* receive a taxable dividend as a result of the corporation's purchase of vehicles for the use of the stockholder *Marvin T. Blackwell, et al.*, T.C. Memo., Docket #52701, Aug. 9, 1956; see also *H. L. McBride, et al.*, 23 T.C. 901 (1955). However, the corporation did retain title to the vehicles, and the Court's decision was grounded on that fact. The tax effect of the stockholder's *use* of such property is dealt with below.

Where both the corporation and the stockholder benefit, as where a claim is made against both and the corporation's payment in settlement results in the release of the claim against the stockholder, it has been held that the stockholder's escape from personal liability was not a taxable distribution of a dividend by the corporation, *Ruben v. Commissioner*, 97 F.2d 926 (8th Cir., 1938). But cf. *Holloway v. Commissioner*, 203 F.2d 566 (6th Cir., 1953).

Stockholder's Bargain Purchase of Corporate Property. The question is whether the corporation received a fair price for the property sold by it; if so, there is no dividend to the stockholder. Hence, the problem is basically one of fact and the proof thereof. Where the sale price is a fair one, if the amount is substantial it is wise to obtain an appraisal of the property from an unrelated and qualified appraiser.

Where a corporation waived its right to purchase property, thereby enabling the owner to offer it to the stockholders of the waiving corporation, and the stockholders purchased the property, it was held that these stockholders had not received any taxable distribution from the corporation; but the particular facts there involved should be noted, *Morris E. Floyd, et al.,* T.C. Memo., Docket #49815, July 26, 1955.

Stockholder's Bargain Purchases of Shares of Treasury Stock of the Corporation. Three cases directly dealing with this problem are *Joseph Scura,* T.C. Memo., Docket ##56461–2, Aug. 27, 1958; *Elizabeth Susan Strake Trust,* 1 T.C. 1131 (1943); and *Waldheim v. Commissioner,* 244 F.2d 1 (1957).

In *Scura,* the court held that since the sales were made in numbers of shares *disproportionate* to the stockholdings of the purchasers, the excess of the value of the shares over the purchase price was taxable as a dividend. In *Strake,* the sales were disproportionate to the purchasers' stock holdings, but this circumstance was not cited as controlling, the court holding that the excess was taxable as a dividend because, *in purpose and effect,* the transaction was an implement for the distribution of a part of corporate earnings. The *Waldheim* case, involving similar facts, held that the *effect* of the transaction justified a finding that the excess was taxable as a dividend.

Although in each of the three foregoing treasury stock cases a disproportionate distribution was involved, only in the *Scura* case was this factor specifically stated to be determinative of the issue. It may be that the question of a dividend will never arise where treasury stock is sold on a pro rata basis, and that only in the non pro rata cases will the application of the "purpose and effect" test be made by the Internal Revenue Service or the court. The "purpose and effect" test has, however, been employed by the courts in cases involving bargain sales of stock of other corporations and of newly issued preferred stock and it should, therefore, be considered in any case of a bargain purchase from a corporation of shares of its treasury stock.

Corporate Property Used by Stockholder. In two cases in which corporation property was occupied rent-free by stockholders, the stockholders were held taxable upon the rental value of the property, but as ordinary income and not as dividend income, *Henry T. Roberts,* T.C. Memo., Docket #9807, Aug. 24, 1948, and *Charles A. Frueauff,* 30 B.T.A. 449 (1934). Strangely, no reported case has been found in which a stockholder using a corporation's property has been held taxable upon the rental value of such property as being essentially equivalent to a dividend. Despite the absence of court decisions in this field, however, it is believed unsafe to conclude that such transactions will not give rise to income taxable either as a dividend or as ordinary income.

Income of Corporation Diverted to Stockholders. Where it is found that stockholders have received income belonging to their corporation, the minimum penalty is a double tax, both on the corporation and on the stockholders, plus interest on any deficiencies so found.

Where such an issue might possibly be raised by the Internal Revenue Service, do all that is possible to establish that the income in question is in fact earned by the stockholders' activities as individuals or is derived from property owned by them individually, and be prepared with proof of such facts to submit in answer to any allegation of the Internal Revenue Service that such income belonged to the corporation.

Other Transactions Which May Be Held To Be Essentially Equivalent to the Distribution of a Dividend. To sum up; whenever a person receives, directly or indirectly, cash, property or other benefit flowing from a corporation in which he is a stockholder, there is danger that the Internal Revenue Service will allege that he has received a distribution essentially equivalent to a dividend, taxable as such. If the transaction is one not covered by any provision of the Internal

Revenue Code dealing specifically with exchanges of property or distributions taxable as dividends, it may nevertheless be necessary, in order successfully to meet such an allegation, to establish that the:

1. Corporation received adequate value in exchange for what it parted with, or
2. Property and/or income in question was that of the taxpayer and not that of the corporation.

Distribution Taxable as a Dividend Is Limited to Amount of Earnings and Profits. Despite any grounds which might exist for a finding that a transaction constitutes a distribution essentially equivalent to a dividend, no amount in excess of the corporation's earnings and profits can be taxable as a dividend, Section 316 of the 1954 Code, but cf. Sec. 312(j).

Corporation's Payments to Stockholders, Claimed by It as Deductible Interest on Indebtedness. Court decisions involving the question whether payments to stockholders, claimed by the corporation as deductible interest, are essentially equivalent to dividends and hence not deductible, are very numerous.

The basic question is, in every instance: Was the corporation indebted to the stockholder?

If so, then the interest payable on such debt is deductible by the corporation, otherwise, it is not. In either event, the creditor-stockholder will have received taxable income, whether the income be held to be interest or dividends.

The determination whether the alleged indebtedness of the corporation is in fact a debt due the stockholder or a capital investment by the stockholder depends upon *all* the facts, including the intention of both parties, the corporation and the stockholder, as evidenced by their statements and their acts. These include:

1. The form of evidence of the alleged debt
   a. Promissory notes
   b. "Debentures"
   c. "Preferred stock"

    d. Other instruments

    e. Book entries only

2. Terms of the instrument, or debt, as to maturity, installment payments, interest, and security;

3. Subsequent payments of principal and interest;

4. Extent to which percentage of shares held corresponds with percentage of alleged debt due each stockholder.

The effect given by the courts to these and other factors in determining whether to recognize an alleged indebtedness as such, is digested in the numerous cases involving this issue, in Part II, Chapter 3 of this book.

In addition to the foregoing, the courts have, of late, placed increasing weight upon the significance of what is now often referred to as "thin capitalization." [9] By this is meant an excessively small capitalization, in comparison with the amount of the corporation's indebtedness to its stockholders.

The "Do's and Don't's" to be observed in order to insure deduction of interest on a corporation's indebtedness held by its stockholders may be inferred from the foregoing, amplified by reference to the above-mentioned digest of court decisions; the decisions themselves; and the book cited. The most important of these "Do's and Don't's" include the following:

1. Make sure that there are minutes of a meeting of the Board of Directors authorizing the incurring of the indebtedness, its terms, and the issuance of promissory notes or other evidence of such indebtedness.

2. See to it that there is an issuance and delivery to creditor of promissory notes or other evidence of indebtedness, preferably not designated as "debentures" or "preferred stock." If "debentures" are issued, their terms should include fixed maturity date or dates, preferably installment payments if debt is not payable in a short time, and a fixed interest rate. The designation of an instrument as a certificate of shares of preferred stock, no matter what the actual terms of the instrument, is almost certain to result in difficulties in obtaining a deduction

---

[9] Martin M. Lore, *op. cit.*

for "interest" payments due with respect thereto, and the use of the name "debenture" is very likely to have the same effect.

3. If no instrument is given to the creditor in evidence of the indebtedness, it is vital that there be evidence, in the form of correspondence, at least, that the amount claimed as an indebtedness is such in fact. It is preferable to have a written agreement as to the terms of the debt.

4. Payments on account of principal and interest should be made as agreed; otherwise, there should be correspondence showing a request for extension of time for such payment, and reasons therefor, and the granting of such extension.

Two other factors must be considered:

1. Relationship between per cent of share holdings and "debt" holdings of each stockholder.

2. "Thin capitalization," which might be cured, for example, by a transfer of a portion of earnings to capital, or a contribution of cash or property to the corporation's capital, with or without the corporation's issuance of additional shares of stock.[10]

Payments Claimed by Corporation as Other Expenses. As might be expected, the deduction of items other than "interest" may likewise be questioned by the Internal Revenue Service.

There are many payments to stockholders which may be questioned, including:

1. Compensation for services
2. Rents
3. Royalties

Here the question is simply this: Does the entire amount paid, or accrued, constitute fair consideration for a benefit received by the corporation? If so, it is deductible, unless it constitutes cost of an asset which must be capitalized.

[10] *Ibid.,* pp. 201-4.

This makes the problem one of valuation and appraisal, whether it be a question of determining how much is "a reasonable allowance for . . . compensation for . . . services actually rendered," or the fair amount to be paid for rents, for royalties for the use of patents, or for any other service rendered or goods supplied to a corporation by a stockholder, Section 162 (a) of the 1954 Code and Regulations thereunder.

To the extent that the amount received by the stockholder is held to be excessive, the deduction thereof may be disallowed to the corporation, as being "essentially equivalent to a dividend," or merely disallowed as unallowable under the statute. Hence, if the payee happens to be a stockholder of the corporation, it is essential, if such a result is to be avoided, to be in a position to prove the value of the consideration received, or to be received, by the corporation in exchange for the payment made, or to be made, for rendering the services, making available the property, or supplying the goods to the corporation.

Finally, whenever any transaction is contemplated which might conceivably be alleged by the Internal Revenue Service to result in a dividend, you will find it useful to satisfy yourself as to the answers to the following questions:

1. Does the "essentially equivalent to a dividend" issue lurk in any proposed step?
2. Is there more than one practicable way to accomplish the desired end result?
3. Which of the available ways will it be best to use to obtain the desired tax treatment?
4. Once a given way is decided upon, what should be done to insure the successful carrying out of your intentions and your ability to prove the essential facts which may be needed to establish the desired tax consequences?

APPENDIX

BIBLIOGRAPHY

ALEXANDER, JOHN H., and LANDIS, WILLIAM B., JR. "Bail-outs and the Internal Revenue Code of 1954," *Tax Counselor's Quarterly*, Vol. 2, No. 1 (December, 1958), p. 37.

ANDREWS, WILLIAM D. " 'Out of Its Earnings and Profits': Some Reflections on the Taxation of Dividends," *Harvard Law Review*, Vol. 69, No. 8 (June, 1956), p. 1403.

AYERS, ALLAN F., JR. "Taxable Distributions (Other Than in Liquidations or Reorganizations)," *Proceedings of the New York University Fourteenth Annual Institute on Federal Taxation*. Albany: Matthew Bender & Co., Inc., 1956, p. 633.

AYERS, ALLAN F., JR., and REPETTI, PETER J. "Boot Distributions Under the '54 Tax Code," *Notre Dame Lawyer*, Vol. 32, No. 3 (May, 1957), p. 414.

BITTKER, BORIS I. "Corporate Dividends and Other Nonliquidating Distributions in Cash, Property, Stock, and Obligations," *Howard Law Journal*, Vol. 5, No. 1 (January, 1959), p. 46.

———. "Taxation of Stock Redemptions and Partial Liquidations," *Cornell Law Quarterly*, Vol. 44, No. 3 (Spring, 1959), p. 299.

BRAFFORD, WILLIAM CHARLES. "Constructive Receipt of Dividends by Stockholders of a Closely Held Corporation," Parts I and II, *Kentucky Law Journal*, Vol. 46, No. 4 (Summer, 1958), p. 515, and Vol. 47, No. 1 (Fall, 1958), p. 17.

———. "Constructive Receipt of Dividends," Part III, *Kentucky Law Journal*, Vol. 47, No. 3 (Spring, 1959), p. 378.

BRODSKY, SAMUEL. "Partial Liquidation: Definition of Partial Liquidation and Rules for Determining Termination of a Business," *Proceedings of the New York University Fifteenth Annual Institute on Federal Taxation*. Albany: Matthew Bender & Co., Inc., 1957, p. 539.

———. "Stock Dividends, Stock Rights and Recapitalizations," *Proceedings of the New York University Fourteenth Annual Institute on Federal Taxation*. Albany: Matthew Bender & Co., Inc., 1956, p. 647.

BROWN, LEON B. "Selected Problems in Stock Redemptions," *Proceedings of the Tax Institute of the University of Southern California School of Law. Major Tax Planning for 1959*. Albany: Matthew Bender & Co., Inc., 1959, p. 171.

CHOMMIE, JOHN C. "Section 346(a)(2): The Contraction Theory," *Tax Law Review*, Vol. 11, No. 4 (May, 1956), p. 407.

"Current Trends in the Taxation of Stock Distributions," Note, *St. John's Law Review*, Vol. 33, No. 2 (May, 1959), p. 339.

DANZIG, AARON L. "Problems in Effecting Tax-Free Split-Ups, Split-Offs and Spin-Offs," *Proceedings of the New York University Thirteenth Annual Institute on Federal Taxation.* Albany: Matthew Bender & Co., Inc., 1955, p. 783.

DEAN, STEPHEN T. "Redemptions: Dividend or Capital Gain; Death Taxes, Related Corporations," *Proceedings of the New York University Thirteenth Annual Institute on Federal Taxation.* Albany: Matthew Bender & Co., Inc., 1955, p. 547.

"Determination of Whether Corporate Withdrawals Constitute Loans or Dividends," Note, *North Carolina Law Review*, Vol. 36, No. 4 (June, 1958), p. 540.

DIAMOND, LEO A. " 'Brother-Sister Corporations'—Sale of Stock or Other Assets, and Other Problems," *Proceedings of the Tax Institute of the University of Southern California School of Law. Major Tax Planning for 1959.* Albany: Matthew Bender & Co., Inc., 1959, p. 109.

"Disguised Dividends: A Comprehensive Survey," Comment, *UCLA Law Review*, Vol. 3, No. 2 (February, 1956), p. 207.

FROST, F. DANIEL, and BURNS, DONALD T. "Current Tax Problems While Operating as a Corporation," *Proceedings of the Tax Institute of the University of Southern California School of Law. Major Tax Planning for 1958.* Albany: Matthew Bender & Co., Inc., 1958, p. 117.

GRAHAM, ROBERT F. "Redemption Problems—The Holsey and Zipp Cases," *TAXES—The Tax Magazine*, Vol. 36, No. 12 (December, 1958), p. 925.

GUTKIN, SIDNEY A., and BECK, DAVID. *Tax Avoidance vs. Tax Evasion.* New York: The Ronald Press Co., 1958.

HOLZMAN, ROBERT S. *Arm's Length Transactions.* New York: The Ronald Press Co., 1958.

———. *Sound Business Purpose.* New York: The Ronald Press Co., 1958.

"Income Tax Hazards of Life Insurance Funded Stock Redemption Agreements in Close Corporations," Note, *University of Pittsburgh Law Review*, Vol. 20, No. 1 (Fall, 1958), p. 66.

KAMANSKI, CHARLES W. P. "Partial Liquidation—Section 346," *Proceedings of the Tax Institute of the University of Southern California School of Law. Major Tax Planning for 1959.* Albany: Matthew Bender & Co., Inc., 1959, p. 137.

LORE, MARTIN M. *Thin Capitalization.* New York: The Ronald Press Co., 1958.

LYONS, MARVIN. "Corporate Separations Under the 1954 Code," *Proceedings of the Eighth Annual Tulane Tax Institute.* Indianapolis: The Bobbs-Merrill Co., Inc., 1959, p. 574.

MACLEAN, CHARLES C., JR. "Problems of Reincorporation and Related Proposals of the Subchapter C Advisory Group," *Tax Law Review*, Vol. 13, No. 4 (May, 1958), p. 407.

MANNING, ELLIOTT. " 'In Pursuance of the Plan of Reorganization': The Scope of the Reorganization Provisions of the Internal Revenue Code," *Harvard Law Review*, Vol. 72, No. 5 (March, 1959), p. 881.

MOSS, ARTHUR H. "How To Determine Whether Corporate Distributions

Are 'Essentially Equivalent to a Dividend,'" *Journal of Taxation*, Vol. 4, No. 2 (February, 1956), p. 66.

REILING, HERMAN T. "The Law of Income Taxation and Corporate Distributions," *Notre Dame Lawyer*, Vol. 31, No. 2 (March, 1956), p. 147.

RINGLE, FRED M., SURREY, STANLEY S., and WARREN, WILLIAM C. "Attribution of Stock Ownership in the Internal Revenue Code," *Harvard Law Review*, Vol. 72, No. 2 (December, 1958), p. 209.

SHAW, T. T. "Effect of Boot in Tax-Free Acquisitions and Distributions," *Proceedings of the New York University Thirteenth Annual Institute on Federal Taxation*. Albany: Matthew Bender & Co., Inc., 1955, p. 731.

SINGER, ALLEN M. "Tax Consequences of Stock Redemptions for Shareholders Whose Stock Is Not Redeemed," *Oregon Law Review*, Vol. 38, No. 1 (December, 1958), p. 1.

SPEAR, HARVEY M. "Stockholder Problems Subsequent to Tax-Free Split-Ups, Split-Offs and Spin-Offs," *Proceedings of the New York University Thirteenth Annual Institute on Federal Taxation*. Albany: Matthew Bender & Co., Inc., 1955, p. 795.

SURREY, STANLEY S., and WARREN, WILLIAM C. "Deductible Expense or Non-Deductible Dividend Distribution," *Federal Income Taxation, Cases and Materials*. Brooklyn, N. Y.: Foundation Press, Inc., 1955, pp. 1000-1024.

TRITT, CLYDE E. "Corporate Distributions of Property," *Proceedings of the Tax Institute of the University of Southern California School of Law. Major Tax Planning for 1957*. Albany: Matthew Bender & Co., Inc., 1957, p. 69.

YOUNG, ANDREW B. "Preferred Stock Bail-Outs: Statutory Restrictions: Pitfalls and Continuing Opportunities Under the 1954 Code (Section 306)," *Proceedings of the New York University Fifteenth Annual Institute on Federal Taxation*. Albany: Matthew Bender & Co., Inc., 1957, p. 431.

INDEX TO LAWS, REGULATIONS, AND RULINGS

Laws Cited

Internal Revenue Code of 1954 *

* See also pp. 253-55.

Internal Revenue Code of 1939 *

Revenue Acts of 1928, 1932, 1934, 1936, 1938

Revenue Act of 1926

Revenue Act of 1924

Revenue Act of 1921

Revenue Act of 1918

Regulations Cited

Internal Revenue Code of 1954

* See also pp. 253–55.

Rulings Cited

CASES CITED

GENERAL INDEX

See also pages 39–41 and 253–55.